THIRD EDITION

Learning by Doing

A Handbook for Professional Learning Communities at Work®

Richard DuFour

Rebecca DuFour

Robert Eaker

Thomas W. Many

Mike Mattos

With Karen Power

Solution Tree | Press

a division of
Solution Tree

555 North Morton Street
Bloomington, IN 47404
800.733.6786 (toll free) / 812.336.7700
FAX: 812.336.7790

email: CanadaOrders@SolutionTree.com
SolutionTree.com/ca

Visit **go.SolutionTree.com/ca/PLCbooks** to download the free reproducibles in this book.

Printed in the United States of America

Library of Congress Cataloging-in-Publication Data

Names: DuFour, Richard, 1947-2017, author. | DuFour, Rebecca Burnette,
     author. | Eaker, Robert E., author. | Many, Thomas W., author. | Mattos,
     Mike (Mike William), author.
Title: Learning by doing : a handbook for professional learning communities
     at work / Richard DuFour, Rebecca DuFour, Robert Eaker, Thomas W. Many,
     Mike Mattos ; contributor, Karen Power.
Other titles: Learning by doing (Canadian version)
Description: Third edition, Canadian version. | Bloomington, IN : Solution
     Tree Press, 2020. | Includes bibliographical references and index.
Identifiers: LCCN 2019032328 (print) | LCCN 2019032329 (ebook) | ISBN
     9781949539479 (paperback) | ISBN 9781949539486 (ebook)
Subjects: LCSH: School improvement programs--Canada. | Group work in
     education--Canada. | Team learning approach in education--Canada. |
     Educational leadership--Canada. | Professional learning
     communities--Canada. | Teachers--In-service training--Canada.
Classification: LCC LB2822.84.C2 L39 2020 (print) | LCC LB2822.84.C2
     (ebook) | DDC 371.2/070971--dc23
LC record available at https://lccn.loc.gov/2019032328
LC ebook record available at https://lccn.loc.gov/2019032329

Solution Tree
Jeffrey C. Jones, CEO
Edmund M. Ackerman, President

Solution Tree Press
President and Publisher: Douglas M. Rife
Associate Publisher: Sarah Payne-Mills
Managing Production Editor: Kendra Slayton
Art Director: Rian Anderson
Content Development Specialist: Amy Rubenstein
Senior Production Editor: Suzanne Kraszewski
Proofreader: Evie Madsen
Text and Cover Designer: Rian Anderson
Compositor: Laura Cox
Editorial Assistant: Sarah Ludwig

*I dedicate my contributions to this revision to
the memories of Rick and Becky DuFour.
I thank Bob Eaker, Mike Mattos, and
Tom Many for continuing to lead and support
all of us in our pursuit of learning by doing.*

Acknowledgments

For this special Canadian edition, thank you to the teachers and leaders in Canadian schools and districts who were so willing to share their stories for our new case studies. It is a daunting task to be asked to be the "case" that would lead to solutions. These authentic Canadian stories provided evidence and celebration that the Professional Learning Community at Work process is alive and well in Canada. To my work family, Solution Tree, and especially editor Sarah Payne-Mills, who patiently provided editing guidance and support, thank you, thank you, thank you!

—Karen

We must acknowledge the tremendous support we have received for this project from the Solution Tree family. Suzanne Kraszewski is the skillful editor who polished our prose; Rian Anderson created the cover and designed layouts for the book. We are grateful for the enthusiasm and energy they devoted to the book's development.

In addition, each of us owes a tremendous debt of gratitude to Jeff Jones, the CEO of Solution Tree. Jeff is more than a publisher. He is one of the most ethical, service-oriented business leaders we know. He has been an ardent advocate for spreading the professional learning community (PLC) process across North America and the world, and his passion and skill have given our ideas a platform we could not have built on our own. Finally, he is a friend in every sense of the word. Every author should have the opportunity to work with a publisher like Jeff Jones. More importantly, everyone should know the joy of having someone like him for a friend.

—Rick, Becky, Bob, Tom, and Mike

Table of Contents

Chapter 1

Chapter 2

Chapter 3

Building the Collaborative Culture of a Professional Learning Community. . .   55

Chapter 4

Creating a Results Orientation in a Professional Learning Community   81

Chapter 5

Establishing a Focus on Learning   103

Chapter 10

Implementing the PLC Process Districtwide **213**

Conclusion

The Fierce Urgency of Now **235**

References and Resources **241**

Index **261**

About the Authors

Richard DuFour, EdD, was a public school educator for thirty-four years, serving as a teacher, principal, and superintendent. During his nineteen-year tenure as a leader at Adlai E. Stevenson High School in Lincolnshire, Illinois, Stevenson was one of only three U.S. schools to win the United States Department of Education Blue Ribbon Award on four occasions and the first comprehensive high school to be designated a New America High School as a model of successful school reform. He received his state's highest award as both a principal and superintendent.

A prolific author and sought-after consultant, Dr. DuFour is recognized as one of the leading authorities on helping school practitioners implement the Professional Learning Communities at Work® process in their schools and districts.

Dr. DuFour was presented the Distinguished Scholar Practitioner Award from the University of Illinois, and was the 2004 recipient of the National Staff Development Council's Distinguished Service Award.

Visit www.allthingsplc.info to learn more about Dr. DuFour's work.

Rebecca DuFour served as a teacher, school administrator, and central office coordinator. As a former elementary principal, she helped her school earn state and national recognition as a model professional learning community (PLC). Becky was one of the featured principals in the 2001 *Video Journal of Education* program, "Leadership in an Age of Standards and High Stakes"; and she was the lead consultant and featured principal in the 2003 program "Elementary Principals as Leaders of Learning." She was coauthor of numerous books, articles, and a video series on the topic of PLCs.

Serving as a consultant for more than decade, Becky brought over thirty years of professional experience to her work with educators around the world who are implementing the PLC process in their own organizations.

Becky was the recipient of the Distinguished Alumni Award of Lynchburg College.

Visit www.allthingsplc.info to learn more about Becky's work.

Robert Eaker, EdD, is professor emeritus at Middle Tennessee State University, where he also served as dean of the College of Education and as the university interim vice president and provost. Dr. Eaker is a former fellow with the National Center for Effective Schools Research and Development. He has written widely on the issues of effective teaching, effective schools, and schools and school districts functioning as professional learning communities.

Dr. Eaker is a frequent speaker at national, regional, and state meetings and regularly consults with school districts throughout North America.

Visit www.allthingsplc.info to learn more about Dr. Eaker's work.

Thomas W. Many, EdD, works with teachers, administrators, school boards, parents, and other education stakeholders on organizational leadership, implementation and change, and PLC at Work strategies and concepts.

Dr. Many's long and distinguished career includes twenty years of experience as a superintendent. He has also served as a classroom teacher, learning centre director, curriculum supervisor, principal, and assistant superintendent.

As former superintendent of Kildeer Countryside Community Consolidated School District 96 in Illinois, Dr. Many used the tenets of the PLC at Work process to ensure high levels of learning for all students. He played a key role in preparing elementary and middle-grade students to enter Adlai E. Stevenson High School, a nationally recognized PLC. Under Dr. Many's leadership, student achievement in District 96 improved every year for twelve consecutive years. More than 95 percent of all students now meet or exceed state standards. The district has been especially effective in helping students with special needs improve their academic performance. It has become recognized as one of the premier elementary school districts in the United States. A dedicated PLC practitioner, he is a compelling and sought-after speaker.

Dr. Many has written numerous articles and has coauthored books.

To learn more about Dr. Many's work, visit www.allthingsplc.info and follow @tmany96 on Twitter.

Mike Mattos is an internationally recognized author, presenter, and practitioner who specializes in uniting teachers, administrators, and support staff to transform schools by implementing the response to intervention (RTI) and PLC processes. Mike co-created the RTI at Work™ model, which builds on the foundation of the PLC at Work process by using team structures and a focus on learning, collaboration, and results to drive successful outcomes to successfully create systematic, multitiered systems of support to ensure high levels of learning for all students.

He is former principal of Marjorie Veeh Elementary School and Pioneer Middle School in California. At both schools, Mike helped create powerful PLCs, improving learning for all students. In 2004, Marjorie Veeh, an elementary school with a large population of youth at risk, won the California Distinguished School and National Title I Achieving School awards.

A National Blue Ribbon School, Pioneer is among only thirteen schools in the United States selected by the GE Foundation as a Best-Practice Partner and is one of eight schools chosen by Richard DuFour to be featured in the video series *The Power of Professional Learning Communities at Work: Bringing the Big Ideas to Life*. Based on standardized test scores, Pioneer ranks among the top 1 percent of California secondary schools and, in 2009 and 2011, was named Orange County's top middle school. For his leadership, Mike was named the Orange County Middle School Administrator of the Year by the Association of California School Administrators.

To learn more about Mike's work, visit http://mattos.info/Welcome.html and follow @mikemattos65 on Twitter.

Karen Power is a consultant and former teacher, principal, superintendent, and senior advisor for professional learning and leadership. Karen has implemented the Professional Learning Communities at Work process both as a principal and as a superintendent, and, for several years as a consultant, she has supported collaborative work in schools to meet the needs of students.

Karen's work focuses on school improvement, leadership coaching, and professional learning community implementation, as well as instruction, assessment, and evidence-based decisions for long-term sustainability.

In 2010, 2011, and 2012, Karen was selected as one of Canada's Top 100 Most Powerful Women in the Public Sector by the Women's Executive Network. She also received the national *Reader's Digest* Leadership in Education Award and was named one of the Outstanding People in the Atlantic Region by Atlantic Canada's *Progress* magazine. She is the coauthor of *Leading With Intention: Eight Areas for Reflection and Planning in Your PLC at Work*.

Karen has served on the Greater Moncton United Way Board, Moncton Rotary Board, Horizon Health Network Board of Directors, and Canadian Education Association Board. Karen holds a master's degree in school administration.

Karen divides her time between New Brunswick, Canada, and Jensen Beach, Florida, with her husband, Wayne. She has two grown daughters, Sandra and Elizabeth, who have provided her with endless opportunities for learning, love, and lots of fun.

To learn more about Karen's work, visit https://karenpower.blog, Karen's weekly blog for school improvement.

To book Robert Eaker, Thomas W. Many, Mike Mattos, or Karen Power for professional development, contact pd@SolutionTree.com.

Preface
Learning by Doing
for the Canadian Context

By Karen Power

It has been a privilege and an honour to revisit *Learning by Doing: A Handbook for Professional Learning Communities at Work, Third Edition* and create this Canadian version. Adding Canadian case studies to the beginning of each chapter led me to many compelling conversations with amazing Canadian educators and leaders. Thinking about our geographic language and cultural differences has reminded me of the pride that I have as a Canadian. Knowing that many of you reading this will be living in small and perhaps isolated communities created even more urgency for me to help build common understanding of the need for all of us to collaborate around learning and results. Being aware of the political conversations happening in many provinces and territories about education helped me deepen my own wisdom about the need for educators to improve schools and not wait for others to do it for us. And, this is what "learning by doing" is all about. I am so appreciative of the opportunity to add my voice to the collective *we* of our expert authors Richard DuFour, Rebecca DuFour, Robert Eaker, Thomas Many, and Mike Mattos.

I first stumbled across Richard DuFour and Robert Eaker's (1998) book *Professional Learning Communities at Work* in the late 1990s. I was a school principal in need of direction. I wasn't confident in knowing all that had to be done to improve the school. The book led me to developing a successful, collaborative school culture that was focused on learning and results. Later in my career, I became a superintendent and continued to do the work in our thirty-eight schools. Today, as a PLC at Work coach, author, and presenter for Solution Tree, I am still learning and doing, and I appreciate this opportunity to support continuous school improvement through the PLC process in Canada.

In chapter 1 (page 9), I share Canadian context in To Present a Compelling Argument That Canadian Educators Have a Moral Imperative to Improve Their Individual and Collective Practice (page 16). As we know, there is no federal department of education in Canada. The ten provinces and three territories are responsible for establishing policy, curriculum, legislation, and funding for education. As I researched and interviewed educators in Canada, I continued to be reminded that, despite our unique governance model, Canadians want the same thing: for each and every student to be

Canadians want the same thing: for each and every student to be successful.

successful. Many schools are achieving this through the PLC at Work process. Here are a few excellent examples.

- Some First Nations schools in British Columbia are participating in a collaborative PLC initiative, which includes collective meetings involving cohorts of principals and grade-level groups of teachers from interested First Nation schools located throughout the province (First Nations Schools Association of British Columbia, n.d.; B. Kavanagh, personal communication, May 16, 2019).

- In Quebec, over two hundred schools have created their own professional network and are learning and implementing the PLC process (Lucie and André Chagnon Foundation, n.d.; F. Masse, personal communication, 2019).

- There are schools or districts in all provinces that are focused on the four PLC critical questions. There is evidence of various implementation stages, but the good news is that schools are working at improving their practice. On the AllThingsPLC website (n.d.b; www.allthingsplc.info), the number of Canadian schools who are now model PLCs continues to grow.

- The Ontario essential outcomes for school principals includes a statement expectation for leadership of collaborative learning communities. Other boards and district are embracing this language in writing (Institute for Education Leadership, 2013).

- Many regions of our northern lands are successfully implementing the PLC process including the Cree School Board, the Tłı̨chǫ Community Services Agency, and the Commission scolaire francophone des TNO. In fact, the Cree School Board's (2018) organizational values state, "We are different from one another but work well together" and "we need each other to succeed." These two values represent the focus that they have put on implementing the PLC process.

As Canadians, are we ready to forge a stronger commitment to a process that will help us improve learning for each student? I believe we are and so do many educators, parents, and students across this country. In a 2012 public survey conducted by the Canadian Education Association, 76 percent of respondents felt that there was a need for educators to find a new way of "handling differences in student abilities," 70 percent agreed that different ways were needed for "reducing different outcomes among different groups of students," and 67 percent stated that it was time for educators to find different ways for "deciding what is important for students to learn" (p. 8). All three of these concerns are answered when you work through the four critical questions of the PLC process.

Early Childhood Education is not universally supported in Canada, and this creates many inequities in the level of school readiness, health of our young children, and parent expectations about school. In UNICEF's first-ever global report on pre-primary education, it revealed that children enrolled in at least one year of programming before primary school are more likely to develop the critical skills they need to succeed in school, and are less likely to repeat grades or drop out of school (UNICEF, 2019).

Canada currently has 532,000 children between the ages of two and four. Children not in pre-primary education are missing critical development opportunities and are at risk of suffering deep inequalities from the start, the report notes. Canada has a higher rate of pre-primary education than lower-income countries, where only one in five young children are enrolled. However, Canada ranks a disappointing twenty-second out of thirty-eight peer countries in equality of access. Most wealthy countries invest, on average, 5–6 percent of their annual budgets on early childhood education while Canada spends less than 3 percent. (UNICEF, 2019). This is one more reason that Canadian educators must have deep understanding of the most effective practices to succeed with their students like implementing the PLC process with fidelity.

As Canadian schools continue to strive to become more inclusive in our practices, the expectations on our educators to be able to respond appropriately with differentiated instruction, timely interventions within the classrooms, and appropriate skills and knowledge to meet the needs of each student seem daunting. Again, this is the shared work of a collaborative team using the PLC process.

I trust that you will learn from the Canadian examples and context that has been added to the third edition of *Learning by Doing* and that you will continue to deepen your understanding of the need for continuous collaboration focused on learning and results.

Canadian educators must have deep understanding of the most effective practices to succeed with their students like implementing the PLC process with fidelity.

Introduction to the Third Edition

The first edition of this book began with a simple sentence: "We learn best by doing." This axiom certainly applies to our own work. Since the publication of the first edition of *Learning by Doing: A Handbook for Professional Learning Communities at Work®* in 2006, we have made presentations to more than one hundred thousand educators, served on dozens of panels, worked with several districts on a long-term basis to assist with their implementation of the Professional Learning Community at Work (PLC) process, and participated in ongoing dialogue with educators on AllThingsPLC (www.allthingsplc.info). This continuing work with teachers, principals, and central office staff from schools and districts throughout North America and beyond has given us a deeper understanding of the challenges they face as they attempt to implement the PLC process in their organizations.

In 2010, we shared our deeper understanding in the second edition of *Learning by Doing*. That edition addressed such key concepts as reciprocal accountability, districtwide implementation of the PLC process, the dangerous detours and seductive shortcuts that undermine effective implementation, and a detailed five-point continuum of each element of the PLC process to help educators assess their progress on the PLC journey.

We learn best by doing.

What's New in This Edition

We remain proud of the second edition of *Learning by Doing*, but since it was published in 2010, we have learned a lot, individually and collectively, and we have written extensively about the PLC process. As we reflected on our learning, we soon recognized several areas of the second edition that needed updating and a few significant issues that we had not adequately addressed. In this third edition, we address those issues and expand on others. New additions and expanded topics to this revised edition include the following.

- **We have added two new chapters:** One new chapter focuses on the importance of team-developed common formative assessments. In our work with schools and educators, we have come to recognize that developing assessments is a fork in the road for many schools on their PLC journey. The path that educators take determines in large part whether their schools will become high-performing PLCs or settle for "PLC lite." The new material on creating common formative assessments in this edition will help you travel the right path.

We have also added a chapter on staffing issues in PLCs. We have heard educators express their frustration with the disruption of the collaborative team process that occurs when colleagues leave the team and they must bring new members on board. In this edition, we address keys to hiring staff members who will be a good fit for the PLC process, how to provide effective orientation for them, and how to do a better job of retaining educators.

- **We include more information about successful implementation and common mistakes:** We now have a deeper understanding both of how to implement the PLC process successfully districtwide and the common mistakes districts make when implementation has little impact on student achievement. In this edition, we compare and contrast the strategies that high-impact and low-impact districts use.

- **We address proficiency:** We have come to recognize that clarifying essential outcomes demands developing an agreed-on understanding of what proficient work looks like. Too often we have seen teams leave the issue of proficiency unaddressed. We provide examples of the kind of clarity regarding proficiency that is a prerequisite to a guaranteed and viable curriculum.

- **We offer suggestions for integrating deeper knowledge into the curriculum and teacher-made assessments:** Most provinces and territories recognize the need for all students to develop core competencies such as thinking critically and being able to explain their thinking to solve problems. In the past, assessments typically relied on low-level questions that primarily focus on recall of information rather than probing for deeper knowledge. Canadian educators must focus on requiring deeper learning on the part of their students and on creating assessments that will allow students to demonstrate that deeper knowledge.

- **We comprehensively address the issue of systemic intervention:** We are thrilled that Mike Mattos, one of the leading experts on intervention, has become an integral part of our team. Although we addressed the issue of systematic interventions in previous editions, Mike addresses the issue of systematic intervention more fully in this edition.

- **We provide even more tools for your work:** It has become evident to us that educators benefit from having explicit protocols and tools to guide their work as they move through the various steps on the PLC journey. Throughout this edition, we include proven protocols, tools, and sample products from high-performing PLCs and districts.

- **We provide a broader research base:** In this edition, we have updated the research base that supports the PLC process with more than one hundred new references.

- **We focus on immediate steps:** In previous editions, we attempted to present a compelling rationale for why schools should operate as PLCs. The PLC process has become so widely accepted as the best strategy for improving schools that in this edition, we place a much greater emphasis on taking immediate steps to begin implementation of the process itself.

A Move From Interest to Commitment

It has been gratifying to witness the growing interest in the PLC at Work process since Rick and Bob published their groundbreaking book on PLCs in 1998, *Professional Learning Communities at Work: Best Practices for Enhancing Student Achievement*. It has been frustrating, however, that more educators have not moved from interest to commitment. As Art Turock, the author of several books on self-motivation observes, "There is a difference between interest and commitment. When you are interested in something, you do it only when it is convenient. When you are committed to something, you accept no excuses, only results" (personal communication, September 30, 2015).

Our colleagues Ken Williams and Canadian educator Tom Hierck (2015) frame the issue another way. To paraphrase their approach, they observe that many educators are "flirting" with PLCs, observing the process from afar but not taking positive steps to move forward. Other educators are "dating" PLCs. They are dabbling in the work and curious about its potential, but they leave their options open so that they can break up when the next hot thing comes along. Still other educators are "engaged" to the PLC process because they have made a commitment to engage fully in the work and are striving to get better at it. As Williams and Hierck (2015) put it, these educators have "put a ring on it" (p. 96). Finally, we would extend their analogy to say that some educators are "married" to the PLC process. This is the way of life they have chosen, and they would never return to their old way of doing things. Their schools continue to flourish even if key leaders leave because the PLC process is so deeply embedded in the culture of their school it has become "the way we do things around here."

It is time for educators to move from an interest in the PLC process to a commitment to the process where there are no excuses for failing to move forward. It is time to progress from flirting with PLCs to marrying the process. It is time to move from thinking about PLCs and talking about PLCs to *doing* what PLCs actually do and getting better at it. The moral imperative for engaging fully in this process has never been stronger, and we do not apologize for presenting this book as what it is intended to be: a demand for action from educators at all levels.

The first edition supported schools and teams engaged in the PLC process by providing helpful tools and templates in two formats—within the pages of the book and on a compact disc that was included with the book. In the second edition, we moved many of the tools and templates online so that we could revise, update, and add to them on an ongoing basis. This edition features the most up-to-date online resources along with some new tools and templates, including Canadian examples. Please visit **go.SolutionTree.com/ca/PLCbooks** to download the free reproducibles and access materials related to this book. We also invite educators to visit AllThingsPLC (www .allthingsplc.info) to access research, case studies, strategies, and tools and to share materials they have created to help them in their work.

It is time for educators to move from an interest in the PLC process to a commitment to the process where there are no excuses for failing to move forward.

The Format

We continue with the format that we introduced in the second edition. Starting in chapter 2 (page 25), each chapter of this handbook includes seven parts.

- Part One: The Case Study

- Part Two: Here's How

- Part Three: Here's Why

- Part Four: Assessing Your Place on the PLC Journey

- Part Five: Tips for Moving Forward

- Part Six: Questions to Guide the Work of Your Professional Learning Community

- Part Seven: Dangerous Detours and Seductive Shortcuts

Part One: The Case Study

Each chapter opens with a case study describing some of the issues and challenges that have arisen in a school or district that is attempting to implement the PLC process. We are pleased that nine Canadian schools or districts honoured us with their stories. They represent the very real issues educators must grapple with and resolve if they are to bring the PLC process to life in their schools and districts. Readers may be tempted to skip the case studies and move quickly to solutions; we urge you to resist that temptation. A critical step in assessing alternative solutions to any problem is to come to an understanding and appreciation of the problem itself. We hope you will take the time to consider each case study carefully, reflect on the issues it presents, and generate possible strategies for addressing those issues prior to studying the rest of the chapter. Engaging in this reflective process with your colleagues will further strengthen your learning.

Part Two: Here's How

In our work with schools, we have found that *how* questions come in at least two varieties. One type represents a sincere and genuine solicitation of guidance from inquirers who are willing to act, and the other typically comes in waves as a series of "Yeah, but . . ." questions. For example, after listening to an explanation of the PLC process, a teacher or administrator responds:

- "Yeah, but . . . how are we supposed to find time to collaborate?"

- "Yeah, but . . . how can we give students extra time and support for learning when our schedule will not allow it?"

- "Yeah, but . . . how can this work in a school this big (or small, or poor, or urban, or rural, or suburban, or low achieving and, therefore, too despondent, or high achieving and, therefore, too complacent)?"

- "Yeah, but . . . how can we make this happen with our ineffective principal (or unsupportive central office, or adversarial teacher professional organization)?"

These questions are less of a search for answers on how to implement the PLC process successfully and more of a search for a reason to avoid implementation. As Peter Block (2003) says, "Asking 'How?' is a favourite defense against taking action" (p. 11). Block (2003) goes on to say, "We act like we are confused, like we don't understand. The reality is that we *do* understand—we get it, but we don't like it" (pp. 47–48). Our own work with schools has confirmed that a group that is determined not to act can always find a justification for inaction. Questions about how can have a positive impact only if those asking are willing to act on the answers. We challenge those who read this book to begin with the attitude that you are seeking a solution for every obstacle instead of looking for an obstacle in every solution.

Therefore, the Here's How sections in this book are written for those who seek ideas, insights, and information regarding how the PLC process comes alive in the real world of schools. Part two of each chapter describes how educators bring a particular PLC element to life in their school. It presents exemplars for schools to use as a model as they work through the challenges of moving from concept to action.

We fully recognize that there is no precise recipe for school improvement (blending two parts collaboration with one part formative assessment does not work). We also understand that even the most promising strategies must be customized for the specific context of each district and each school. The most effective improvement models are those that staff have *adapted* to fit the situation in their schools and communities. In these schools and districts "leaders use an array of strategies and tactics to accommodate the contextual realities in which they operate" (Mourshed, Chijioke, & Barber, 2010, p. 62). Therefore, the Here's How sections do not presume to present the answer to problems posed in the case study, because it is the dialogue about and the struggle with those problems at the school and district levels that result in the deepest learning and greatest commitment for teachers and administrators. Our hope is that this book can serve as a tool that educators can use to initiate the dialogue and to engage in the struggle.

Even the most promising strategies must be customized for the specific context of each district and each school.

Part Three: Here's Why

Informing others about how something can be done does not ensure they will be persuaded to do it. In fact, we are convinced that one of the most common mistakes school administrators make in the implementation of improvement initiatives is to focus exclusively on *how* while being inattentive to *why*. Leaders at all levels must be prepared to anticipate and respond to the inevitable questions and concerns that arise when educators are called on to engage in new practices. We have included part three in each chapter to offer useful tools—research, reasoning, and rationale—to help clarify why the initiative should be undertaken.

Throughout the book we have provided a concise summary of research to assist in the consideration of the why question for a specific recommended action. Our review of research draws on, but is not limited to, the research base on education. We examine findings from studies in organizational development, change processes, leadership, effective communication, and psychology because the challenges facing contemporary leaders demand that they look outside the narrow scope of their professional field for answers. We recommend that staff members be encouraged to review the summaries of research and to identify any research that refutes or contradicts it. In every case, the weight of the evidence should be apparent to all who consider it.

Part Four: Assessing Your Place on the PLC Journey

In each chapter of this handbook, we'll ask you to reflect on the current conditions in your school or district and assess the alignment of those conditions with the principles and practices of a PLC.

The assessment will present a five-point continuum.

1. **Pre-initiating stage:** The school has not yet begun to address this PLC principle or practice.

2. **Initiating stage:** The school has made an effort to address this principle or practice, but the effort has not yet begun to impact a critical mass of staff members.

3. **Implementing stage:** A critical mass of staff members is participating in implementing the principle or practice, but many approach the task with a sense of compliance rather than commitment. There is some uncertainty regarding what needs to be done and why it should be done.

4. **Developing stage:** Structures are being altered to support the changes and resources are being devoted to moving them forward. Members are becoming more receptive to the principle, practice, or process because they have experienced some of its benefits. The focus has shifted from, "Why are we doing this?" to "How can we do this more effectively?"

5. **Sustaining stage:** The principle or practice is deeply embedded in the culture of the school. It is a driving force in the daily work of staff. It is deeply internalized, and staff would resist attempts to abandon the principle or practice.

The continuum in each chapter is based on the premise that it is easier to get from point A to point B if you know where point B is and can recognize it when you get there. The sustaining stage of the continuum explains point B in vivid terms. It describes the better future your school is moving toward on its PLC journey. A journey from A to B, however, also requires some clarity regarding the starting point. The continuum is also a tool to help educators assess the current position of their school or team so that they can move forward purposefully rather than fitfully.

This continuum can be administered across a district, school, or team. Many districts have converted it to an electronic format and used simple survey tools, such as SurveyMonkey, to gather information on staff perceptions. Whatever format you use, we recommend that the process begins by asking each individual to make anonymous, independent, and candid assessments and to offer evidence and anecdotes to support his or her conclusions on each characteristic presented.

Once members complete their individual assessments, the results should be compiled and shared with all participants. Staff members can then analyze the results and use them to begin dialogue to clarify the current reality of their team, school, or district. Participants should be particularly attentive to discrepancies in responses and explore reasons for the differences. Groups have a tendency to gloss over disagreements. One person contends the school is in the pre-initiating stage while another contends it is developing, and to avoid discussion, they merely compromise and settle for the initiating stage. Avoid that temptation. Delve into one another's thinking to see if you can clarify discrepancies and establish common ground.

Part Five: Tips for Moving Forward

Each chapter includes specific suggestions and strategies to assist with the implementation of particular PLC processes. The primary purpose of this handbook is to encourage people to act, to learn by doing. Random actions, however, do nothing to enhance the capacity of a staff to function as a PLC. The challenge facing leaders is to identify purposeful and focused actions that contribute to the goal of improved learning for students and staff alike. Part five offers insight regarding which actions to take and which to avoid. It identifies tactics that offer the greatest leverage for implementing PLC processes and presents research-based and practitioner-proven tips for pursuing those tactics effectively.

Part Six: Questions to Guide the Work of Your Professional Learning Community

PLC team members engage in *collective* inquiry: they learn how to learn together. But only when they focus this collective inquiry on the right questions do they develop their capacity to improve student and adult learning.

It has been said that the leader of the past knew how to tell. The leader of the future, however, will have to know how to ask. Those who lead the PLC process should not be expected to have all the answers and tell others what they must do. Leaders should instead be prepared to ask the right questions, facilitate the dialogue, and help build shared knowledge. Part six offers some of the right questions educators should consider as they work to drive the PLC process deeper into the culture of their schools and districts.

Part Seven: Dangerous Detours and Seductive Shortcuts

It is the *process* of learning together that helps educators build their capacity to create a powerful PLC. One of the most common mistakes that they make on the journey is to seek ways to circumvent that process. This section alerts readers to the some of the most common ways educators have attempted to avoid actually doing the work of a PLC so they won't fall victim to those mistakes.

It is the process of learning together that helps educators build their capacity to create a powerful PLC.

A Companion Book

This third edition of *Learning by Doing* is intended to offer a comprehensive rationale for implementing the PLC process, the research that supports the various elements of the process, common mistakes people make in implementation, and specific strategies and tools for overcoming those mistakes. The key word in this description is *comprehensive*. We recognize that there may be readers who get stuck on a specific problem who are looking for a quick answer to help them move forward. Therefore, we have created a companion book to this third edition, *Concise Answers to Frequently Asked Questions About Professional Learning Communities at Work* (Mattos, DuFour, DuFour, Eaker, & Many, 2016), in an effort to meet their needs as well. This guide on the side is arranged in a question-and-answer format by topic for easy reference. For example, if you are looking for what the research indicates is the best way to organize teams, or how a school counselor could contribute to the PLC's collaborative process, or countless other specific questions, this book is the place to find what you need to know.

A Journey Worth Taking

Despite the popularity of the term *professional learning community*, the *practices* of a PLC continue to represent the road less traveled in public education. Many teachers and administrators prefer the familiarity of their current path, even when it becomes apparent that it will not take them to their desired destination. We recognize it is difficult to pursue an uncharted path, particularly when it is certain to include inevitable bumps and potholes along the way. We do not argue that the PLC journey is an easy one, but we know with certainty that it is a journey worth taking. We have seen the evidence of improved learning and heard the testimonials of teachers and principals who have been renewed by establishing common ground, clear purpose, effective monitoring, and collaborative processes that lead to better results. They describe a heightened sense of professionalism and a resurgence of energy and enthusiasm that committed people have generated while working together to accomplish what could not be done alone. As Robert Evans (1996) writes:

We do not argue that the PLC journey is an easy one, but we know with certainty that it is a journey worth taking.

> Anyone part of such a process, or anyone who has seen first-rate teachers engage in reflective practice together, knows its power and excitement. Opportunities to collaborate and to build knowledge can enhance job satisfaction and performance. At their best, they help schools create a self-reflective, self-renewing capacity as learning organizations. (p. 232)

The following chapters will not eliminate the bumps and potholes of the PLC journey, but they will offer some guidance as to how educators can maneuver their way around and through the rough spots on the road. It has been said that the journey of a thousand miles begins with a single step. For those new to the PLC process, we urge you to take that step. And for those already on the journey, we hope the content in this new edition will assist your next steps. Let us begin together.

CHAPTER 1

A Guide to Action for Professional Learning Communities at Work

We learn best by doing. We have known this to be true for quite some time. More than 2,500 years ago Confucius observed, "I hear and I forget. I see and I remember. I do and I understand." Most educators acknowledge that our deepest insights and understandings come from action, followed by reflection and the search for improvement. After all, most educators have spent four or five years *preparing* to enter the profession —taking courses on content and pedagogy, observing students and teachers in classrooms, completing student teaching under the tutelage of a veteran teacher, and so on. Yet almost without exception, they admit that they learned more in their first semester of *teaching* than they did in the four or five years they spent *preparing* to enter the profession. This is not an indictment of higher education; it is merely evidence of the power of learning that is embedded in the work.

Our profession also attests to the importance and power of learning by doing when it comes to educating our students. We want students to be *actively engaged* in *hands-on authentic exercises* that promote *experiential learning*. How odd, then, that a profession that pays such homage to the importance of learning by doing is so reluctant to apply that principle when it comes to developing its collective capacity to meet students' needs. Why do institutions created for and devoted to learning not call on the professionals within them to become more proficient in improving the effectiveness of schools by actually doing the work of school improvement? Why have we been so reluctant to learn by doing?

What Are Professional Learning Communities?

Since 1998, we have published many books and videos with the same two goals in mind: (1) to persuade educators that the most promising strategy for meeting the challenge of helping all students learn at high levels is to develop their capacity to function as a professional learning community and (2) to offer specific strategies and structures to help them transform their own schools and districts into PLCs.

It has been interesting to observe the growing popularity of the term *professional learning community*. In fact, the term has become so commonplace and has been used so ambiguously to describe virtually any loose coupling of individuals who share a common interest in education that it is in danger of losing all meaning. This lack of precision is an obstacle to implementing PLC processes because, as Mike Schmoker (2004a) observes, "clarity precedes competence" (p. 85). Thus, we begin this handbook with an attempt to clarify our meaning of the term. To those familiar with our past work, this step may seem redundant, but we are convinced that redundancy can be a powerful tool in effective communication, and we prefer redundancy to ambiguity.

We have seen many instances in which educators assume that a PLC is a program. For example, one faculty told us that each year they implemented a new program in their school. In the previous year it had been PLC, the year prior to that it had been Understanding by Design, and the current year it was differentiated instruction. They had converted the names of the various programs into verbs, and the joke on the faculty was that they had been "PLCed, UBDed, and DIed."

The PLC process is not a program. It cannot be purchased, nor can it be implemented by anyone other than the staff itself. Most importantly, it is ongoing—a continuous, never-ending process of conducting schooling that has a profound impact on the structure and culture of the school and the assumptions and practices of the professionals within it.

We have seen other instances in which educators assume that a PLC is a meeting—an occasional event when they meet with colleagues to complete a task. It is not uncommon for us to hear, "My PLC meets Wednesdays from 9:00 a.m. to 10:00 a.m." This perception of a PLC is wrong on two counts. First, *the PLC is the larger organization and not the individual teams that comprise it.* While collaborative teams are an essential part of the PLC process, the sum is greater than the individual parts. Much of the work of a PLC cannot be done by a team but instead requires a schoolwide or districtwide effort. So we believe it is helpful to think of the school or district as the PLC and the various collaborative teams as the building blocks of the PLC. Second, once again, the PLC process has a pervasive and ongoing impact on the structure and culture of the school. If educators meet with peers on a regular basis only to return to business as usual, they are not functioning as a PLC. So the PLC process is much more than a meeting.

Other educators have claimed they are members of a PLC because they engage in dialogue based on common readings. The entire staff reads the same book or article, and then members meet to share their individual impressions of what they have read. But a PLC is more than a book club. Although collective study and dialogue are crucial elements of the PLC process, the process requires people to *act* on the new information.

So, what is a PLC? We argue that it is an ongoing process in which educators work collaboratively in recurring cycles of collective inquiry and action research to achieve better results for the students they serve. PLCs operate under the assumption that the key to improved learning for students is continuous job-embedded learning for educators. The following section examines the elements of the PLC process more closely.

It is helpful to think of the school or district

better results

Three Big Ideas That Drive the Work of a PLC

There are three big ideas that drive the work of the PLC process. The progress a district or school experiences on the PLC journey will be largely dependent on the extent to which these ideas are considered, understood, and ultimately embraced by its members.

A Focus on Learning

The first (and the biggest) of the big ideas is based on the premise that *the fundamental purpose of the school is to ensure that all students learn at high levels (grade level or higher)*. This focus on and commitment to the learning of each student is the very essence of a *learning* community.

The fundamental purpose of the school is to ensure that all students learn at high levels.

When a school or district functions as a PLC, educators within the organization embrace high levels of learning for all students as both the reason the organization exists and the fundamental responsibility of those who work within it. In order to achieve this purpose, the members of a PLC create and are guided by a clear and compelling vision of what the organization must become in order to help all students learn. They make collective commitments clarifying what each member will do to create such an organization, and they use results-oriented goals to mark their progress. Members work together to clarify exactly what each student must learn, monitor each student's learning on a timely basis, provide systematic interventions that ensure students receive additional time and support for learning when they struggle, and extend their learning when students have already mastered the intended outcomes.

A corollary assumption is that if the organization is to become more effective in helping all students learn, the adults in the organization must also be continually learning. Therefore, structures are created to ensure staff members engage in job-embedded learning as part of their routine work practices.

There is no ambiguity or hedging regarding this commitment to learning. Whereas many schools operate as if their primary purpose is to ensure that students are *taught* or are merely provided with *an opportunity* to learn, PLCs are dedicated to the idea that their organization exists to ensure that all students actually acquire the essential knowledge, skills, and dispositions of each unit, course, and grade level. Every potential organizational practice, policy, and procedure is assessed on the basis of this question: Will this ensure higher levels of learning for our students? All the other characteristics of a PLC flow directly from this epic shift in assumptions about the purpose of the school.

A Collaborative Culture and Collective Responsibility

The second big idea driving the PLC process is that in order to ensure all students learn at high levels, *educators must work collaboratively and take collective responsibility for the success of each student*. Working collaboratively is not optional, but instead is an expectation and requirement of employment. Subsequently, the fundamental structure

In order to ensure all students learn at high levels, educators must work collaboratively and take collective responsibility for the success of each student.

of a PLC is the collaborative teams of educators whose members work *interdependently* to achieve *common goals* for which members are *mutually accountable*. These common goals are directly linked to the purpose of learning for all. The team is the engine that drives the PLC effort and the primary building block of the organization.

It is difficult to overstate the importance of collaborative teams in the improvement process. It is even more important, however, to emphasize that collaboration does not lead to improved results unless people are focused on the right work. Collaboration is a means to an end, not the end itself. In many schools, staff members are willing to collaborate on a variety of topics—as long as the focus of the conversation stops at their classroom door. In a PLC, *collaboration* represents a systematic process in which teachers work together interdependently in order to *impact* their classroom practice in ways that will lead to better results for their students, for their team, and for their school.

Working together to build shared knowledge on the best way to achieve goals and meet the needs of those they serve is exactly what *professionals* in any field are expected to do, whether it is curing the patient, winning the lawsuit, or helping all students learn. Members of a *professional* learning community are expected to work and learn together.

A Results Orientation

The third big idea that drives the work of PLCs is the need for a *results orientation*. To assess their effectiveness in helping all students learn, educators in a PLC focus on results—evidence of student learning. They then use that evidence of learning to inform and improve their professional practice and respond to individual students who need intervention or enrichment. Members of a PLC recognize that all of their efforts must ultimately be assessed on the basis of results rather than intentions. Unless their initiatives are subjected to ongoing assessment on the basis of tangible results, they represent random groping in the dark rather than purposeful improvement. As Peter Senge and colleagues (Senge, Ross, Smith, Roberts, & Kleiner, 1994) conclude, "The rationale for any strategy for building a learning organization revolves around the premise that such organizations will produce dramatically improved results" (p. 44).

This constant search for a better way to improve results by helping more students learn at higher levels leads to a cyclical process in which educators in a PLC:

- Gather evidence of current levels of student learning

- Develop strategies and ideas to build on strengths and address weaknesses in that learning

- Implement those strategies and ideas

- Analyze the impact of the changes to discover what was effective and what was not

- Apply new knowledge in the next cycle of continuous improvement

The intent of this cyclical process is not simply to learn a new strategy, but instead to create conditions for perpetual learning—an environment in which innovation and experimentation are viewed not as tasks to be accomplished or projects to be completed but as ways of conducting day-to-day business, *forever*. Furthermore, participation in this process is not reserved for those designated as leaders; rather, it is a responsibility of every member of the organization.

This focus on results leads each team to develop and pursue measurable improvement goals for learning that align with school and district goals. It also drives teams to create a series of common formative assessments that are administered to students multiple times throughout the year to gather ongoing evidence of student learning. Team members review the results from these assessments in an effort to identify and address program concerns (areas of learning where many students are experiencing difficulty). They also examine the results to discover strengths and weaknesses in their individual teaching in order to learn from one another. Very importantly, the assessments are used to identify students who need additional time and support for learning. We will make the case that frequent common formative assessments represent one of the most powerful tools in the PLC arsenal.

The PLC Process Requires a Culture That Is Simultaneously Loose and Tight

The PLC process empowers educators to make important decisions and encourages their creativity and innovation in the pursuit of improving student and adult learning. As you read through this text you will discover that when a school functions as a PLC, teachers collectively make many of the important decisions including:

- What to teach

- The sequencing and pacing of content

- The assessments used to monitor student learning

- The criteria they will use in assessing the quality of student work

- The norms for their team

- The goals for their team

Teachers working in teams have primary responsibility for analyzing evidence of student learning and developing strategies for improvement. Each teacher is free to use the instructional strategies that he or she feels will be most effective in helping students learn. Teachers have the authority to make all of these important decisions because these aspects of the PLC process are said to be "loose."

At the same time, however, there are elements of the PLC process that are "tight," that is, they are nondiscretionary and everyone in the school is required to adhere to those elements. The tight elements of the PLC process are listed in the feature box on page 14.

Tight Elements in a PLC

1. Educators work collaboratively rather than in isolation, take collective responsibility for student learning, and clarify the [com]mitments they make to each other about how they will [work t]ogether.

[The fun]damental structure of the school becomes the collabo[rative te]am in which members work interdependently to achieve [common] goals for which all members are mutually accountable.

[The team] establishes a guaranteed curriculum, unit by unit, [so that stud]ents have access to the same knowledge and skills [regardless] of the teacher to whom they are assigned.

[The team de]velops common formative assessments to frequently [gather evide]nce of student learning.

[The school ha]s created systems of intervention and extension [to ensure stu]dents who struggle receive additional time and [support for lea]rning in a way that is timely, directive, diagnostic, [and systematic] and students who demonstrate proficiency can [extend their l]earning.

[Th]e team uses evidence of student learning to inform and improve the individual and collective practice of its members.

Intervention

The debate that has raged about whether or not school improvement should be top-down and driven by administrative mandates or bottom-up and left to the discretion of individuals or groups of teachers has been resolved. Neither top-down nor bottom-up works. Top-down fails to generate either the deep understanding of or commitment to the improvement initiative that is necessary to sustain it. The laissez-faire bottom-up approach eliminates the press for change and is actually associated with a decrease in student achievement (Marzano & Waters, 2009). High-performing PLCs avoid the too-tight/too-loose trap by engaging educators in an improvement process that empowers them to make decisions at the same time that they demand adherence to core elements of the process (DuFour & Fullan, 2013). We will reference this simultaneously loose and tight culture throughout this book.

The Importance of Effective Communication

The keys to creating a PLC culture that is simultaneously loose and tight are first, getting tight about the right things (see the feature box), and then communicating what is tight clearly, consistently, and unequivocally. Marcus Buckingham (2005) contends that the "one thing" leaders of any organization must know to be effective is the importance of clarity. Powerful communication is simple and succinct, driven by a few key ideas, and is repeated at every opportunity (Collins, 2001; Pfeffer & Sutton, 2000). Leaders must realize, however, that the most important element in communicating is congruency between their actions and their words. It is not essential that leaders are eloquent or clever; it is imperative, however, that they demonstrate consistency between what they say and what they do (Collins & Porras, 1994; Covey, 2006; Erkens & Twadell, 2012; Fullan, 2011; Kanold, 2011; Kouzes & Posner, 1987). When leaders' actions are inconsistent with what they contend are their priorities, those actions overwhelm all other forms of communication (Kotter, 1996).

One of the most effective ways leaders communicate priorities is by what they pay attention to (Kouzes & Posner, 2003; Peters & Austin, 1985). As a leader, how you use your time each day speaks volumes about what you value (Spiller & Power, 2019). Subsequent chapters provide specific examples of leaders communicating what is valued by creating systems and structures to promote priorities, monitoring what is essential, reallocating time, asking the right questions, responding to conflict in strategic ways, and celebrating evidence of collective commitments moving the school closer to its vision.

The need for clear communication is so vital to the PLC process that we present a continuum of effective communication and worksheet at the conclusion of this chapter for your consideration (pages 22–24).

Why Don't We Apply What We Know?

As we have shared our work in support of PLCs with educators from around the world, we have become accustomed to hearing the same response: "This just makes sense." It just makes sense that a school committed to helping all students learn at high levels would focus on learning rather than teaching, would have educators work collaboratively, would ensure students had access to the same curriculum, would assess each student's learning on a timely basis using consistent essential outcomes for proficiency, and would create systematic interventions and extensions that provide students with additional time and support for learning. It just makes sense that we accomplish more working collaboratively than we do working in isolation. It just makes sense that we would assess our effectiveness in helping all students learn on the basis of results—tangible evidence that they have actually learned. It just makes sense! In fact, we have found little overt opposition to the characteristics of a PLC.

So why don't schools *do* what they already *know* makes sense? In *The Knowing-Doing Gap: How Smart Companies Turn Knowledge Into Action*, Jeffrey Pfeffer and Robert Sutton (2000) explore what they regard as one of the great mysteries of organizational management: the disconnect between knowledge and action. They ask, "Why does knowledge of what needs to be done so frequently fail to result in action or behavior that is consistent with that knowledge?" (Pfeffer & Sutton, 2000, p. 4).

Learning by Doing is intended to help educators close the knowing-doing gap by transforming their schools into PLCs. More specifically, it is designed to accomplish the following six objectives.

1. To help educators develop a common vocabulary and a consistent understanding of key PLC processes

2. To present a compelling argument that Canadian educators have a moral imperative to improve their individual and collective practice

Learning by Doing is intended to help educators close the knowing-doing gap by transforming their schools into PLCs.

3. To help Canadian educators assess the current reality in their own schools, regions, and districts

4. To offer tools, templates, protocols, and sample products to help educators on their journey

5. To eliminate excuses for inaction and convince educators that the best way to become more effective in the PLC process is to begin doing what PLCs do

To Help Educators Develop a Common Vocabulary and a Consistent Understanding of Key PLC Processes

Canadian educator Michael Fullan (2005) observes that "terms travel easily . . . but the meaning of the underlying concepts does not" (p. 67). Terms such as *professional learning community*, *collaborative team*, *goal*, *formative assessments*, and scores of others have indeed traveled widely in educational circles. They are prevalent in the lexicon of contemporary "educationese." If pressed for a specific definition, however, many educators would be stumped. It is difficult enough to bring these concepts to life in a school or district when there is a shared understanding of their meaning. It is impossible when there is no common understanding and the terms mean very different things to different people within the same organization.

Developmental psychologists Robert Kegan and Lisa Laskow Lahey (2001) contend that the transformation of both individuals and organizations requires new language. They write, "The places where we work and live are, among other things, places where certain forms of speech are promoted and encouraged, and places where other ways of talking are discouraged or made impossible" (Kegan & Lahey, 2001, p. 7). As educators make the cultural shift from traditional schools and districts to PLCs, a new language emerges. Therefore, we have highlighted and defined key terms used in implementing PLC processes to assist in building shared knowledge of both critical vocabulary and the concepts underlying the terms. We have also included an online glossary at **go.SolutionTree.com/ca/PLCbooks** that readers can freely download and distribute. We hope it will add to the precision and clarity of the emerging language that accompanies the transformation of traditional schools and districts into high-performing PLCs.

We have included an online glossary at go.SolutionTree.com /ca/PLCbooks that readers can freely download and distribute.

To Present a Compelling Argument That Canadian Educators Have a Moral Imperative to Improve Their Individual and Collective Practice

Across a widely varied geography, from sea to sea to sea, Canadian educators work with diverse populations to achieve a common goal—to increase student learning. From fly-in-only northern communities and the small east coast and west coast fishing villages to the shores of the Great Lakes and the busy streets of populated cities, students are learning:

> While there are a great many similarities in the provincial and territorial education systems across Canada, there are significant differences in curriculum, assessment, and accountability policies among the jurisdictions that express the geography, history, language, culture, and corresponding specialized needs of the populations served. The comprehensive, diversified, and widely accessible nature of the education systems in Canada reflects the societal belief in the importance of education. (Council of Ministers of Education, Canada, n.d.)

As stated in the preface, there is no federal department of education in Canada and no integrated national system of education. Thirteen jurisdictions, departments, or ministries of education are establishing policy and setting the stage of the organization, delivery, and assessment of all things education. This filters down to school boards or district education councils who add their unique perspectives to what is going to happen in schools and classrooms.

Canada's education is culturally rich and diversified with French and English school boards as well as Catholic school boards (in six provinces and territories). As a country, Canada is described globally as a *melting pot*, with immigrants from all parts of the world living and studying in Canada. Geographically speaking, Canada is the second largest country in the world, but the population does not spread out evenly across the country. Two of every three Canadians live within 100 km of the border of its southern neighbour, the United States (World Population Review, 2019).

The only federally funded schools in Canada are found within indigenous communities. Indigenous Services Canada (part of the federal government of Canada) provides funding for students who "ordinarily live on reserve, are 4 to 21 years of age, and are enrolled in and attending an eligible elementary or secondary program" (Council of Ministers of Education, Canada, n.d.). The governing of the schools, however, including all decisions around what is taught, how students are assessed and supported, and who teaches in the schools are local community decisions. From the 2016 Canadian Census, we know that more than 1.67 million people in Canada identify themselves as indigenous people. This is the fastest-growing population in Canada, growing by 42.5 percent between 2006 and 2019; the youngest population in Canada, 44 percent, are under the age of twenty-five in 2016 (Statistics Canada, 2016).

How does this all work? Despite the complexity of education in Canada, there is much to celebrate (see OECD, 2014, 2018; Statistics Canada, 2017).

- Every three years, Canadian students participate in the international PISA (Programme for International Student Assessment) assessment. In 2015 (OECD, 2018):
  - Canada ranked fifth in science among the Organisation for Economic Co-operation and Development (OECD) countries, tied

Despite the complexity of education in Canada, there is much to celebrate.

with Finland and surpassed only by Singapore, Japan, and Estonia, according to the report involving 540,000 students from around the world

- ◆ When it comes to mathematics and reading, fifteen-year-old students in Canada also performed well above the OECD average. Only Singapore surpassed Canada in reading

- ◆ Canada was also one of the highest-performing countries when it came to equity between boys and girls

- ◆ Only China outperformed Canada on the Financial Literacy Assessment

- ▪ At the university level, Canada has the world's highest proportion of working-age adults who have been through higher education—55 percent compared with an average in OECD countries of 35 percent.

- ▪ In addition to PISA, every three years, eighth graders across Canada participate in the Pan-Canadian Assessment (PCAP) for reading, mathematics, and science. In 2016, 27,000 students from 1,500 schools participated, and 88 percent of eighth graders were reading at the level expected.

- ▪ More students are graduating than ever before with a rate of 87 percent in 2015.

- ▪ Canada has a higher rate of adults continuing their education than other OECD countries (58 percent compared to 50 percent).

- ▪ Indigenous Services Canada is implementing programs and services to transform and improve the quality of teaching and outcomes for students in Canadian on-reserve schools.

- ▪ Every province or territory provides kindergarten programs, whether full-day or half-day, mandatory, or voluntary. Eight provide full-day kindergarten for all five-year-olds (Newfoundland, Prince Edward Island, Nova Scotia, New Brunswick, Quebec, Ontario, British Columbia, and the Northwest Territories).

- ▪ Provincial and territorial governments are increasingly moving to support inclusive education to ensure how we develop and design our schools, classrooms, programs, and activities allow all students to learn together (see Inclusive Education Canada, 2017).

- ▪ Canada has a high level of migrants in the school population with more than one-third of students in Canada from families where both parents are from another country. These children integrate rapidly enough and perform at the same high level as their classmates.

Andreas Schleicher, the OECD's education director, says Canada's "big uniting theme is equity" (as cited in Marchildon, 2017). Despite the different policies in individual provinces, there is a common commitment to an equal chance in school.

Despite Canada's lack of a federal system, the thirteen jurisdictions are united in providing a more equitable system than seen in many countries. The variation in scores caused by socioeconomic differences is only 9 percent in Canada. For comparison, it is 17 percent in Singapore and 20 percent in France (see figure 1.1 in OECD, 2012). This is another example of how the concept of equity in education positively affects Canada's scores. The country as a whole does not have the same underachievement issues poverty often causes (Coughlan, 2017; OECD, 2012).

Canadian educators are accomplishing a great deal with a more diverse population than any previous generation. They warrant respect. However, they also must recognize that the need to help every student succeed in school has never been greater: the consequences of failure in the K–12 system have never been more dire. Consider the implications for students who are unsuccessful in the K–12 system.

Canadian educators are accomplishing a great deal with a more diverse population than any previous generation.

- Students who fail school are three times more likely to be unemployed (Breslow, 2012).

- These students are more likely to live in poverty, earning an annual salary of $20,241 or less (Breslow, 2012).

- Nearly 1.2 million Canadian children younger than the age of eighteen now live in poverty (Statistics Canada, 2017).

- High school dropouts in Canada earn 80 percent of what a graduate earns (Conference Board of Canada, 2019).

- Female dropouts will live an average of ten and a half fewer years than females who graduate from high school. Male dropouts will live an average of thirteen fewer years than males who graduate from high school. The gap for both sexes is widening (Tavernise, 2012).

- High school dropouts are sixty-three times more likely to be incarcerated (Breslow, 2012).

- On average, each high school dropout costs taxpayers $292,000 over his or her lifetime (Breslow, 2012).

- The average age of young Canadians (age twenty to twenty-four) who continue studying or go to work is about the same (43 percent versus 44 percent), and 13 percent are neither employed nor in school (Statistics Canada, 2017).

- Canada's average for completing a university education for twenty-five- to sixty-four-year-olds was 31 percent, a rate just above the OECD figure at 29 percent (Statistics Canada, 2017).

- Forty-percent of indigenous people in Canada, between the ages of twenty to twenty-four, do not have high school diplomas compared to 13 percent of nonindigenous people of the same age (Statistics Canada, 2013).

Considering these statistics, we know that educators must view every student as if he or she were their own child and provide the same education they would want for their own (DuFour, 2015). In Canada and other OECD countries, employment prospects increase with educational attainment. In 2016, Canada's employment rate for adults ages twenty-five to sixty-four who had not completed a high school diploma was 58 percent. In Canada, as well as in other OECD countries overall, the 2015 employment rates among people ages twenty-five to sixty-four years old were clearly highest among individuals who had a college or university credential (Statistics Canada, 2019).

To Help Canadian Educators Assess the Current Reality in Their Own Schools, Regions, and Districts

A key step in any effective improvement process is an honest assessment of the current reality—a diligent effort to determine the truth.

For many educators, however, school improvement initiatives have been plagued by uncertainty and confusion regarding both the current status of their school and what they hope it will become. As a result, efforts to reform their schools have too often been characterized by random stops and starts, rather than by purposeful progression on a path of improvement. A key step in any effective improvement process is an honest assessment of the current reality—a diligent effort to determine the truth. Educators will find it easier to move forward to where they want to go if they first agree on where they are.

Even when teachers and administrators make a good faith effort to assess their schools, they face significant obstacles. All schools have cultures: the assumptions, beliefs, expectations, and habits that constitute the norm for a school and guide the work of the educators within it. Perhaps it is more accurate, however, to say that educators *do not* have school cultures, but rather that the school cultures have *them*. Teachers and administrators are typically so immersed in their traditional ways of doing things that they find it difficult to step outside of those traditions to examine conventional practices from a fresh, critical perspective. Therefore, this handbook, and particularly the continua presented throughout, are designed not only to offer specific examples of PLC practices but also to help educators make a frank and honest assessment of current conditions in their schools.

To Offer Tools, Templates, Protocols, and Sample Products to Help Educators on Their Journey

As we have worked in our own schools and assisted many hundreds of others, we have found that providing the right tools, templates, protocols, and sample products can help make the complex simpler and increase the self-efficacy of educators. We have attempted to gather these useful instruments in one place so that readers can access what they need at different points in the process. We hope that they are helpful, but they are not carved in stone. Feel free to adapt and modify them to make them fit your unique situations.

To Eliminate Excuses for Inaction and Convince Educators That the Best Way to Become More Effective in the PLC Process Is to Begin Doing What PLCs Do

Our greatest hope in developing this handbook is that it will help educators take immediate and specific steps to close the knowing-doing gap in education by implementing the PLC processes in their own schools and districts. There has never been greater consensus regarding what educators can do to improve their schools. As a profession we know with certainty that more students learn at higher levels when their schools are committed to high levels of learning for each student; when educators have worked collaboratively to clarify the knowledge, skills, and dispositions students are to acquire as a result of each unit, course, and grade level; when student learning is monitored on an ongoing basis; when the school has a systematic process for providing students with extra time and support when they struggle and extended learning when they are proficient; and when educators work together to use transparent evidence of student learning to inform and improve their individual and collective practice. Conversely, there is simply no credible evidence that schools are more effective when educators work in isolation and the questions of what students learn, how they are assessed, and what happens when they struggle are left to the randomness of the individual teacher to whom they have been assigned.

Our greatest hope in developing this handbook is that it will help educators take immediate and specific steps to close the knowing-doing gap.

When professionals know better, they have an obligation to do better. Our profession now clearly knows better. The weight of the evidence from research, our professional organizations, high-performing districts and schools, and common sense have made it clear that schools are more effective when they operate as PLCs. It is time for educators to act on what they know. The question confronting most schools and districts is not, "What do we need to know in order to improve?" but rather, "Will we turn what we already know into action?"

When professionals know better, they have an obligation to do better.

Perhaps the greatest insight we have gained in our work with school districts in Canada, the United States, and throughout the world is that organizations that take the plunge and actually begin *doing* the work of a PLC develop their capacity to help all students learn at high levels far more effectively than schools that spend years *preparing* to become PLCs through reading or even training. Canadian author and educator Michael Fullan along with his coauthor Joanne Quinn, who has studied school improvement efforts from around the world, came to a similar conclusion. He argues that educators must move quickly from conversations about mission and vision to action because "it is learning by purposeful doing that counts most" (Fullan & Quinn, 2016, p. 21).

This book is not meant to be a study guide: it is emphatically an action guide. Developing the collective capacity of educators to create high-performing PLCs demands more than book studies and workshops. It demands "the daily habit of *working together*, and you can't learn this from a workshop or course. You need to learn by doing it and having mechanisms for getting better at it on purpose" (Fullan, 2005, p. 69). So let's examine some of the challenges of working together and consider mechanisms for getting better at it.

The Professional Learning Communities at Work® Continuum: Communicating Effectively

DIRECTIONS: Individually, silently, and *honestly* assess the current reality of your school's implementation of each indicator listed in the left column. Consider what evidence or anecdotes support your assessment. This form may also be used to assess district or team implementation.

We understand the purpose and priorities of our school because they have been communicated consistently and effectively.

Indicator	Pre-Initiating	Initiating	Implementing	Developing	Sustaining
The school has established a clear purpose and priorities that have been effectively communicated. Systems are in place to ensure action steps aligned with the purpose and priorities are implemented and monitored.	There is no sense of purpose or priorities. People throughout the school feel swamped by what they regard as a never-ending series of fragmented, disjointed, and short-lived improvement initiatives. Changes in leadership inevitably result in changes in direction.	Key leaders may have reached agreement on general purpose and priorities, but people throughout the organization remain unclear. Furthermore, if asked to explain the priorities of the school or the strategies to achieve those priorities, leaders would have difficulty articulating specifics. Staff members would offer very different answers if pressed to explain the priorities of the school.	There is general understanding of the purpose and priorities of the school, but many staff members have not embraced them. Specific steps are being taken to advance the priorities, but some staff members are participating only grudgingly. They view the initiative as interfering with their real work.	Structures and processes have been altered to align with the purpose and priorities. Staff members are beginning to see benefits from the initiative and are seeking ways to become more effective in implementing it.	There is almost universal understanding of the purpose and priorities of the school. All policies, procedures, and structures have been purposefully aligned with the effort to fulfill the purpose and accomplish the priorities. Systems have been created to gauge progress. The systems are carefully monitored, and the resulting information is used to make adjustments designed to build the collective capacity of the group to be successful.

page 1 of 3

Indicator	Pre-Initiating	Initiating	Implementing	Developing	Sustaining
The leaders in the school communicate purpose and priorities through modeling, allocation of resources, what they celebrate, and what they are willing to confront.	There is no sense of purpose and priorities. Different people in the school seem to have different pet projects, and there is considerable in-fighting to acquire the resources to support those different projects.	Leaders can articulate the purpose and priorities of the school with a consistent voice, but their behaviour is not congruent with their words. The structures, resources, and rewards of the school have not been altered to align with the professed priorities.	The school has begun to alter the structures, resources, and rewards to better align with the stated priorities. Staff members who openly oppose the initiative may be confronted, but those confronting them are likely to explain they are doing someone else's bidding. For example, a principal may say, "The central office is concerned that you are overtly resisting the process we are attempting to implement."	People throughout the school are changing their behaviour to align with the priorities. They are seeking new strategies for using resources more effectively to support the initiative, and are willing to reallocate time, money, materials, and people in order to move forward. Small improvements are recognized and celebrated. Leaders confront incongruent behaviour.	The purpose and priorities of the school are evident by the everyday behaviour of people throughout the school. Time, money, materials, people, and resources have been strategically allocated to reflect priorities. Processes are in place to recognize and celebrate commitment to the priorities. People throughout the school will confront those who disregard the priorities.

Where Do We Go From Here? Worksheet
Communicating Effectively

Indicator of a PLC at Work	What steps or activities must be initiated to create this condition in your school?	Who will be responsible for initiating or sustaining these steps or activities?	What is a realistic timeline for each step or phase of the activity?	What will you use to assess the effectiveness of your initiative?
The school has established a clear purpose and priorities that have been effectively communicated. Systems are in place to ensure action steps aligned with the purpose and priorities are implemented and monitored.				
The leaders in the school communicate purpose and priorities through modeling, allocation of resources, what they celebrate, and what they are willing to confront.				

Learning by Doing © 2020 Solution Tree Press • SolutionTree.com
Visit **go.SolutionTree.com/ca/PLCbooks** to download this free reproducible.

CHAPTER 2
Defining a Clear and Compelling Purpose

Part One

The Case Study: Clarifying Our Purpose

Elizabeth Nowlan woke up with a start from her dream (or, more accurately, her nightmare). It was her first day of school as a principal. They were finally ready to open the brand-new Maplehurst Middle School in Moncton, New Brunswick. In her nightmare, Principal Nowlan had assembled the entire staff to share both her enthusiasm for the three big ideas of a PLC (a focus on learning, a collaborative culture and collective responsibility, and a results orientation) and her plans for bringing the concept to the school. She told the staff that she wanted to develop a mission statement that captured the focus of the school. She presented the following draft to the staff and invited their reaction.

It is our mission to ensure all our students acquire the knowledge and skills essential to achieving their full potential and becoming productive citizens.

As soon as Principal Nowlan finished talking, a teacher challenged the statement. He argued that the mission statement should acknowledge that the extent of student learning was dependent on the student's ability and effort. Another teacher jumped in and added that the word *ensuring* would place too much accountability on the teachers and not enough on the students. Before she knew it, several support staff were chiming in to say that there was too much focus on academics. In order to keep peace at the meeting, Principal Nowlan invited the staff to come up with a new mission statement. Here is what they presented to her:

It is our mission to give each student the opportunity to learn according to his or her ability and to create a school that is attentive to the emotional needs of every student.

Principal Nowlan expressed concern that the statement did not convey a commitment to helping all students learn; instead it merely promised to give them a *chance* to learn.

This led to a discussion that revealed significant differences of opinion, and it was obvious to her that she was not going to convince the staff that her concerns were valid. She asked the staff to vote on which mission statement they liked; she went with the majority vote, which was to accept the teacher-created statement.

As the days turned to weeks, she saw that staff were not buying in to deep implementation of PLC practices. She became increasingly disenchanted with the whole PLC process. After all, she had engaged the staff in clarifying the mission of the school, just as she had been advised to do at the PLC at Work Institute. There was virtually no evidence, however, that this new mission had impacted either teacher practice or student achievement. Her new school was not becoming the school that she envisioned, so she resolved to find another school improvement model.

Now awake in her bed, she promised herself she would not let this nightmare become a reality. She would apply everything that she learned at PLC at Work Institutes and in her reading. In the months leading up to her dream, Principal Nowlan had been busy getting ready for the opening. She hired two great vice principals and they held focus groups with parents and teachers and started to prepare for the opening. Her teachers had mostly come from the two K–8 schools that were now becoming K–5 schools. Her school would be the middle school for both of these schools. Principal Nowlan and her administrative team had done lots of thinking and planning about how to merge these staffs and create a school.

Reflection

Consider Principal Nowlan's nightmare and the way that she went about developing a clear and compelling purpose for the school and her staff. What advice would you give her and her administrative team if you were called on to mentor them as they were beginning to initiate this process with staff?

Part Two

Here's How

In her nightmare, despite her good intentions and initial enthusiasm, Principal Nowlan struggled with two significant factors that adversely impacted her efforts.

1. The process she utilized in attempting to build consensus

2. Her failure to move the dialogue beyond the philosophical debate about the mission of the school to the specific actions needed to move it forward

How would leaders of a high-performing PLC work to build consensus, and what steps would they take to move from dialogue to action?

Create a Guiding Coalition

Those who hope to lead the PLC process must begin by acknowledging that no one person will have the energy, expertise, and influence to lead a complex change process until it becomes anchored in the organization's culture without first gaining the support of key staff members. Robert Marzano, Timothy Waters, and Brian McNulty (2005) refer to this group as the "leadership team." John Kotter (2012) describes them as the "guiding coalition," and Jim Collins (2001) simply reminds leaders that they must first "get the right people on the bus." Although the terminology may vary, according to the Wallace Foundation (2012):

> A broad and longstanding consensus in leadership theory holds that leaders in all walks of life and all kinds of organizations, public and private, need to depend on others to accomplish the group's purpose and need to encourage the development of leadership across the organization. (pp. 6–7)

Principal Nowlan made a mistake in thinking she was personally responsible for selling the faculty on her version of a new mission statement. If a mission is to be truly shared, it must be co-created, not sold, and co-creation requires a process that fully engages others. Before bringing the issue to the full faculty, Principal Nowlan would want to have first worked at developing a small cadre of staff members to serve as her guiding coalition. She should have selected members on the basis of their influence with their peers. Kerry Patterson, Joseph Grenny, David Maxfield, Ron McMillan, and Al Switzler (2008) find that, in most organizations, who supports an idea is typically more important than the quality of the idea itself. Roughly 15 percent of the members of an organization are the "opinion leaders"—people who are so knowledgeable, respected, and trustworthy that their position has a major influence on the rest of the group. Principal Nowlan and her administrative team will want to organize this guiding coalition, work through the issues with its members, build consensus among them that the school's mission must commit to ensuring learning for all, and secure them as allies of and champions for the new mission. Then, there will be a much greater likelihood of winning the faculty's support. The bottom line for principals is this: if you can't persuade a small group of people of the merits of an idea and enlist their help, there is little chance you will persuade the larger group.

If a mission is to be truly shared, it must be co-created, not sold, and co-creation requires a process that fully engages others.

Choose the Right Forum

As we see in the nightmare, in presenting the proposal to the entire staff at one time, Principal Nowlan used a forum—a large group—that was ill suited to the dialogue that facilitates consensus. Most people will have questions when significant change is proposed, and they will want those questions answered before they are willing to give their consent for moving forward. The large-group forum she used in the case study allowed those skeptical of the proposal to dominate the discussion before the idea had been fully considered. A more intimate venue with a small number of staff would have been more effective. Principal Nowlan might ask teachers to meet with her or representatives of the guiding coalition in small groups during a preparation period to engage in this dialogue, particularly if she is willing to cancel an after-school faculty meeting to compensate teachers for their lost time. She might hire enough substitute teachers to free small groups of teachers to meet with her during the school day. As we see, efforts to build support for her idea through a presentation is unlikely to succeed. Building consensus requires conversations not presentations, dialogue not monologue.

Build Shared Knowledge

A cardinal rule of decision making in a professional learning community is that prior to making a decision, people must first build shared knowledge, that is, they must learn together.

The biggest process mistake represented in Principal Nowlan's nightmare was her failure to build shared knowledge among the staff. Although she had apparently learned of concepts and strategies at a PLC at Work Institute and had read books like this one that convinced her of the benefits of a PLC, she did nothing to share that learning with her colleagues in the school. A cardinal rule of decision making in a professional *learning* community is that prior to making a decision, people must first build shared knowledge, that is, they must *learn together*. When all staff members have access to the same information, it increases the likelihood that they will arrive at similar conclusions. Conversely, if uniformed people are asked to make decisions, they will make uninformed decisions. Without access to pertinent information, they resort to debating opinions or retreating to a muddied middle ground.

Working with her guiding coalition, Principal Nowlan and her administrative team might present information to help the staff assess the current reality of the school. For example, she could have presented data to help paint a picture of the school's current reality. In this case, they would gather data from their feeder schools, where the students and staff are coming from. The data picture worksheet (see the reproducible, "A Data Picture of Our School") assists in the gathering and presentation of information to help clarify the existing conditions of the school. Anecdotes and stories about students who were not being successful could also have helped establish what the school experience was like for some students.

In addition, the coalition can present staff with a synthesis of research on characteristics of high-performing schools such as PLCs, clear academic goals for every student, ongoing monitoring of student learning, systematic interventions, and high expectations for student achievement to support the premise that schools are most effective when staff members define their purpose as helping students learn rather than ensuring they are taught. The staff might hear testimonials from other schools that had adopted PLC processes or conducted site visits to see a PLC in action. All this information will help frame a moral imperative by providing a picture of what happens when students do not succeed in the K–12 system, and by challenging the staff to consider if these outcomes would be acceptable for the students in both their personal and professional lives. Time spent up front building shared knowledge results in faster, more effective, and most importantly, more committed action later in the improvement process (Patterson, Grenny, McMillan, & Switzler, 2002).

Arrive at Consensus on Consensus

Principal Nowlan wants to build consensus for a new mission statement. In our work with schools, however, we have found that most schools do not have consensus

A Data Picture of Our School

School Name:

page 1 of 3

Student Achievement Results

Indicator	Year 20__–20__	Year 20__–20__	Year 20__–20__	Facts About Our Data
Based on Our School Assessment Data				
Based on Our District Assessment Data				
Based on Our Provincial or Territorial Assessment Data				
Based on Our National Assessment Data				

Student Engagement Data

Indicator	Year 20__–20__	Year 20__–20__	Year 20__–20__	Facts About Our Data
Average Daily Attendance				
Percentage of Students in Extracurricular Activities				
Percentage of Students Using School's Tutoring Services				
Percentage of Students Enrolled in Most Rigorous Courses Offered				
Percentage of Students Graduating Without Retention				
Percentage of Students Who Drop Out of School				

A Data Picture of Our School

Student Engagement Data (continued)

Indicator	Year 20__-20__	Year 20__-20__	Year 20__-20__	Facts About Our Data
Other Areas in Which We Hope to Engage Students, Such as Community Service				

Discipline

Indicator				
Number of Referrals / Top-Three Reasons for Referrals				
Number of Parent Conferences Regarding Discipline				
Number of In-School Suspensions				
Number of Detentions / Saturday School				
Number of Out-of-School Suspensions				
Number of Expulsions				
Other				

Survey Data

Indicator				
Student Satisfaction or Perception Assessment				
Alumni Satisfaction or Perception Assessment				

A Data Picture of Our School

Survey Data (continued)

Indicator	Year 20__-20__	Year 20__-20__	Year 20__-20__	Facts About Our Data
Parent Satisfaction or Perception Assessment				
Teacher Satisfaction or Perception Assessment				
Administration Satisfaction or Perception Assessment				
Community Satisfaction or Perception Assessment				

Demographic Data

Percent Free and Reduced Lunch				
Percent Mobility				
Percent Special Education				
Percent English as a Second Language				
Percent White (Not of Hispanic Origin)				
Percent Black				
Percent Hispanic				
Percent Asian				
Percent Native American				

page 3 of 3

on when they have consensus. We ask a straightforward question: "How do you define *consensus* when your staff considers a proposal?" The responses we hear vary greatly within the same school. We have established a continuum of consensus based on the typical responses. Consider the following continuum, and select the point at which you feel you have reached agreement on a proposal in your own school.

We have arrived at consensus in our school when we meet five criteria.

1. All of us can embrace the proposal.

2. All of us can endorse the proposal.

3. All of us can live with the proposal.

4. All of us can agree not to sabotage the proposal.

5. We have a majority—at least 51 percent—in support of the proposal.

The most common outcome of this survey is a staff distributed all along the continuum because members do not have consensus on the definition of consensus. Disagreements and allegations are inevitable when a faculty does not understand the criteria that must be met in order to make a collective decision.

We advise staffs to reject all points on the five-point continuum we just presented. In our view, it is difficult to maintain that you have the consent of the group to move forward with a simple majority—a criterion that can disregard the perspective of 49 percent of the group. On the other hand, every other point on the continuum goes beyond consensus when it calls for "all of us" to reach a level of agreement. While it is wonderful to strive for unanimity, there is a difference between unanimity and consensus. In the real world of schools, if all of us must agree before we can act, if any staff member can veto taking action, we will be subjected to constant inaction, a state of perpetual status quo.

A group has arrived at consensus when it meets two criteria.

The definition of consensus that we prefer establishes two simple criteria that must be met in order to move forward when a decision is made. A group has arrived at consensus when it meets two criteria.

1. All points of view have not merely been heard, but have been actively solicited.

2. The will of the group is evident *even to those who most oppose it.*

This definition can, and typically does, result in moving forward with a proposal despite the fact that some members of the organization are against it. However, as Patrick Lencioni (2005) writes, "Waiting for everyone to agree intellectually on a decision is a good recipe for mediocrity, delay, and frustration" (p. 51). An insistence on unanimity conflicts with the action orientation of a PLC.

If the criteria for consensus we recommend had been applied in the case study, Principal Nowlan and a guiding coalition could have engaged in small-group dialogues to address concerns. At some point, however, they would have also presented a specific proposal such as the following:

It is our mission to ensure all our students acquire the knowledge and skills essential to achieving their full potential and becoming productive citizens.

Each small group would then be *randomly* divided into two groups. The first would be asked to work together to create a comprehensive list of all the reasons the faculty should oppose the proposal. The second group would be called on to create a comprehensive list of all the reasons the staff should support the proposal. At this point, personal feelings about the proposal do not come into play. Each staff member is to engage in an intellectual exercise to list all the possible pros and cons regarding the specific idea under consideration.

In the next step of the process, the first group presents all the reasons members listed to oppose the suggestion. Members of the second group are asked to listen attentively until the opposed group has completed its list, and then they are invited to add to that list with other objections that might not have been identified. The process is then repeated with the proponent group announcing its comprehensive list in support of the decision, and the group responsible for listing objections is invited to add to it. If done correctly, no one will know where any staff member stands on the issue personally, but all points of view have now been heard.

The next step is to determine the will of the group. A quick and simple way to do so is to use the *fist to five* strategy. Once everyone is clear on the proposal, and all pros and cons have been offered, each person is asked to indicate a level of support, as shown in the feature box.

A quick and simple way to determine the will of the group is to use the **fist to five** *strategy.*

Fist to Five Strategy

- **Five fingers:** I love this proposal. I will champion it.
- **Four fingers:** I strongly agree with the proposal.
- **Three fingers:** The proposal is okay with me. I am willing to go along.
- **Two fingers:** I have reservations and am not yet ready to support this proposal.
- **One finger:** I am opposed to this proposal.
- **Fist:** If I had the authority, I would veto this proposal, regardless of the will of the group.

The facilitator for the process ensures that everyone understands the issue under consideration and how to express themselves through fist to five. All members of the small group are then asked to express their position simultaneously by raising their hands with the number of fingers best expressing their level of support. Each participant is then able to look around the room to ascertain the support for the proposal. If participants do not support the proposal, or the vote is too close to determine the will of the group at a glance, the proposal does not go forward. Pilot projects may be run, more time can be taken to build shared knowledge, and in time the proposal may be presented again; however, if support is not readily apparent, the criteria of consensus has not been met.

If, however, it is evident by looking around the room that it is the will of the group to move forward (the number of hands with three, four, and five fingers clearly outnumbers those with two, one, and fists), consensus has been reached, and all staff members will be expected to honour the decision.

There are certainly variations on this format. For example, if the technology is available, staff could vote anonymously and have the tally reported instantly. If there are concerns about intimidation, an anonymous paper vote may be necessary as long as the process for counting the votes is accepted as fair by all concerned. It may be prudent to have the teacher professional organization appoint a representative to attend all of the meetings in case concerns emerge about the accuracy of the reporting. But while the format may vary, one thing does not: decision making is easier, more effective, and less likely to end in disputes about process when a staff has a clear operational definition of consensus.

Live Your Mission

The words of a mission statement are not worth the paper they are written on unless people begin to do differently.

As we see in the nightmare, the biggest mistake Principal Nowlan and her staff made was confusing *writing* a mission statement with *living* a mission. No school has ever improved simply because the staff wrote a mission statement. In fact, we have found no correlation between the presence of a written mission statement, or even the wording of a mission statement, and a school's effectiveness as a PLC. The words of a mission statement are not worth the paper they are written on unless people begin to *do* differently.

What can Principal Nowlan and her guiding coalition do to bring the mission to life in their school? First, after engaging staff in building shared knowledge on the specific practices and characteristics of schools where all students were learning at high levels, she might ask them to describe in vivid detail the school they hoped to create. Once the staff could describe that school, the principal and her guiding coalition would lead the staff in a discussion of the specific commitments each member would need to honour in order to become the school they had envisioned. Principal Nowlan and her administrative team will want to model a willingness to make commitments by identifying the specific things they are prepared to do to support the effort to transform the school. She can share her commitments with the staff and ask for their reactions, revisions, and additions. Members of the guiding coalition can then lead the staff in a process to clarify their collective commitments.

Principal Nowlan might also ask the faculty to identify the indicators that should be monitored to assess the progress they will make in creating their agreed-on school. They can establish benchmarks for what they hope to achieve in the first six months, the first year, and the first three years. Each teacher team can be asked to establish specific team goals that, if accomplished, will contribute to achieving schoolwide goals and to moving the school toward the ideal the staff had described.

Of course, all of this dialogue will impact the school only if purposeful steps are taken to demonstrate that they have created the school of their hopes, honoured their commitments, and are achieving their goals through the collective responsibility of every staff member. How is that message best communicated? The most powerful communication is not a function of what is written or said, but rather, once again, what is *done*. As James Autry (2001), author of *The Servant Leader*, wrote:

> Those around you in the workplace—colleagues and employees—
> can determine who you are only by observing what you do. . . .
> the only way you can manifest your character, your personhood,
> and your spirit in the workplace is through your behavior. (p. 1)

Or to paraphrase Ralph Waldo Emerson, what you do stands over you all the while and thunders so loudly that we cannot hear what you say.

Consider seven specific actions the principal and staff might have taken to convey their commitment to improving their school.

1. **Initiating structures and systems to foster qualities and characteristics consistent with a learning-centred school:** When something is truly a priority in an organization, people do not hope it happens; they develop and implement systematic plans to ensure that it happens. For example, if the leadership team was committed to creating a collaborative culture, they could take steps to organize teachers into teams, build time for collaboration into the contractual workday, develop protocols and parameters to guide the work of teams, and so on. True priorities are not left to chance but are carefully and systematically addressed.

2. **Creating processes to monitor critical conditions and important goals:** In most organizations, what gets monitored gets done. A critical step in moving an organization from rhetoric to reality is to establish the indicators of progress to be monitored, the process and timeline for monitoring them, and the means of sharing results with and getting input from people throughout the organization. For example, if the staff agreed student learning was the priority in their school, creating procedures to monitor each student's learning on a timely and systematic basis would be imperative.

3. **Reallocating resources to support the proclaimed priorities:** Marshall McLuhan (1994) observes, "Money talks because money is a metaphor" (p. 136). The actual legal tender may have little intrinsic value, but how it is expended, particularly in times of scarcity, reveals a great deal about what is valued. Money, however, is not the only significant resource in an organization, and in contemporary public education, time is even scarcer than money. Providing teachers with time to collaborate and students who are struggling with additional time and support for learning are prerequisite conditions for a PLC (Battelle for Kids, 2015; Farbman, Goldberg, & Miller, 2014; Fulton & Britton, 2011; NGA & CCSSO, 2008; Robinson, 2010; Tucker, 2014).

    Decisions about the spending of precious resources are some of the most unequivocal ways organizations communicate what is important. If Principal Nowlan and the guiding coalition create a schedule that provides teachers with time to collaborate and students with time for additional support for learning when they experienced difficulty, they will send the message that teacher collaboration and student learning are viewed as priorities in the school.

The questions an organization poses—and the effort and energy spent in the pursuit of answers— not only communicate priorities but also turn members in a particular direction.

4. **Posing the right questions:** The questions an organization poses—and the effort and energy spent in the pursuit of answers—not only communicate priorities but also turn members in a particular direction. In too many schools the prevalent question is, "What is wrong with these students?"—a question that typically has little impact on improving student achievement. Principal Nowlan and her staff can convey their commitment to student learning by devoting time to the pursuit of the four critical questions of the PLC process.

    a. What knowledge, skills, and dispositions should every student acquire as a result of this unit, this course, or this grade level?

    b. How will we know when each student has acquired the essential knowledge and skills?

    c. How will we respond when some students do not learn?

    d. How will we extend the learning for students who are already proficient?

5. **Modeling what is valued:** Example is still the most powerful teacher. If Principal Nowlan and her administrative team hope the staff will make a commitment to high levels of learning for all students, they must demonstrate their own commitment by focusing on learning with laser-like intensity and keeping the issue constantly before the faculty. If they hope to build a culture in which teachers collaborate, they must engage the staff in collaborative decision making and provide the time and support essential for effective collaboration. As one study concluded, "The single most powerful mechanism for creating a learning environment is that the leadership of the organization be willing to model the approach to learning they want others to embrace" (Thompson, 1995, p. 96).

6. **Celebrating progress:** When an organization makes a concerted effort to call attention to and celebrate progress toward its goals, the commitments members demonstrate in day-to-day work, and evidence of improved results, people within the organization are continually reminded of the priorities and what it takes to achieve them. Furthermore, this celebration provides real-life models by which they can assess their own efforts and commitment. If Principal Nowlan uses every opportunity to publicly celebrate positive, forward steps on the journey of school improvement, the faculty will soon learn what was noted, appreciated, and valued in their school.

7. **Confronting violations of commitments:** If Principal Nowlan hopes to convey what is important and valued, she must be prepared to confront those who act in ways that are contrary to the priorities of the school and

the commitments of the staff. Leaders who are unwilling to promote and defend improvement initiatives put those initiatives at risk. A leader of the PLC process cannot verbally commit to a school mission of learning for all but then allow individuals within the organization to act in ways that are counterproductive to this commitment. Not only will allowing these actions negatively impact student learning, but staff members that supported the new school mission will become skeptical because the school leadership is hedging on their commitment. We will address both celebration and confrontation more fully in chapter 9 (page 191).

A leader of the PLC process cannot verbally commit to a school mission of learning for all but then allow individuals within the organization to act in ways that are counterproductive to this commitment.

Part Three

Here's Why

Engaging members of an organization in reflective dialogue about the fundamental purpose of the organization, as Principal Nowlan attempted to do in her dream, can be a powerful strategy for improvement. In fact, the first question any organization must consider if it hopes to improve results is the question of purpose (Drucker, 1992). Why does our organization exist? What are we here to do together? What exactly do we hope to accomplish? What is the business of our business (American Society for Quality, n.d.; Champy, 1995; Senge et al., 1994)?

Research on effective organizations, effective leadership, and effective schools all support the idea that a shared sense of purpose is key to high performance. See "Why Should We Clarify Our Mission?" on page 38 for what the research says about shared purpose.

To close that gap, educators must move beyond writing mission statements to first clarifying the vision, values (that is, collective commitments), and goals that drive the daily workings of the school, and second, align all their practices accordingly.

The Foundation of a PLC

Imagine that the foundation of a PLC rests on the four pillars of mission, vision, values, and goals (see the graphic on page 39). Each of these pillars asks a different question of the educators within the school. When teachers and administrators have worked together to consider those questions and reach consensus regarding their collective positions on each question, they have built a solid foundation for a PLC. Much work remains to be done, for these are just a few of the thousands of steps that must be taken in the never-ending process of continuous improvement. But addressing these questions increases the likelihood that all subsequent work will have the benefit of firm underpinnings. If staff members have not considered the questions, have done so only superficially, or are unable to establish common ground regarding their positions on the questions, any and all future efforts to improve the school will stand on shaky ground.

The foundation of a PLC rests on the four pillars of mission, vision, values, and goals.

Why Should We Clarify Our Mission?

"There is no point in thinking about changes in structure until the school achieves reasonable consensus about its intellectual mission for children" (Newmann & Wehlage, 1996, p. 295).

"Members of great organizations think they are 'on a mission from God. . . . [They] always believe that they are doing something vital, even holy . . . something worthy of their best selves. . . . Their clear collective purpose makes everything they do seem meaningful and valuable'" (Bennis & Biederman, 1997, p. 204).

"In the effective school, there is a clearly articulated mission of the school through which the staff shares an understanding of and a commitment to the school's goals, priorities, assessment procedures, and accountability. . . . The issue of mission is one that must receive substantial discussion" (Lezotte, 2002, pp. 4–5).

"Contrary to popular wisdom, the proper first response to a changing world is NOT to ask, 'How should we change,' but rather, 'What do we stand for and why do we exist?' This should never change. And then feel free to change everything else. Put another way, visionary companies distinguish between their core values and enduring purpose (which should never change) from their operating practices and business strategies (which should be changing constantly in response to an ever-changing world)" (Collins & Porras, 1994, p. xiv).

The Wallace Foundation study of effective district leadership found that district offices that had a positive influence on schools and student achievement established clear purpose that was widely shared (Leithwood et al., 2009).

"The most deeply motivated people—not to mention those that are most productive and satisfied—hitch their desires to a cause larger than themselves. . . . Nothing bonds a team like a shared mission. The more people that share a common cause . . . the more your group will do deeply satisfying and outstanding work" (Pink, 2011, pp. 131, 174)

Research examining successful schools reveals that they share the characteristics of modern high-performance workplaces that foster cultures built on teamwork and shared mission (Anrig, 2013).

A "persuasive and valuable" mission statement "gives people a context for their" actions and empowers them "to support one another's efforts" and fully engage their talents and imagination (Halvorson, 2014, p. 38).

"Leaders need the ability to develop a shared moral purpose and meaning as well as a pathway for attaining that purpose. . . . Great leaders connect others to the reasons they became educators—their moral purpose" (Fullan & Quinn, 2016, p. 17).

Educators who believe that merely clarifying or reaffirming their mission will somehow improve results are certain to be disappointed. In fact, in many schools, developing a mission statement has served as a substitute, rather than a catalyst, for meaningful action. Merely drafting a new mission statement does not automatically change how people act, and therefore writing a mission statement does nothing to close the knowing-doing gap (Pfeffer & Sutton, 2000).

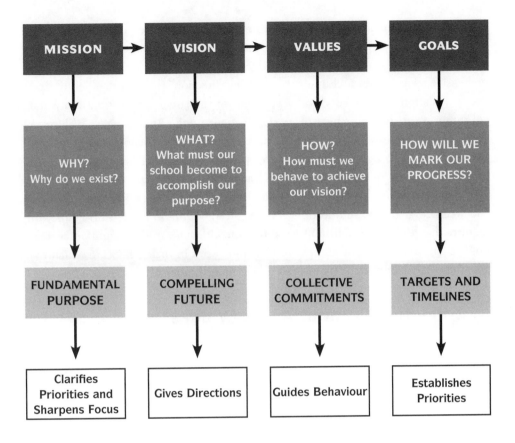

Mission

As we have stressed, the mission pillar asks the question, "Why?" More specifically, it asks, "Why do we exist?" The intent of this question is to help reach agreement regarding the fundamental purpose of the school. This clarity of purpose can help establish priorities and becomes an important factor in guiding decisions. In a learning-centred school ensuring that all students learn must be at the heart of its mission.

"Why do we exist?"

Vision

The vision pillar asks "What?"—that is, "What must we become in order to accomplish our fundamental purpose?" In pursuing this question, a staff attempts to create a compelling, attractive, realistic future that describes what they hope their school will become. Vision provides a sense of direction and a basis for assessing both the current reality of the school and potential strategies, programs, and procedures to improve on that reality. Equally important, a clear vision statement can lead to the creation of a "stop doing" list, comprised of the current school policies and procedures that are misaligned to ensuring higher levels of student learning. Researchers within and outside of education routinely cite the importance of developing shared vision. (See page 41, "Why Should We Describe the School or District We Are Trying to Create?") The conclusion of Burt Nanus (1992) is typical: "There is no more powerful engine driving an organization toward excellence and long-range success than an attractive, worthwhile and achievable vision of the future, widely shared" (p. 3).

"What must we become in order to accomplish our fundamental purpose?"

The very first standard for school administrators drafted by the National Policy Board for Educational Administration (2015) calls on education leaders to "collaboratively develop a shared mission and vision" and to "promote the success of every student by facilitating the development, articulation, implementation and stewardship of a vision of learning that is shared and supported by the school community" (p. 14). A comprehensive review of research finds that "setting direction" through the identification and articulation of a shared vision accounted for the largest proportion of a principal's impact on student achievement (Leithwood, Louis, Anderson, & Wahlstrom, 2004). Several jurisdictions in Canada have expectations for school leaders to work with their staffs to create a vision for the school. The Alberta Learning Leadership Quality Standard, for example, states, "A leader collaborates with the school community to create and implement a shared vision for student success, engagement, learning and well-being" (Alberta Education, n.d., p. 5). The Ontario Leadership Framework requires that leaders, "establish, in collaboration with staff, students, and other stakeholders, an overall sense of purpose or vision for work in their schools to which they are all strongly committed" (Institute for Education Leadership, 2013, p. 12).

Collective Commitments (Values)

In their study of high-performing organizations, Jim Collins and Jerry Porras (1994) find that although creating a vision can be a helpful step in the improvement process, it is never sufficient. Teachers and administrators must also tackle the collective commitments they will make and honour in order to achieve the shared vision for their school or district. The third pillar of the foundation, the values pillar, clarifies these collective commitments. It does not ask, "Why do we exist?" or "What do we hope to become?" Rather, it asks, "How must we behave to create the school that will achieve our purpose?" In answering this question, educators shift from offering philosophical musings on mission or their shared hopes for the school of the future to making commitments to act in certain ways—starting today. Clarity on this topic guides the individual and collaborative work of each staff member and outlines how each person can contribute to the improvement initiative. When members of an organization understand the purpose of their organization, know where it is headed, and then pledge to act in certain ways to move it in the right direction, they don't need prescriptive rules and regulations to guide their daily work. Policy manuals and directives are replaced by commitments and covenants. As a result, members of the organization enjoy greater autonomy and creativity than their more rigidly supervised counterparts.

"How must we behave to create the school that will achieve our purpose?"

Leaders benefit from clearly defined commitments as well. When leaders in traditional hierarchical structures address an employee's inappropriate behaviour and demand change, their rationale tends to be, "Because the rules say we have to do it," or "Because I am the boss, and I said so." If, however, the members of the organization have specified collective commitments, leaders operate with the full weight of the moral authority of the group behind them. Inappropriate behaviour is presented to the offender as a violation of collective commitments, and the leader moves from the role of "boss" to the promoter and protector of what members have declared as important or sacred. Furthermore, the leader is not alone in insisting that collective commitments be honoured. A values-driven culture generates internal accountability in which people throughout the organization create a positive peer pressure to act in accordance with public commitments.

Why Should We Describe the School or District We Are Trying to Create?

"At both school and district levels, administrative tasks essential to teachers' learning and learning communities include building a shared vision and common language about practice" (McLaughlin & Talbert, 2006, p. 80).

"The very best leaders understand that their key task is inspiring a *shared* vision, not selling their own idiosyncratic view of the world" (Kouzes & Posner, 2006, p. 108).

"A vision builds trust, collaboration, interdependence, motivation, and mutual responsibility for success. Vision helps people make smart choices, because their decisions are made with the end result in mind. . . . Vision allows us to act from a proactive stance, moving toward what we want. . . . Vision empowers and excites us to reach for what we truly desire" (Blanchard, 2007, p. 22).

In order for a school to move forward its faculty needs to develop an understood and agreed-on purpose and sense of direction. "If you don't have a common, agreed-upon destination, then everyone is left to his or her own devices to imagine one—a scenario that results in unharnessed and unfocused efforts" (Gabriel & Farmer, 2009, p. 46).

A key responsibility of an educational leader is "developing and delivering a compelling picture of the school's future that produces energy, passion, and action in yourself and others. . . . [A vision is] one of your most potent leadership tools for the development of coherent and sustainable actions" (Kanold, 2011, pp. 6–7).

In identifying five key functions of principals, the Wallace Foundation (2012) listed shaping a vision of academic success as the first of those functions. It concludes, "Effective principals are responsible for establishing a schoolwide vision of commitment to high standards and the success of all students" (p. 5).

"Shared vision emerges from a collaboratively defined understanding of what constitutes worthwhile student learning, with all members of the PLC working together on problems around that common vision" (Fulton & Britton, 2011, p. 14).

A powerful vision results in inspiration, aspiration, and perspiration. It inspires people to rally round a greater purpose. It challenges educators to articulate the school they aspire to create. It leads to action, beginning with building shared knowledge of what it will take to reduce the gap between the current reality of the schools and the school described in the vision (Williams & Hierck, 2015).

"The better people can envision where they are going, the more they can focus on specific initiatives that will make that vision a reality" (Kotter International, 2015, p. 17).

Shared vision emerges when there is clarity of purpose and "continuous collaborative conversations that build shared language, knowledge, and expectations" (Fullan & Quinn, 2016, p. 29).

Finally, achieving agreement about what we are prepared to start *doing*, and then *implementing* that agreement, is, by definition, the key step in closing the knowing-doing gap. We believe that attention to clarifying collective commitments is one of the most important and, regrettably, least utilized strategies in building the foundation of a PLC. There is, once again, considerable evidence in organizational and educational research to support that belief. (See the reproducible, "Why Should We Articulate Collective Commitments?")

Goals

The final pillar of the foundation asks members to clarify the specific goals they hope to achieve as a result of their improvement initiative. The goals pillar identifies the targets and timelines that enable a staff to answer the question, "How will we know if all of this is making a difference?"

"How will we know if all of this is making a difference?"

Goals provide staff members with a sense of their short-term priorities and the steps to achieve the benchmarks. Effective goals foster both the results orientation of a PLC and individual and collective accountability for achieving the results. They help close the gap between the current reality and where the staff hopes to take the school (the shared vision).

Furthermore, goals are absolutely essential to the collaborative team process. We define a team as a group of people working together *interdependently* to achieve a *common goal* for which members are *mutually accountable*. In the absence of a common goal, there can be no true team. Effective goals generate joint effort and help collaborative teams clarify how their work can contribute to schoolwide or districtwide improvement initiatives.

When schools create short-term goals and routinely celebrate as those goals are achieved, they foster a sense of confidence and self-efficacy among the staff. Confidence is merely "the expectation of success" (Kanter, 2005), and when people expect to be successful they are more likely to put forth the effort to ensure it. Thus, goals play a key role in motivating people to honour their commitments so the school moves closer to fulfilling its fundamental purpose of learning for all students. We will have more to say about goals in chapter 4 (page 81), but, once again, educational researchers and organizational theorists consider measurable goals as a key element in improvement.

The key to effective leadership and healthy organizations is clarity regarding the purpose of the organization, the future it is creating, the specific actions members can take immediately to achieve the long-term purpose and make progress on short-term goals, and the indicators of progress it will track (Buckingham, 2005). When educators have addressed each of the four pillars we have referenced in this chapter and arrived at both a shared understanding of and commitment to each pillar, they have the benefit of a solid foundation for all of the future efforts in building their PLCs.

The final document articulating the shared mission, vision, collective commitments, and goals should need not be lengthy. Brevity and specificity are preferred over verbosity.

Why Should We Articulate Collective Commitments?

With the democratization of organizations, especially schools, the leadership function becomes one of creating a "community of shared values" (Lezotte, 1991, p. 3).

"Values describe how we intend to operate, on a day-to-day basis, as we pursue our vision. . . . Values are best expressed in terms of behavior: If we act as we should, what would an observer see us doing? . . . If values are made a central part of the organization's shared vision effort, and put out in full view, they become like a figurehead on a ship: a guiding symbol of the behavior that will help move people toward the vision" (Senge et al., 1994, p. 302).

Both profit and nonprofit organizations should be grounded on "a timeless set of core values and an enduring purpose" (Collins & Porras, 1994, p. xxiv).

"The language of complaint essentially tells us, and others, what it is we can't stand. The language of commitment tells us (and possibly others) what it is we stand for" (Kegan & Lahey, 2001, p. 32).

High-performing districts "tended to rely more on a common culture of values to shape collective action than on bureaucratic rules and controls. The shared values typically focused on improvement of student learning as the central goal" (Elmore, 2000, p. 26).

"Values provide guidelines on how you should proceed as you pursue your purpose and picture of the future. They answer the question . . . 'How?' They need to be clearly described so that you know exactly what behaviors demonstrate that the value is being lived" (Blanchard, 2007, p. 30).

Values must be driven into the policy, the decision making, and ultimately the culture of the organization, otherwise value statements are just words. When values become part of an employee's DNA, they not only guide day-to-day work but also empower employees to act in unique situations (Berry & Seltman, 2008).

"Values represent the *commitments to action* necessary to ensure the vision is realized. . . . In the best PLC cultures, vision and values ultimately become the driving force behind the decision-making process that takes place every day" (Kanold, 2011, p. 13).

To bring a mission statement to life "educators must be willing to transparently communicate their commitment to students as it relates to their stated mission and challenge one another to live up to that commitment" (Muhammad & Hollie, 2012, p. 28).

The key to values impacting the organization in a positive way is that people have to "live by them, reinforce them every day, and not tolerate behavior that is at odds with them" (Bryant, 2014).

Part Four

Assessing Your Place on the PLC Journey

It is important to help your staff build shared knowledge regarding your school's current status in addressing the critical step on the PLC journey of establishing a solid foundation. We have created a tool to assist you in that effort. "The Professional Learning Communities at Work® Continuum: Laying the Foundation" is available on pages 46–48 and at **go.SolutionTree.com/ca/PLCbooks** as a free reproducible. Once your staff have established greater clarity regarding the current status of your PLC foundation, we urge you to turn your attention to the "Where Do We Go From Here?" worksheet that accompanies the continuum (on page 49 and also available for free to download at **go.SolutionTree.com/ca/PLCbooks**). It will prompt you to take the action necessary to close the knowing-doing gap.

Part Five

Tips for Moving Forward: Building the Foundation of a PLC

1 **Move quickly to action:** Remember that you will not progress on the PLC continuum or close the knowing-doing gap until people in the school or district begin to "do" differently. We have seen educators devote years to studying, debating, rewording, and revising different elements of the foundation, thereby giving the illusion of meaningful action. In most instances, a staff should be able to consider and resolve all of the questions of the foundation in a matter of weeks. They may need to return to the foundation in the future to make changes as the vision becomes clearer, the need for additional commitments arises, or new goals emerge. Perfection is not the objective: action is. Once again, the school or district that actually does the work of a PLC will develop its capacity to help all students learn far more effectively than the school or district that spends years preparing to be a PLC.

2 **Build shared knowledge when asking people to make a decision:** Asking uninformed people to make decisions is bound to result in uninformed decisions. Members of a PLC resolve issues and answer important questions by asking, "What information do we need to examine together to make a good decision?" and then building shared knowledge regarding that information. In a profession, decisions should be guided by research-based best practices that will best serve the clients' needs—in this case, our students. Learning together is, by definition, the very essence of a *learning* community. Furthermore, giving people access to the same information increases the likelihood that they will arrive at the same conclusions. All staff should have direct access to user-friendly information on the current reality in their school or district as well as access to summaries of the best practices and best thinking regarding the issue under consideration. School and district leaders must take responsibility for gathering and disseminating this information, but all staff should be invited to present any information for distribution that they feel is relevant.

3 **Use the foundation to assist in day-to-day decisions:** Addressing the foundation of a PLC will impact the school only if it becomes a tool for making decisions. Posting mission statements in the building or inserting a vision statement or goals into a strategic plan does nothing to improve a school. When proposals are considered, the first questions that should be asked are:

- Is this consistent with our purpose?

- Will it help us become the school we envision?

- Are we prepared to commit to do this?

- Will it enable us to achieve our goals?

An honest assessment of these questions can help shorten debate and lead the group to the right conclusion.

4 **Use the foundation to identify existing practices that should be eliminated:** Once your foundation has been established, use it to identify and eliminate any practices that are inconsistent with its principles. As Jim Collins (2001) writes:

Most of us have an ever-expanding "to do" list, trying to build momentum by doing, doing, doing—and doing more. And it rarely works. Those who build good to great companies, however, made as much use of "stop doing" lists as "to do" lists. They had the discipline to stop doing all the extraneous junk. (p. 139)

5 **Translate the vision of your school into a teachable point of view:** Effective leaders create a "teachable point of view": a succinct explanation of the organization's purpose and direction that can be illustrated through stories that engage others emotionally and intellectually (Tichy, 1997). They have a knack for making the complex simple in ways that give direction to those in the organization (Collins, 2001). They use simple language, simple concepts, and the power of common sense (Pfeffer & Sutton, 2000). Develop a brief teachable point of view that captures the vision of your school in a message that is simple, direct, and jargon free. Practice presenting the vision until articulating it becomes second nature.

The Professional Learning Communities at Work® Continuum: Laying the Foundation

DIRECTIONS: Individually, silently, and *honestly* assess the current reality of your school's implementation of each indicator listed in the left column. Consider what evidence or anecdotes support your assessment. This form may also be used to assess district or team implementation.

We have a clear sense of our collective purpose, the school we are attempting to create to achieve that purpose, the commitments we must make and honour to become that school, and the specific goals that will help monitor our progress.

Indicator	Pre-Initiating	Initiating	Implementing	Developing	Sustaining
Shared Mission It is evident that learning for all is our core purpose.	The purpose of the school has not been articulated. Most staff members view the mission of the school as teaching. They operate from the assumption that although all students should have the opportunity to learn, responsibility for learning belongs to the individual student and will be determined by his or her ability and effort.	An attempt has been made to clarify the purpose of the school through the development of a formal mission statement. Few people were involved in its creation. It does little to impact professional practice or the assumptions behind those practices.	A process has been initiated to provide greater focus and clarity regarding the mission of learning for all. Steps are being taken to clarify what, specifically, students are to learn and to monitor their learning. Some teachers are concerned that these efforts will deprive them of academic freedom.	Teachers are beginning to see evidence of the benefits of clearly established expectations for student learning and systematic processes to monitor student learning. They are becoming more analytical in assessing the evidence of student learning and are looking for ways to become more effective in assessing student learning and providing instruction to enhance student learning.	Staff members are committed to helping all students learn. They demonstrate that commitment by working collaboratively to clarify what students are to learn in each unit, creating frequent common formative assessments to monitor each student's learning on an ongoing basis, and implementing a systematic plan of intervention when students experience difficulty. They are willing to examine all practices and procedures in light of their impact on learning.

Indicator	Pre-Initiating	Initiating	Implementing	Developing	Sustaining
Shared Vision We have a shared understanding of and commitment to the school we are attempting to create.	No effort has been made to engage staff in describing the preferred conditions for the school.	A formal vision statement has been created for the school, but most staff members are unaware of it.	Staff members have participated in a process to clarify the school they are trying to create, and leadership calls attention to the resulting vision statement on a regular basis. Many staff members question the relevance of the vision statement, and their behaviour is generally unaffected by it.	Staff members have worked together to describe the school they are trying to create. They have endorsed this general description and use it to guide their school improvement efforts and their professional development.	Staff members can and do routinely articulate the major principles of the school's shared vision and use those principles to guide their day-to-day efforts and decisions. They honestly assess the current reality in their school and continually seek more effective strategies for reducing the discrepancy between that reality and the school they are working to create.
Collective Commitments (Shared Values) We have made commitments to each other regarding how we must behave in order to achieve our shared vision.	Staff members have not yet articulated the attitudes, behaviours, or commitments they are prepared to demonstrate in order to advance the mission of learning for all and the vision of what the school might become.	Administrators or a committee of teachers have created statements of beliefs regarding the school's purpose and its direction. Staff members have reviewed and reacted to those statements. Initial drafts have been amended based on staff feedback. There is no attempt to translate the beliefs into the specific commitments or behaviours that staff will model.	A statement has been developed that articulates the specific commitments staff have been asked to embrace to help the school fulfill its purpose and move closer to its vision. The commitments are stated as behaviours rather than beliefs. Many staff object to specifying these commitments and prefer to focus on what other groups must do to improve the school.	Staff members have been engaged in the process to articulate the collective commitments that will advance the school toward its vision. They endorse the commitments and seek ways to bring them to life in the school.	The collective commitments are embraced by staff, embedded in the school's culture, and evident to observers of the school. They help define the school and what it stands for. Examples of the commitments are shared in stories and celebrations, and people are challenged when they behave in ways that are inconsistent with the collective commitments.

page 2 of 3

Indicator	Pre-Initiating	Initiating	Implementing	Developing	Sustaining
Common School Goals We have articulated our long-term priorities, short-term targets, and timelines for achieving those targets.	No effort has been made to engage the staff in establishing school improvement goals related to student learning.	Goals for the school have been established by the administration or school improvement team as part of the formal district process for school improvement. Most staff would be unable to articulate a goal that has been established for their school.	Staff members have been made aware of the long-term and short-term goals for the school. Tools and strategies have been developed and implemented to monitor the school's progress toward its goals. Little has been done to translate the school goal into meaningful targets for either collaborative teams or individual teachers.	The school goal has been translated into specific goals that directly impact student achievement for each collaborative team. If teams are successful in achieving their goals, the school will achieve its goal as well. Teams are exploring different strategies for achieving their goals.	All staff members pursue measurable goals that are directly linked to the school's goals as part of their routine responsibilities. Teams work interdependently to achieve common goals for which members are mutually accountable. The celebration of the achievement of goals is part of the school culture and an important element in sustaining the PLC process.

Where Do We Go From Here? Worksheet
Laying the Foundation

Indicator of a PLC at Work	What steps or activities must be initiated to create this condition in your school?	Who will be responsible for initiating or sustaining these steps or activities?	What is a realistic timeline for each step or phase of the activity?	What will you use to assess the effectiveness of your initiative?
Shared Mission It is evident that learning for all is our core purpose.				
Shared Vision We have a shared understanding of and commitment to the school we are attempting to create.				
Collective Commitments (Shared Values) We have made commitments to each other regarding how we must behave in order to achieve our shared vision.				
Common School Goals We have articulated our long-term priorities, short-term targets, and timelines for achieving those targets.				

Write value statements as behaviours rather than beliefs: "We believe in the potential and worth of each of our students" is a morally impeccable statement; however, it offers little insight into what a staff is prepared to do to help each student realize that potential. Another difficulty with belief statements is their failure to assign specific, personal responsibility. A staff may agree with the statement, "We believe in a safe and orderly environment," but feel it is the job of the administration to create such an environment. Simple, direct statements of what we commit to do are preferable to the most eloquent statements of our beliefs. For example, "We will monitor each student's learning on a timely basis and provide additional time and support for learning until the student becomes proficient" helps to clarify expectations far more effectively than assertions about the potential of every student.

Focus on yourself rather than others: In our work with schools, we have found that educators rarely have difficulty in articulating steps that could be taken to improve their schools, but they call on others to do them. Parents need to be more supportive, students need to be more responsible, the district needs to reduce class size, the province or territory needs to provide more funding, and so on. This external focus on what others must do fails to improve the situation and fosters a culture of dependency and resignation (Sparks, 2007). Furthermore, we cannot make commitments on the behalf of others. We can only make them for ourselves. Members of a PLC have an internal focus that acknowledges that there is much within their sphere of influence that could be done to improve their school. They create a culture of self-efficacy and optimism by concentrating on what is within their collective power to do.

Recognize that the process is nonlinear: Although we present the four pillars sequentially, the process of clarifying purpose, vision, collective commitments, and goals is nonlinear, nonhierarchical, and non-sequential. Working on the foundation is cyclical and interactive. Writing purpose and vision statements can help shape commitments and goals, but it is not until those commitments are honoured and goals are achieved that purpose and vision become more real, clearer, and more focused.

Remember it is what you do that matters, not what you call it: Henry Mintzberg (1994) advises, "Never adopt a technique by its usual name . . . call it something different so that you have to think it through for yourself and work it out on your own terms" (p. 27). When concepts take on a label, they accumulate baggage. People get the impression that a proposal represents the latest fad, or they settle for a superficial understanding rather than really engaging in an assessment of the underlying ideas. There are schools and districts throughout Canada that call themselves professional learning communities yet demonstrate none of the characteristics of a PLC. There are schools that could serve as model PLCs that are unfamiliar with the term. We are not advocating that faculties be asked to vote to become a PLC or take a PLC pledge. In fact, it may be more helpful to never use the term. What is important is that we first engage staff members in building shared knowledge of certain key assumptions and critical practices and then call on them to act in accordance with that knowledge.

Part Six

Questions to Guide the Work of Your Professional Learning Community

To assess your effectiveness in building a solid foundation for a PLC, ask . . .

1. Have we created a guiding coalition to help implement and sustain our PLC?

2. Have we established an understood and accepted working definition of when we have reached consensus?

3. Did we build shared knowledge throughout the organization before asking people to make a decision?

4. Did we engage in dialogue rather than monologue—conversations rather than presentations—to provide people throughout the organization with ample opportunity to ask their questions and raise their concerns?

5. Have we created a process to allow dissenting points of view to be heard in a nonacrimonious way?

6. Have the staff embraced the premise that the purpose of their school is to ensure high levels of learning for all students?

7. Have the staff established the conditions they must create in the school to help all students learn at high levels?

8. Have the staff translated their aspirations for the school and their desire to help all students learn at high levels into collective commitments about how each individual can contribute to the school's vision and mission?

9. Have the staff established the school's short-term and long-term goals to serve as benchmarks of progress on their PLC journey?

10. Has the discussion to clarify the mission, vision, values (collective commitments), and goals led to specific actions designed to move the school closer to its vision?

11. Has the school initiated structural changes and reallocated resources to support the new vision?

12. Has the school created a process for monitoring progress toward the vision?

13. Are the four critical questions of a PLC driving the work of people throughout the school?

14. Do we celebrate our progress, model our commitments, and confront violations of the commitments?

Part Seven

Dangerous Detours and Seductive Shortcuts

Beware of mission statements that hedge on the collective commitment to promote high levels of learning for all students. References to "providing students with an opportunity to learn" or "helping each student learn according to the best of his or her ability" are subtle ways of distancing a school from a focus on the achievement of each student. Educators must do more than give students the chance to learn: they must align their practices to promote learning. They must reject the fixed mindset that attributes accomplishments to innate ability or dispositions that cannot be enhanced. They must instead embrace the *growth* mindset—the belief that students can cultivate their ability and talent through their own additional effort and the support of their educators (Dweck, 2006).

Educators must do more than give students the chance to learn: they must align their practices to promote learning.

Do not equate writing a mission statement with establishing shared purpose for your school. Shared purpose is ultimately revealed by what you do. The completion of a mission statement does not indicate that your work is over, but rather that it has just begun. The tenets of a mission statement must be translated into specific, actionable steps that bring the mission to life. Remember the advice of Jim Collins (1996), who wrote:

> [Leaders] spend too much time drafting, wordsmithing, and redrafting vision statements, mission statements, values statements, purpose statements, aspiration statements, and so on. They spend nowhere near enough time trying to align their organizations with the values and visions already in place. . . . When you have superb alignment, a visitor could drop into your organization from another planet and infer the vision without having to read it on paper. (p. 19)

Final Thoughts

The consideration of the questions of purpose, vision, commitments, and goals can help a staff lay the foundation for a professional learning community, but important work remains to be done. The fundamental structure and the engine that drives the PLC process is not the individual educator but a collaborative team. In the next chapter we examine how to create genuine collaborative *teams* rather than congenial groups.

CHAPTER 3
Building the Collaborative Culture of a Professional Learning Community

Part One

The Case Study: Are We Engaged in Collaboration or "Co-blaboration"?

Principal Randy Kerr was puzzled. He knew that building a collaborative culture at Tisdale Middle and Secondary School in Saskatchewan was the key to improving student achievement. He could cite any number of research studies to support his position. In the past, his school division had mandated that every school implement a PLC culture. Despite this mandate, students were not experiencing the benefit of the collaboration.

As principal, Kerr had promoted this collaboration and had taken a number of steps to support teachers working together. He organized each team and provided time for teachers to collaborate. He trained staff in the skills they needed, and he emphasized the importance of collaboration at almost every faculty meeting. Teachers were meeting regularly as expected. He felt that he was doing the right work, but to his dismay and bewilderment, every academic indicator of student achievement that the school monitored had remained essentially the same.

Principal Kerr continued to read and learn more about the PLC process. As he observed collaborative team meetings, he noticed that the teachers seemed to enjoy working together, but they needed to focus their discussions more on student learning. He recognized that, in order for students to be successful, his teams would have to move from meeting because of compliance to actually understanding the *why* of the PLC process. They would have to develop a common understanding of *what* they are collaborating about.

He invested in professional development for the staff and created opportunities for all teachers to work together to develop their mission, vision, and collective commitments. Even though he wasn't seeing the results of this effort as fast as he wanted, he hoped that if the teachers continued to build common understanding of why the collaborative work was important, they would eventually see a difference in student achievement.

Part Two

Here's How

The situation in this school reflects one of the most pervasive problems in building PLCs. Many educators have gradually, sometimes grudgingly, come to acknowledge that collaborating with one's colleagues is preferable to working in isolation. Slowly, structures have been put in place to support collaboration. Staff members are increasingly assigned to teams, given time for collaboration during their contractual day, and provided with training to assist them as they begin the challenge of working together. Administrators and teachers alike take pride that the goal has been accomplished: professionals in the building are collaborating with each other on a regular basis. The anticipated gains in student achievement, however, often fail to materialize.

We cannot stress this next point too emphatically: the fact that teachers collaborate will do nothing to improve a school. The pertinent question is not, "Are they collaborating?" but rather, "What are they collaborating about?" Collaboration is not a virtue in itself, and building a collaborative culture is simply a means to an end, not the end itself. The purpose of collaboration—to help more students achieve at higher levels—can only be accomplished if the professionals engaged in collaboration are focused on the *right work*.

The purpose of collaboration— to help more students achieve at higher levels— can only be accomplished if the professionals engaged in collaboration are focused on the right work.

What is the right work that would occupy the collaborative efforts of a team committed to higher levels of learning for all students? Once again, we return to the four questions that drive the work of a PLC.

1. **What is it we want our students to learn?** Have we identified the essential knowledge, skills, and dispositions each student is to acquire as a result of each unit of instruction?

2. **How will we know if each student has learned it?** Are we using formative assessment in our classrooms on an ongoing basis? Are we gathering evidence of student learning through one or more team-developed common formative assessments for each unit of instruction?

3. **How will we respond when some students do not learn it?** Can we identify students who need additional time and support by the student, by the

essential outcome, and for every unit of instruction? Do we use evidence of student learning from common formative assessments to analyze and improve our individual and collective instructional practice?

4. **How can we extend and enrich the learning for students who have demonstrated proficiency?** Can we identify students who have reached identified learning targets to extend their learning?

Principal Kerr must first form an alliance with key staff members to help build a deeper understanding of the real purpose of their collaboration and then create supports and parameters to guide staff dialogue to the right topics. He must do more than assign people to teams and hope for the best. If Principal Kerr is to build the capacity of the staff to function as members of high-performing teams, he must demonstrate reciprocal accountability by providing those teams with the focus, support, and resources to be successful.

Clarifying Key Terms

Educators who are asked to work in collaborative teams will continue to struggle unless they come to a shared understanding of key terms. Principal Kerr must clarify that in asking educators to work in teams, he is asking them to work interdependently to achieve a common goal for which members are mutually accountable. Furthermore, since a school's mission is to ensure high levels of learning, the team's goals must be explicitly and directly tied to that purpose. A collection of teachers does not truly become a team until members must rely on one another to accomplish a goal that none could achieve individually. We will have more to say about the importance of goals in the next chapter.

In asking teachers to collaborate, Principal Kerr is asking them to engage in a systematic process in which they work together, interdependently, to analyze and impact their professional practice in order to improve individual and collective results. A systematic process is a combination of related parts, organized into a whole in a methodical, deliberate, and orderly way, toward a particular aim. It is not intended to be invitational or indiscriminate. Those who develop systematic practices do not hope things happen a certain way; they create specific structures to ensure certain steps are taken.

A deeper understanding of the meaning and purpose of teams and collaboration could help the educators in this school recognize that they have not been focusing on the right work in the right way.

A collection of teachers does not truly become a team until members must rely on one another to accomplish a goal that none could achieve individually.

Creating Meaningful Teams

One of the ways Principal Kerr can support teachers in the effort to create high-performing collaborative teams is to ensure that each staff member is assigned to a meaningful team. It is important for principals to recognize that the task of building a collaborative culture requires more than bringing random adults together in the hope they will discover a topic of conversation. The fundamental question in organizing teams is, "Do team members have a shared responsibility for responding to the four critical questions in ways that enhance students' learning?"

Much work will remain in terms of helping teams develop their capacity to improve student learning, but that outcome is far more difficult to achieve without organizing teams appropriately.

Examining Possible Team Structures

Let's examine some possible team structures that support meaningful collaboration.

Same Course or Grade Level

The best team structure for improving student achievement is simple: a team of teachers who teach the same course or grade level.

The best team structure for improving student achievement is simple: a team of teachers who teach the same course or grade level. These teachers have a natural common interest in exploring the critical questions of learning. Furthermore, there is considerable research that indicates that this structure is best suited for the ongoing professional learning that leads to improved student achievement (Gallimore, Ermeling, Saunders, & Goldenberg, 2009; Little, 2006; Robinson, 2010; Saphier, King, & D'Auria, 2006; Stigler & Hiebert, 2009; Wei, Darling-Hammond, Andree, Richardson, & Orphanos, 2009). In some instances, however, a single person may be the only teacher of a grade level or content area (such as in very small schools or courses outside of the core curriculum). How does the only first-grade teacher or the only art teacher in a school become a member of a meaningful collaborative team?

Vertical Teams

Vertical teams link teachers with those who teach content above and below their students. For example, the sole first-grade teacher could join the kindergarten and second-grade teacher to create the school's primary team. The team members would work together to:

- Clarify the essential outcomes for students in kindergarten, first grade, and second grade

- Develop assessments for the students in each grade level

- Analyze the results of each assessment

- Offer suggestions for improving results

- Take collective responsibility for each other's students during a common block of time designated for intervention and enrichment

In this structure, each teacher has the benefit of two *critical friends* who can offer suggestions for improvement as the team examines indicators of student achievement. Furthermore, when teachers examine evidence indicating students are having difficulty in a particular skill in the grade level beyond the one they are teaching, they can make adjustments to their own instruction, pacing, and curriculum to better prepare students for that content.

Vertical teams can also cut across schools. A middle school band director, for example, could join the high school band director to create a vertical team responsible for creating a strong band program. An elementary school art teacher could work with the middle school art teacher to clarify the prerequisite skills students should have acquired as they enter the middle school art program. The K–12 vertical team format can be a powerful tool for strengthening the program of an entire district.

Virtual Teams

Proximity is not a prerequisite for an effective collaborative team. Teachers can use technology to create powerful partnerships with colleagues across the district, province, territory, or world. As Ken Blanchard (2007) concludes in his study of effective organizations, "There is no reason that time and distance should keep people from interacting as a team. With proper management and the help of technology, virtual teams can be every bit as productive and rewarding as face-to-face teams" (p. 173). Any teacher with access to a computer can create a virtual team of colleagues who teach the same course or grade level by using Skype to engage in real-time dialogue with a colleague, Google Docs to share files, and remote conferencing services such as GoToMeeting, Webex, Zoom, or Mikogo to see each other's desktops. Using technology, the team members can clarify what students should learn, develop common pacing guides, create common assessments, and share information regarding the learning of their students. Principals in the same district can facilitate the process by coordinating with their colleagues to provide a common planning period for singleton teachers in different schools. For example, all of the elementary physical education teachers in the district could become a team to answer the critical questions of learning related to their content area of expertise.

Furthermore, educators in Canada are supported by their teacher professional organizations, school districts, and a variety of organizations that champion online collaboration. In its 2015 research document "Shifting Minds 3.0," Canadians for 21st Century Learning and Innovation (C21) states, "the transformative view [of improving schools] is that learning is a social process, with students and teachers working in partnership with each other and with experts beyond school, supported by digital technologies." With great distances between schools in many parts of Canada, it could be very easy for educators to feel isolated in their work. Virtual teams should be considered as a way to provide a collaborative structure.

The ubiquity and easy access to technology means every teacher is able to engage in powerful collaboration even without the benefit of having a colleague in the building who teaches the same content.

Interdisciplinary Teams

The interdisciplinary team model used in the case-study school can be an effective structure for collaboration, but only if certain steps are taken to change the nature of the conversation. If teachers share no common content or objectives, they will inevitably turn their attention to the one thing they do have in common: their students. A seventh-grade team's discussions regarding Johnny's behaviour and Mary's attitude can be appropriate and beneficial, but at some point the team must clarify the knowledge, skills, and dispositions Johnny and Mary are to acquire as a result of their seventh-grade experience.

Proximity is not a prerequisite for an effective collaborative team.

In an interdisciplinary structure, each team in the school should be asked to create an overarching curricular goal that members will work together interdependently to achieve.

Therefore, in an interdisciplinary structure, each team in the school should be asked to create an overarching curricular goal that members will work together interdependently to achieve. For example, Principal Kerr could make staff aware of the power of nonfiction writing to improve student achievement in mathematics, science, social studies, and reading (Reeves, 2006). He could then ask each grade-level team to develop a goal to increase student achievement by becoming more effective in the instruction of nonfiction writing. The seventh-grade team would confront a series of questions as members worked together to achieve this goal, such as:

- How can we integrate nonfiction writing into each of our different subject areas?

- What criteria will we use to assess the quality of student writing?

- How will we know if we are applying the criteria consistently?

- What are the most effective ways to teach nonfiction writing?

- Is there a team member with expertise in this area who can help the rest of us become more effective?

- How will we know if our students are becoming better writers?

- How will we know if the focus on writing is impacting achievement in our respective courses?

- What strategies will we put in place for students who struggle with nonfiction writing?

- How can we enrich the learning experience for students who are already capable writers?

- Are there elements of the seventh-grade curriculum we can eliminate or curtail to provide the necessary time for greater emphasis on nonfiction writing?

Principal Kerr could also foster a greater focus on learning if he created a schedule that allowed teachers to meet in content-area teams as well as in grade-level teams. Once again, research finds the grade level or course structure to be the most conducive to meaningful dialogue and the continuing professional learning of a team. Middle schools make a mistake when they put all their eggs in the interdisciplinary basket. A seventh-grade mathematics teacher can certainly benefit from conversations with colleagues who teach language arts, social studies, or science, but just as certainly, that mathematics teacher can also benefit from conversations with other mathematics teachers. The best middle schools utilize both team structures to focus on and improve the academic achievement of their students.

Logical Links

Specialist teachers can become members of grade-level or course-specific teams that are pursuing outcomes linked to their areas of expertise. A physical education teacher can join a sixth-grade team in an effort to help students learn percentages. Each day he or she could help students learn to calculate the percentage of free throws they made in basketball or their batting averages. A music teacher we know joined the fourth-grade team and wrote a musical based on key historical figures students were required to learn that year. A special education teacher joined a biology team because of the difficulties her students were experiencing in that course. She disaggregated the scores of students with special needs on each test and became a consultant to the team on supplementary materials, instructional strategies, and alternative assessments to help special education students achieve the intended outcomes of the course. She then worked as a member of the special education team to help her colleagues recognize the specific biology skills and concepts that were causing difficulty for students in special education. She provided colleagues with resources and ideas for supporting students in those areas during their resource period with their special education teacher.

Specialist teachers can become members of grade-level or course-specific teams that are pursuing outcomes linked to their areas of expertise.

Team Structures

- **Same-course or grade-level teams** are those in which, for example, all the geometry teachers or all the second-grade teachers in a school form a collaborative team.

- **Vertical teams** link teachers with those who teach content above or below their students.

- **Virtual teams** use technology to create powerful partnerships with colleagues across the district, province, territory, or world.

- **Interdisciplinary teams** found in middle schools and small high schools can be an effective structure if members work interdependently to achieve an overarching curricular goal that will result in higher levels of student learning.

- **Logical links** put teachers together in teams that are pursuing outcomes linked to their areas of expertise.

In short, teachers should be organized into structures that allow them to engage in meaningful collaboration that is beneficial to them and their students. Once again, the fundamental question in organizing teams is this: "Do team members have a shared responsibility for responding to the four critical questions in ways that enhance students' learning?" The effectiveness of any particular team structure will depend on the extent to which it supports teacher dialogue and action aligned with those questions.

Teachers should be organized into structures that allow them to engage in meaningful collaboration that is beneficial to them and their students.

Making Time for Collaboration

Reciprocal accountability demands that leaders who ask educators to work in collaborative teams provide those educators with time to meet during their contractual day. We believe it is insincere for any district or school leader to stress the importance of collaboration and then fail to provide time for it. One of the ways in which organizations demonstrate their priorities is allocation of resources, and in schools, one of the most precious resources is time. Thus, school and district leaders must provide teachers with time to do the things they are being asked to do.

We also recognize that many districts face real-world constraints in providing time for collaboration. Releasing students from school so that teachers can collaborate may

School and district leaders must provide teachers with time to do the things they are being asked to do.

create childcare hardships for some families. In fact, we have seen several instances where community pressure has put an end to collaborative time for teachers. In almost every instance, it was not the fact that teachers were collaborating that sparked the opposition, but that the strategy for providing time for collaboration created problems for families. Other districts have paid teachers to extend their school day to provide time for collaboration, but often that time is lost when money gets tight. Furthermore, this strategy conveys the message that collaboration is an add-on to the teacher workday rather than an integral part of teaching. Hiring substitute teachers to give teacher teams time to work together is a possible strategy but may be cost prohibitive in some districts—and it gives teachers the added burden of creating plans for the substitute. Furthermore, teachers and administrators alike are often reluctant to lose precious instructional time so that teachers can meet in teams. Nonetheless, we have worked with school districts throughout Canada that have been able to create regularly scheduled weekly time for collaboration within real-world parameters: they bring teachers together during their contractual day while students are on campus, in ways that do not cost money and that result in little or no loss of instructional time.

The issue of finding time for collaboration has been addressed effectively—and often—in the professional literature and is readily available for those who are sincerely interested in exploring alternatives. Learning Forward alone has addressed the issue hundreds of times in its publications, and AllThingsPLC (www.allthingsplc .info) lists more than two hundred schools that have created time for teachers to collaborate in ways that don't require the school to be shut down, cost money, or result in significant loss of instructional time. The following strategies do not form a comprehensive list; rather, they illustrate some of the steps schools and districts have taken to create the prerequisite time for collaboration.

Common Preparation

Build the master schedule to provide daily common preparation periods for teachers of the same course or department. Each team should then designate one day each week to engage in collaborative, rather than individual, planning.

Parallel Scheduling

Schedule common preparation time by assigning the specialists (physical education teachers, librarians, music teachers, art teachers, instructional technologists, guidance counselors, foreign language teachers, and so on) to provide lessons to students across an entire grade level at the same time each day. The team should designate one day each week for collaborative planning. Some schools build back-to-back specials classes into the master schedule on each team's designated collaborative day, thus creating an extended block of time for the team to meet. Specials teachers must also be given time to collaborate.

Adjusted Start and End Time

Gain collaborative time by starting the workday early or extending the workday one day each week. In exchange for adding time to one end of the workday, teachers get the time back on the other end of that day. A U.S. example of this is included here. For example, on Tuesdays, the entire staff of Adlai E. Stevenson High School in

Lincolnshire, Illinois, begin their workday at 7:30 a.m. rather than the normal 7:45 a.m. start time. From 7:30 to 8:30 a.m., the entire faculty engages in collaborative team meetings. Classes, which usually begin at 8:05 a.m., are delayed until 8:30 a.m. on Tuesdays. Students who can arrange for their own transportation arrive to school then. Buses run their regular routes so that no parent is inconvenienced, and students are delivered to the school at 7:40 a.m. Administrative and noninstructional staff supervise students upon their arrival in a variety of optional activities (such as breakfast, library and computer research, open gym, study halls, and tutorials) until classes begin. To make up for the twenty-five minutes of lost instructional time, five minutes is trimmed from five of the eight fifty-minute class periods. The school day ends at the usual time (3:25 p.m.), and again buses run on their regular schedules. Because they began work fifteen minutes early (7:30 rather than 7:45 a.m.), Stevenson teachers are free to leave fifteen minutes earlier than the normal conclusion of their workday (3:30 rather than 3:45 p.m.). By making these minor adjustments to the schedule one day each week, the entire faculty is guaranteed an hour of collaborative planning without extending their workday or workweek by a single minute. While this is an example from the United States, the concepts can and have been applied to schools in Canada.

Shared Classes

Combine students across two different grade levels or courses into one class for instruction. While one teacher or team instructs the students, the other team engages in collaborative work. The teams alternate instructing and collaborating to provide equity in learning time for students and teams. Some schools coordinate shared classes so older students adopt younger students and serve as mathematics and literacy buddies, tutors, and mentors during shared classes.

Group Activities, Events, and Testing

Teacher teams coordinate activities that require student supervision rather than instructional expertise, such as watching an instructional DVD or video, conducting resource lessons, reading aloud, attending assemblies, or testing. Nonteaching staff members supervise students while teachers engage in team collaboration.

Banked Time

Over a designated period of days, extend the instructional minutes beyond the required school day. After you have banked the desired number of minutes, end the instructional day early to allow for faculty collaboration and student enrichment. For example, in a middle school, the traditional instructional day ends at 3:00 p.m., students board buses at 3:20 p.m., and the teachers' contractual day ends at 3:30 p.m. The faculty may decide to extend the instructional day until 3:10 p.m. By teaching an extra ten minutes for nine days in a row, they bank ninety minutes. On the tenth day, instruction stops at 1:30 p.m., and the entire faculty has collaborative team time for two hours. The students remain on campus and are engaged in clubs, enrichment activities, assemblies, and so on that a variety of parent and community partners sponsor and that the school's nonteaching staff cosupervise.

In-Service and Faculty Meeting Time

Schedule extended time for teams to work together on staff development days and during faculty meeting time. Rather than requiring staff to attend a traditional whole-staff in-service session or sit in a faculty meeting while directives and calendar items are read aloud, shift the focus and use of these days and meetings so team members have extended time to learn with and from each other.

Making Time for Collaboration

- Provide common preparation time.
- Use parallel scheduling.
- Adjust start and end times.
- Share classes.
- Schedule group activities, events, and testing.
- Bank time.
- Use in-service and faculty meeting time wisely.

Clarifying the Right Work

One of the most important ways in which Principal Kerr could support his teams and increase the likelihood of their success is to ensure they are clear on the nature of the work to be done. It is not difficult to assign teachers into meaningful teams and provide them with time to collaborate. But educators arrive at the fork in the road in the PLC process when they determine how they will use that collaborative time. Once again, merely assigning teachers to groups will not improve a school, and much of what passes for collaboration among educators is more aptly described as *co-blaboration*, a term David Perkins (2003) coined. Ineffective or unproductive team meetings create cynicism and only serve to sour teachers' attitudes toward teaming while simultaneously reinforcing the norms of isolation so prevalent in our schools (Boston Consulting Group, 2014). Those who hope to improve student achievement by developing the capacity of staff to function as a PLC must create and foster the conditions that move educators from mere work groups to high-performing collaborative teams.

Those who hope to improve student achievement by developing the capacity of staff to function as a PLC must create and foster the conditions that move educators from mere work groups to high-performing collaborative teams.

In a PLC, the process of collaboration is specifically designed to impact educator practice in ways that lead to better results. Over and over again, we have seen schools in which staff members are willing to collaborate about any number of things—dress codes, tardy policies, the appropriateness of holiday parties—provided they can return to their classrooms and continue to do what they have always done. Yet in a PLC, the reason teachers are organized into teams, the reason they are provided with time to work together, and the reason they are asked to focus on certain topics and complete specific tasks is so that when they return to their classrooms they will possess and utilize an expanded repertoire of skills, strategies, materials, assessments, and ideas in order to impact student achievement in a more positive way.

Therefore, one of the most important elements of reciprocal accountability that district and school leaders must address is establishing clear parameters and priorities that guide teamwork toward the goal of improved student learning. The "Critical Issues for Team Consideration" worksheet (pages 66–67) is a useful tool toward that end. First, it directs the team's attention to issues that impact practice and, thus, student achievement. Second, it calls on the team to generate products that flow directly from the dialogue and decisions regarding those issues. Those products, in turn, are crucial to helping Principal Kerr monitor the progress of teams. Even if teams are doing the right work, they may not be doing the work well. Principals Kerr must put a process in place to monitor each team's work—the *products* of their work (the quality of what they produce), their *processes* (how they do their work), and most important, the *results* of their work (the effects of their work on student learning). Without a process for monitoring teams, the principal will not know when a team is struggling and will be unable to fulfill his or her responsibilities of helping each team succeed in what members are being called on to do (Eaker & Sales, 2016).

Creating the position of team leader is another way Principal Kerr can support teams' work. Team leaders serve as the liaison between the principal and the faculty. He should meet with these leaders regularly; practice, clarify, and rehearse how leaders can lead the team through each of the eighteen critical issues (pages 66–67); and share problems, concerns, and successes (Eaker & Sales, 2016).

Principal Kerr might have avoided some of the initial confusion regarding how teams were expected to use their time had he presented them with the "Critical Issues for Team Consideration" worksheet and then worked with the team leaders to help them establish a timeline for the completion of team products. Imagine if the principal and staff had created the following timeline to guide the dialogue of teams.

By the end of . . .

- The second week of school we will present our team norms

- The fourth week of school we will present our team SMART goal

- The sixth week of school we will present our list of the essential knowledge, skills, and dispositions our students will acquire during this semester

- The eighth week of school we will present our first common assessment

- The tenth week of school we will present our analysis of the results from the common assessments, including areas of strength and strategies for addressing areas of concern

Clearly established expectations and timelines are a tremendous benefit to teams. Members lose no time debating "Why are we here?" or focusing on the trivial because they have been guided toward conversations specific to teaching and learning. Furthermore, by gathering and reviewing team products on a regular basis with team leaders, Principal Kerr can monitor the teams' progress without micromanaging them. We highly recommend that principals and team leaders use the "Critical Issues for Team Consideration" worksheet or a similar tool to help clarify exactly what collaborative teams are expected to do by when and to monitor the progress they are making.

One of the most important elements of reciprocal accountability that district and school leaders must address is establishing clear parameters and priorities that guide teamwork toward the goal of improved student learning.

Critical Issues for Team Consideration

Team Name:

Team Members:

Use the following rating scale to indicate the extent to which each statement is true of your team.

1	2	3	4	5	6	7	8	9	10

Not True of Our Team　　　　　**Our Team Is Addressing This**　　　　　**True of Our Team**

1. _____We have identified team norms and protocols to guide us in working together.

2. _____We have analyzed student achievement data and established SMART goals to improve on this level of achievement we are working interdependently to attain (SMART goals are specific and strategic, measurable, attainable, results oriented, and time bound. SMART goals are discussed at length on pages 83–84).

3. _____Each team member is clear on the knowledge, skills, and dispositions (that is, the essential learning) that students will acquire as a result of our course or grade level and each unit within the course or grade level.

4. _____We have aligned the essential learning with provincial or territorial curriculum expectations and the high-stakes assessments required of our students.

5. _____We have identified course content and topics we can eliminate to devote more time to the essential curriculum.

6. _____We have agreed on how to best sequence the content of the course and have established pacing guides to help students achieve the intended essential learning.

7. _____We have identified the prerequisite knowledge and skills students need in order to master the essential learning of each unit of instruction.

8. _____We have identified strategies and created instruments to assess whether students have the prerequisite knowledge and skills.

9. _____We have developed strategies and systems to assist students in acquiring prerequisite knowledge and skills when they are lacking in those areas.

10. _____We have developed frequent common formative assessments that help us determine each student's mastery of essential learning.

11. _____We have established the proficiency essential outcome we want each student to achieve on each skill and concept examined with our common assessments.

12. _____We use the results of our common assessments to assist each other in building on strengths and addressing weaknesses as part of an ongoing process of continuous improvement designed to help students achieve at higher levels.

13. _____We use the results of our common assessments to identify students who need additional time and support to master essential learning, and we work within the systems and processes of the school to ensure they receive that support.

14. _____We have agreed on the criteria we will use in judging the quality of student work related to the essential learning of our course, and we continually practice applying those criteria to ensure we are consistent.

15. _____We have taught students the criteria we will use in judging the quality of their work and provided them with examples.

16. _____We have developed or utilized common summative assessments that help us assess the strengths and weaknesses of our program.

17. _____We have established the proficiency essential outcome we want each student to achieve on each skill and concept examined with our summative assessments.

18. _____We formally evaluate our adherence to team norms and the effectiveness of our team at least twice each year.

Establishing Collective Commitments to Enhance the Effectiveness of Teams

If teachers are to work collaboratively to clarify the essential learning for their courses and grade levels, write common assessments, and jointly analyze the results, they must overcome the fear that they may be exposed to their colleagues and principals as ineffective.

A reluctance to change their traditional classroom practices is not the only reason educators tend to drift away from substantive conversations about teaching and learning if parameters are not in place to guide their work. Conversations about the trivial are safer. If teachers are to work collaboratively to clarify the essential learning for their courses and grade levels, write common assessments, and jointly analyze the results, they must overcome the fear that they may be exposed to their colleagues and principals as ineffective. After all, you were hired for your professional expertise, but what if the results from a common assessment demonstrate that while your colleagues' students are successful, your students are not? We have seen evidence that some teachers would prefer not to know their strengths and weaknesses in relation to their colleagues' because it is not worth the risk of being exposed and vulnerable.

In his review of the dysfunctions of a team, Patrick Lencioni (2003) contends that the first and most important step in building a cohesive and high-performing team is the establishment of vulnerability-based trust. Individuals on effective teams learn to acknowledge mistakes, weaknesses, failures, and the need for help. They also learn to recognize and value the strengths of other team members and are willing to learn from one another.

The fear of vulnerability leads to the second team dysfunction: avoidance of productive conflict. Dysfunctional teams prefer artificial harmony to insightful inquiry and advocacy. As a result, they avoid topics that require them to work interdependently. Even decisions that would appear to require joint effort fail to generate genuine commitment from individuals on the team. Members settle for the appearance of agreement rather than pushing each other to pledge to honour the agreement through their actions. The avoidance of conflict and lack of commitment lead to yet another dysfunction of a team: avoidance of accountability. Team members are unwilling to confront peers who fail to work toward team goals or to honour team decisions. Finally, since members are unwilling to commit to purpose, priorities, and decisions, and are unwilling to hold each other accountable, they inevitably are inattentive to results. When groups demonstrate the five dysfunctions of a team—the inability to (1) establish trust, (2) engage in honest dialogue regarding disagreements, (3) make commitments to one another, (4) hold each other accountable, and (5) focus on results—the team process begins to unravel (Lencioni, 2003).

Leaders can help teams avoid these dysfunctions in several ways. First, and very importantly, they can model vulnerability, enthusiasm for meaningful exploration of disagreements, articulation of public commitments, willingness to confront those who fail to honour decisions, and an unrelenting focus on and accountability for results. For example, Principal Kerr could acknowledge that he made a mistake in his initial approach to creating high-performing teams and admit that he needs the help of the faculty in altering the team process so that it benefits students. He could invite open dialogue about specific proposals to refocus teams on matters impacting learning and help build shared knowledge regarding the advantages and disadvantages of each proposal. He could make commitments to the staff regarding what he is prepared to do to support their efforts and address their concerns. He could demonstrate his commitment to the decisions they reach by confronting those who violate them. Finally, he could clarify the indicators they would monitor as a school to maintain their focus on results.

Furthermore, Principal Kerr could help staff members engage in professional dialogue designed to address the dangers of a dysfunctional team. Teams benefit not only from clarity regarding the purpose of their collaboration but also from clarity regarding how they will work together and what is expected of each member. Once again, simply putting people in groups does not ensure a productive, positive experience for participants. Most educators can remember a time when they worked in a group that was painfully inefficient and excruciatingly ineffective. But teams increase their likelihood of performing at high levels when they clarify their expectations of one another regarding procedures, responsibilities, and relationships.

All groups establish norms—ground rules or habits that govern the group—regardless of whether or not they take the time to reflect on and articulate the norms they prefer for their team. But when individuals work through a process to create explicitly stated norms, and then commit to honour those norms, they increase the likelihood they will begin to function as a collaborative team rather than as a loose collection of people working together.

Teams increase their likelihood of performing at high levels when they clarify their expectations of one another regarding procedures, responsibilities, and relationships.

Team norms are not intended to serve as rules but rather as collective commitments: public agreements shared among the members (Kegan & Lahey, 2001). Effective teams do not settle for "sorta" agreements; they identify the very specific commitments members have made to each other.

Here again, learning community members will begin the challenging task of articulating collective commitments for each team by building shared knowledge regarding best practices and strategies for implementing those practices. For example, one study of high-performing teams (Druskat & Wolff, 2001) finds that members consistently demonstrated high emotional intelligence in the following characteristics.

- **Perspective taking:** Members are willing to consider matters from the other person's point of view.

- **Interpersonal understanding:** Members demonstrate accurate understanding of other group members' spoken and unspoken feelings, interests, and concerns.

- **Willingness to confront:** Members speak up when an individual violates commitments, but they confront the person in a caring way aimed at building consensus and shared interpretations of commitments.

- **Caring orientation:** Members communicate positive regard, appreciation, and respect. A close personal relationship is not a prerequisite of an effective team, but mutual respect and validation are critical.

- **Team self-evaluation:** The team is willing and able to evaluate its effectiveness.

- **Feedback solicitation:** The team solicits feedback and searches for evidence of its effectiveness from external sources as part of a process of continuous improvement.

- **Positive environment:** The team focuses on staying positive—positive affect, positive behaviour, and the pursuit of positive outcomes. Members cultivate positive images of the group's past, present, and future.

- **Proactive problem solving:** Members actively take the initiative to resolve issues that stand in the way of accomplishing team goals.

- **Organizational awareness:** Members understand their connection to and contribution to the larger organization.

- **External relationships:** The team establishes relationships with others who can support their efforts to achieve their goals.

We also recommend that team members have an honest and open dialogue about the expectations they bring to the process by asking each other to reflect on and discuss his or her past experience with groups. Ask each participant to describe a time when he or she was a member of a group, committee, task force, or so on that proved to be a negative experience. Then ask each participant to explain the specific behaviours or conditions that made it so negative. Next, invite each participant to describe a personal experience in which he or she felt the power and synergy of an effective team. Record the answers, and turn the group's attention to identifying commitments that would avoid the negative and promote the positive aspects of team membership if all participants pledged to honour those norms.

We offer the following six tips for creating norms.

1. **Each team should create its own norms:** Asking a committee to create norms all teams should honour is ineffective. Norms are collective commitments that members make to each other, and committees cannot make commitments for us. Furthermore, norms should reflect the experiences, hopes, and expectations of a specific team's members.

2. **Norms should be stated as commitments to act or behave in certain ways rather than as beliefs:** The statement, "We will arrive to meetings on time and stay fully engaged throughout the meeting," is more powerful than, "We believe in punctuality."

3. **Norms should be reviewed at the beginning and end of each meeting for at least six months:** Norms only impact the work of a team if they are put into practice over and over again until they become internalized. Teams should not confuse writing norms with living norms.

4. **Teams should formally evaluate their effectiveness at least twice a year:** This assessment should include exploration of the following questions.

   - Are we adhering to our norms?

   - Do we need to establish a new norm to address a problem occurring on our team?

   - Are all members of the team contributing to its work?

   - Are we working interdependently to achieve our team goal?

5. **Teams should focus on a few essential norms rather than creating an extensive laundry list:** Less is more when it comes to norms. People do not need a lot of rules to remember, just a few commitments to honour.

6. **One of the team's norms should clarify how the team will respond if one or more members are not observing the norms:** Violations of team norms must be addressed. Failure to confront clear violations of the commitments members have made to each other will undermine the entire team process. We will address the issue of how to confront violations in chapter 9 (page 191).

When done well, norms can help establish the trust, openness, commitment, and accountability that move teams from the trivial to the substantive. No team should work without the benefit of these clearly defined collective commitments. Neglecting to establish norms that clarify expectations is one of the major reasons teams fail (Blanchard, 2007).

When done well, norms can help establish the trust, openness, commitment, and accountability that move teams from the trivial to the substantive.

Leaders can and should take each of the purposeful steps presented in this chapter: creating teams on the basis of a common responsibility for pursuing the critical questions of learning, providing them with time to collaborate, guiding them to the most powerful questions that impact learning, asking teams to create specific products that should flow naturally from the dialogue of a team focused on the right work, and helping them create collective commitments that facilitate the trust, openness, and clarity of expectations essential to effective teams. Those steps can help create the structure for meaningful team dialogue; however, two more critical steps must be taken to help turn the focus of the team to improved student learning.

1. Collaborative teams must develop and pursue SMART goals.

2. Individual teachers and teams must have access to relevant and timely information.

These steps will be addressed in subsequent chapters.

Part Three

Here's Why

Why is it so important to organize a staff into collaborative teams in which people work together interdependently to achieve common goals rather than continuing the longstanding tradition of teacher isolation? The very reason any organization is established is to bring people together in an organized way to achieve a collective purpose that cannot be accomplished by working alone. As Jeffrey Pfeffer and Robert Sutton (2000) write, "Interdependence is what organizations are all about. Productivity, performance, and innovation result from *joint* action, not just individual efforts and behavior" (p. 197). The degree to which people are working together in a coordinated, focused effort is a major determinant of the effectiveness of any organization, and the inability to work interdependently has been described as the "biggest opponent" and the "mortal enemy" of those who confront complex tasks in their daily work (Patterson et al., 2008, p. 192). Certainly, there are few tasks more complex than accomplishing something that has never been done—helping all students learn at high levels.

The very reason any organization is established is to bring people together in an organized way to achieve a collective purpose that cannot be accomplished by working alone.

Furthermore, the collaborative team has been cited repeatedly in organizational literature as the most powerful structure for promoting the essential interdependence of an effective enterprise. Experts on effective teams offer very consistent advice regarding the benefits of teams (see the reproducible, "Why Should We Use Teams as Our Basic Structure?").

As we mentioned earlier in the chapter, simply organizing people into teams does not improve a school. Steps must be taken to ensure that those team members engage in collaboration on the issues that most impact student learning. Education research has repeatedly linked collaborative cultures with school improvement. In fact, the case for teachers working together collaboratively is so compelling that we are not aware of any credible research explicitly opposed to the concept (see page 74, "Why Should We Collaborate?").

We have, however, heard individuals oppose providing educators with time to collaborate. They typically frame their objection by arguing the time a teacher spends collaborating with colleagues is time that could have been spent teaching students and, thus, represents unproductive time. Once again, research from both organizational development and education refute that position. Effective organizations and effective schools build time for reflection and dialogue into every process. The goal is not merely to do more of what we have always done (regardless of its effectiveness) but to create a culture of continuous improvement and to discover ways to become better at achieving our purpose, forever (Black, Harrison, Lee, Marshall, & Wiliam, 2004; Champy, 1995; Collins & Porras, 1994; Darling-Hammond, 1996; Dolan, 1994; Goldsmith, 1996; Kouzes & Posner, 1987; Schein, 1996).

Common sense advises, however, that collaborative time can be squandered if educators do not use that time to focus on issues most directly related to teaching and learning. Canadian Michael Fullan's (2001) caution should be self-evident: "Collaborative cultures, which by definition have close relationships, are indeed powerful, but unless they are focusing on the right things they may end up being powerfully wrong" (p. 67).

Effective leaders will direct the work of teams to the critical questions, because those are the conversations that have the biggest impact on student achievement. Clarifying what students must learn, monitoring each student's learning, responding to students who need additional time and support for learning, and challenging students who have already mastered the intended outcomes are the most critical tasks in a school. It is imperative, therefore, that educators work together interdependently to become more skillful in these critical areas and that these questions become the priority within and among collaborative teams.

School and district leaders should also be prepared to provide the research rationale regarding why collaborative teams should establish the norms or collective commitments to clarify their expectations of one another and guide their collective efforts (see page 75, "Why Should We Create Norms?").

Why Should We Use Teams as Our Basic Structure?

"Empowered teams are such a powerful force of integration and productivity that they form the basic building block of any intelligent organization" (Pinchot & Pinchot, 1993, p. 66).

"Teams are recognized as a critical component of every enterprise—the predominant unit for decision making and getting things done. . . . Working in teams is the norm in a learning organization" (Senge et al., 1994, pp. 354–355).

Teams "bring together complementary skills and experience that . . . exceed those of any individual on the team." Teams are more effective in problem solving, "provide a unique social dimension that enhances . . . work," motivate, and foster peer pressure and internal accountability (Katzenbach & Smith, 1993, p. 18).

In the most innovative organizations teaming *is* the culture. Today's leaders must therefore build a culture where teaming is expected and begins to feel natural (Edmonson, 2013).

"The ability to develop and support high-functioning teams schoolwide is essential to ensuring improved and inspired learning for all learners—adults or children" (D'Auria, 2015, p. 54).

"A team can make better decisions, solve more complex problems, and do more to enhance creativity and build skills than individuals working alone. . . . They have become the vehicle for moving organizations into the future. . . . Teams are not just nice to have. They are hard-core units of the production" (Blanchard, 2007, p. 17).

"Educators work alone more than any other professionals in modern America. Most professions have come to recognize the value of teamwork as a better way to way to understand and solve 'problems of practice.' . . . Fortunately, there appears to be new interest in forms of collaboration among educators. . . . 'Professional learning communities' are increasingly popular" (Wagner, 2007).

"Influencers increase the capacity of others by asking them to work in teams with interdependent relationships. . . . We increase capacity when we work together rather than in isolation" (Patterson et al., 2008, p. 183).

"We now have compelling evidence that when teachers team up with their colleagues they are able to create a culture of success in schools, leading to teaching improvements and student learning gains. The clear policy and practice implication is that teaching is a team sport" (Fulton & Britton, 2011, p. 4).

Why Should We Collaborate?

"The single most important factor for successful school restructuring and the first order of business for those interested in increasing the capacity of their schools is building a collaborative internal environment" (Eastwood & Louis, 1992, p. 215).

When groups, rather than individuals, are seen as the main units for implementing curriculum, instruction, and assessment, they facilitate development of shared purpose for student learning and collective responsibility to achieve it (Newmann & Wehlage, 1995, p. 38).

"[High-achieving schools] build a highly collaborative school environment where working together to solve problems and to learn from each other become cultural norms" (WestEd, 2000, p. 12).

"The key to ensuring that every child has a quality teacher is finding a way for school systems to organize the work of qualified teachers so they can collaborate with their colleagues in developing strong learning communities that will sustain them as they become more accomplished teachers" (National Commission on Teaching and America's Future, 2003, p. 7).

"Collaboration and the ability to engage in collaborative action are becoming increasingly important to the survival of public schools. Indeed, without the ability to collaborate with others, the prospect of truly repositioning schools . . . is not likely" (Schlechty, 2009, p. 237).

"It is time to end the practice of solo teaching in isolated classrooms" (Fulton, Yoon, & Lee, 2005, p. 4).

Teacher collaboration in strong professional learning communities improves the quality and equity of student learning, promotes discussions that are grounded in evidence and analysis rather than opinion, and fosters collective responsibility for student success (McLaughlin & Talbert, 2006).

"Quality teaching is not an individual accomplishment, it is the result of a collaborative culture that empowers teachers to team up to improve student learning beyond what any one of them can achieve alone" (Carroll, 2009, p. 13).

High-performing, high-poverty schools build deep teacher collaboration that focuses on student learning into the culture of the school. Structures and systems are set up to ensure teachers work together rather than in isolation, and the point of their collaboration is to improve instruction and ensure all students learn (Chenoweth, 2009).

Teachers should be provided with more time for collaboration and embedded professional development during the school day and year. . . . Expanding time for collaboration during the school day "facilitates the development of effective professional learning communities among teachers" (Farbman et al., 2014, p. 25).

"When teachers work together on collaborative teams, they improve their practice in two important ways. First, they sharpen their pedagogy by sharing specific instructional strategies for teaching more effectively. Second, they deepen their content knowledge by identifying the specific outcomes students must master. In other words, when teachers work together they become better teachers" (Many & Sparks-Many, 2015, p. 83).

"We must stop allowing teachers to work alone, behind closed doors and in isolation in the staffrooms and instead shift to a professional ethic that emphasizes collaboration. We need communities within and across schools that work collaboratively to diagnose what teachers need to do, plan programs and teaching interventions and evaluate the success of the interventions" (Hattie, 2015b, p. 23).

Why Should We Create Norms?

Teams improve their ability to grapple with the critical questions when they clarify the norms that will guide their work. These collective commitments represent the "promises we make to ourselves and others, promises that underpin two critical aspects of teams—commitment and trust" (Katzenbach & Smith, 1993, p. 60).

Explicit team norms help to increase the emotional intelligence of the group by cultivating trust, a sense of group identity, and belief in group efficacy (Druskat & Wolff, 2001).

"When self-management norms are explicit and practiced over time, team effectiveness improves dramatically, as does the experience of team members themselves. Being on the team becomes rewarding in itself—and those positive emotions provide energy and motivation for accomplishing the team's goals" (Goleman, Boyatzis, & McKee, 2004, p. 182).

Norms can help clarify expectations, promote open dialogue, and serve as a powerful tool for holding members accountable (Lencioni, 2005).

Referring back to the norms can help "the members of a group to 're-member,' to once again take out membership in what the group values and stands for; to 'remember,' to bring the group back into one cooperating whole" (Kegan & Lahey, 2001, p. 194).

Inattention to establishing specific team norms is one of the major reasons teams fail (Blanchard, 2007).

Part Four

Assessing Your Place on the PLC Journey

It is important to help your staff build shared knowledge regarding your school's current status in addressing the critical step on the PLC journey of building a collaborative culture. We have created a tool to assist you in that effort. "The Professional Learning Communities at Work® Continuum: Building a Collaborative Culture Through High-Performing Teams" is available at **go.SolutionTree.com/ca/PLCbooks** as a free reproducible. Once your staff have established greater clarity regarding the current status of your collaborative teams, we urge you to turn your attention to the "Where Do We Go From Here?" worksheet that accompanies the continuum (also available for free to download at **go.SolutionTree.com/ca/PLCbooks**). It will prompt you to take the action necessary to close the knowing-doing gap.

Part Five

Tips for Moving Forward: Building a Collaborative Culture Through High-Performing Teams

1 **Create meaningful teams:** Ensure that teams are created on the basis of shared responsibility for pursuing the critical questions of teaching and learning with a particular group of students; for example, by course or by grade level.

2 **Make time for collaboration:** Work with staff to find creative ways to provide more time for team collaboration, including ways of using existing time more effectively.

3 **Develop widespread leadership:** Disperse leadership more widely by identifying team leaders for any team with more than three people. Meet with team leaders on a regular basis to identify problematic areas of the process, and develop strategies for resolving those problems.

4 **Make decisions on the basis of evidence:** Ask teams to build shared knowledge—to learn together—as they approach each new task in the collaborative process.

5 **Build the capacity of teams to succeed in the PLC process by providing them with essential tools:** Make supporting research, templates, protocols, exemplars, worksheets, and timelines available to teams to assist them in each step of the process.

6 **Continually assess the progress of teams:** Monitor the work of each team through ongoing assessment of their products, regular meetings with team leaders, and formal self-evaluations. Respond immediately to a team that is having difficulty.

7 **Lead by example:** Building-level leadership teams should model everything being asked of the collaborative teams, including meeting on a regular basis, staying focused on issues with the greatest impact on student achievement, establishing and honouring collective commitments, and working toward SMART goals.

8 **Provide for cross-team collaboration:** Create procedures to ensure teams are able to learn from one another.

9 **Expand the knowledge base available to teams:** Look for ways to link teams with relevant resources inside and outside of your building.

10 **Celebrate teams:** Make teams the focus of recognition and celebration (see chapter 9, page 191). Take every opportunity to acknowledge the efforts and accomplishments of teams.

Part Six

Questions to Guide the Work of Your Professional Learning Community

To promote a collaborative culture in your school or district, ask:

1. Have we organized our staff into collaborative teams?

2. Have teams been organized on the basis of common courses and common grade levels whenever possible?

3. If we have used the interdisciplinary team structure, have team members identified specific and overarching student-achievement goals, and do they use those goals to guide their work?

4. Have specialist teachers and singleton teachers found meaningful collaborative teams?

5. Have we avoided assigning people to teams whose disparate assignments make it difficult, if not impossible, to focus on the critical questions of learning?

6. Have we provided time for teachers to meet in their collaborative teams on a regular basis?

7. Do teams focus on the critical questions of learning identified on the "Critical Issues for Team Consideration" worksheet?

8. Are teams asked to submit specific products according to a designated timeline? Do these products reflect their focus on the critical questions?

9. What systems are in place to monitor the teams' work and effectiveness on a timely basis?

10. Has every team developed explicit norms that clarify the commitments members have made to one another regarding how they will work together as a team?

11. Do team members honour the norms they have established? Have they established a process for responding when a member fails to honour the norms?

12. Have we given teams the knowledge base, time, and support essential for their effectiveness?

Part Seven

Dangerous Detours and Seductive Shortcuts

Unless educators are working interdependently to achieve a common goal for which members are mutually accountable, they are not a team.

Many schools and districts are organizing educators into what are simply groups rather than teams. Unless educators are working interdependently to achieve a common goal for which members are mutually accountable, they are not a team.

Beware of artificial teams. We have seen schools create "the leftover team" that combines unrelated singleton teachers under the pretext that they will function as a collaborative team. The likelihood that this disparate group will actually function as a collaborative team is extremely remote. Work with singletons to make them members of meaningful teams, even if the team is vertical or virtual and includes members outside of the building.

Most importantly, remember that a collaborative team will have no impact on student achievement unless its members are co-laboring on the right work. Systems must be in place to clarify what teams are to accomplish, monitor their progress, and provide assistance when they struggle.

Final Thoughts

A collaborative culture does not simply emerge in a school or district: leaders *cultivate* collaborative cultures when they develop the capacity of their staff to work as members of high-performing teams. People throughout the organization, however, must always remember that collaboration is a means to an end—to higher levels of learning—rather than the end itself. The end in a PLC is higher levels of learning for all students. Chapter 4 addresses the challenge of focusing on prerequisite requirements essential to effective teams—working interdependently on a common SMART goal for which members are mutually accountable.

CHAPTER 4

Creating a Results Orientation in a Professional Learning Community

Part One

The Case Study: Creating a Results Orientation at the School, Team, and Teacher Levels

Time was not on Greg Kushnir's side as the first experience he was having with his new staff was two days prior to student arrival. You see, he was the principal of the brand-new school, Esther Starkman School in Edmonton, Alberta. Coming from two previous schools where he had led the PLC process, he was excited about the challenges ahead and had so many things that he wanted to share and build with his staff. Two days would not be enough time to address all the challenges ahead, but he was confident that he and his leadership team would be able to create a shared belief in the three big ideas of PLCs within those two days.

When the doors opened that first day, Principal Kushnir led a discussion on how a focus on learning, collaboration, and results (the three big ideas of a PLC) would be the guiding principles of their work. The teachers discussed the difference between a school focused on teaching rather than learning, and, collectively, the teachers agreed that this was the school that they wanted to create. Principal Kushnir also helped teachers develop a common understanding of the real work of collaborative teams. He knew that as the teams met during the year, it would be important for them to focus on answering the four critical questions of PLCs in order achieve their collective mission of "high levels of learning for all." And, at this first meeting, Principal Kushnir started to help teachers understand the need for the school to be evidence-based in its thinking, to really focus on results as stated in the three big ideas. With all of this knowledge, the school year started and the staff were off to work.

It was a sunny Monday morning in March. Principal Kushnir was feeling pretty good about all they had collectively accomplished as a staff to date when he ran into one of his teachers in the staff room. Ms. Aujla had been to a teacher conference and shared with Principal Kushnir that she had had a frustrating conversation with colleagues from her former school. She explained that as they talked about their collaborative team effort in each of their schools, it was clear to see that, in both schools, teams were collaborating, but it wasn't easy to see how deep that collaboration was at either school. This conversation bothered Principal Kushnir. How could this be? All of his teachers had been working as part of a collaborative team answering the four critical questions. Ms. Aujla should have been able to clearly articulate the difference between the work of her team and the superficial sharing done by the teachers at another school. At the next leadership team meeting Principal Kushnir posed the following questions.

- Do we really know what is happening at each of our team's collaborative meetings?

- How do we know that the work of the collaborative teams is translating into improved teacher practice and student achievement? In other words, how do we know we are truly focused on results?

Principal Kushnir knew that unless the teachers became very interested in improving results, the work of their collaborative teams would represent a culture of PLC lite.

Reflection

How does a school or system create a results orientation among leaders and teachers—the very people who are called on to improve results?

Part Two

Here's How

We have repeatedly listed a results orientation as one of the characteristics of a professional learning community. However, organizations do not focus on results: the people within them do—or they do not. There is little evidence to suggest that centralized formal strategic planning creates such an orientation. In fact, one comprehensive study of strategic planning over a thirty-year period chronicled its failure to impact results (Mintzberg, 1994).

If formal, district-led strategic planning processes do not create a results orientation, will handing the improvement process over to schools be a more effective alternative? The Consortium on Productivity in the Schools (1995) answered that question with a resounding, "no," and concludes:

> Site based management cannot overcome lack of clear goals and goal overloading. . . . Site based management does not substitute for the lack of stable, limited, and well-defined goals for schools. . . .

Otherwise the agendas of site based school improvement drift into non-academic and administrative matters. (pp. 46–47)

The challenge for Principal Kushnir and for any leader who hopes to improve student achievement by creating a results orientation is to engage all members of the organization in establishing goals that, if achieved, will result in higher levels of student learning. We have found that the best way to help people throughout a school district to truly focus on results is to insist that every collaborative team establish SMART goals that align with school and district goals.

Creating Clarity About SMART Goals

Once again we begin with what should now be a familiar refrain: "Clarity precedes competence."

Before teams can create SMART goals, members must be in agreement about the meaning of the term. It is another of those terms that can mean many different things to different people within an organization. While district and school goals tend to be broad goal statements, the SMART goal acronym (Conzemius & O'Neill, 2014) provides much-needed clarity for the kinds of goals teams pursue. Goals are SMART when they are:

- Strategic (aligned with the organization's goals) and specific

- Measurable

- Attainable

- Results oriented

- Time bound (specifying when the goal will be achieved)

Principal Kushnir should help his staff develop confidence in their ability to develop SMART goals. Leadership teams at district, region, or school levels must demonstrate reciprocal accountability by providing each collaborative team with:

- The rationale as to why they are so important in the PLC process

- Tools and templates for establishing SMART goals

- Examples and nonexamples of SMART goals

- Criterion for assessing the quality of the SMART goals they develop

- Tips for developing good SMART goals

Principal Kushnir's leadership team would also need to develop plans for monitoring each collaborative team's SMART goals and providing assistance whenever a team struggles to complete the task.

We have found that the best way to help people throughout a school district to truly focus on results is to insist that every collaborative team establish SMART goals that align with school and district goals.

SMART Goals Are

Strategic and specific

Measurable

Attainable

Results oriented

Time bound

Aligning Team SMART Goals to School and District Goals

A district or school that has stipulated that its fundamental mission is to help all students learn at high levels could adopt such ongoing goals as these.

- We will help all students successfully complete every course and every grade level and demonstrate proficiency on local, provincial, national, and international assessments.

- We will eliminate the gaps in student achievement that are connected to ethnic or cultural origins, language, socioeconomic status, and gender.

These broad overarching district goals can then be translated into school goals. For example:

- We will reduce the failure rate in each grade level (or course) in our school.

- We will increase the percentage of students meeting or exceeding proficiency on district, provincial, or territorial as well as national and international assessments in each course or grade level in our school.

- We will increase the number of students who have access to and succeed in the most rigorous curriculum we offer.

The critical step in this process is to then ensure that each collaborative team translates one or more of the school goals into a SMART goal that drives the work of the team. As we discussed earlier, the definition of a team is a group of people working interdependently *to achieve a common goal* for which members are held mutually accountable. Thus, by definition, team members must be working toward a shared goal, and since the mission of the district and school is to improve student learning, that goal should focus specifically and directly on evidence of student learning.

Team SMART goals aligned to the school goals should stipulate both the past level of performance and the improvement goal for the indicator being monitored. For example:

- **Our reality**—Last year 76 percent of the first-grade students scored at the proficient or advanced levels in mathematics, as measured by our district's end-of-year mathematics assessment.

- **Our SMART goal**—By the end of this school year, at least 81 percent of the first-grade students will score at the proficient or advanced levels in mathematics as measured by our district's end-of-year mathematics assessment.

- **Our reality**—Last year, 68 percent of the ninth-grade English students earned a final grade of C or better.

- **Our SMART goal**—By the end of this school year, at least 75 percent of the ninth-grade English students will earn a final grade of C or better.

- **Our reality**—Last year, 89 percent of the eighth-grade science students scored at the proficient or advanced levels in science, as measured by our province or territory's eighth-grade science assessment.

- **Our SMART goal**—By the end of this school year, at least 93 percent of the eighth-grade science students will score at the proficient or advanced levels in science as measured by our province or territory's eighth-grade science assessment.

- **Our current reality**—Last year, 35 percent of the students in our school enrolled in at least one advanced placement (AP) course. Seventy-three percent of those students scored 3, 4, or 5 (passing scores) on the end-of-course national AP exams.

- **Our SMART goal**—This year, 48 percent of the students in our school will enroll in at least one AP course. At least 75 percent of those students will score 3, 4, or 5 (passing scores) on the end-of-course national AP exams.

Balancing Attainable Goals With Stretch Goals

When building a results-oriented culture, leaders must find a balance between the attainable goals teams feel they can achieve in the short term and stretch goals—goals so ambitious they could not possibly be achieved unless practices within the organization change significantly (Tichy, 1997). Stretch goals have also been referred to as BHAGs: Big Hairy Audacious Goals (Collins & Porras, 1994). Attainable goals are intended to document incremental progress and build momentum and self-efficacy through short-term wins. Stretch goals are intended to inspire, to capture the imagination of people within the organization, to stimulate creativity and innovation, and to serve as a unifying focal point of effort.

Stretch goals are effective only if they stimulate action, if people begin to behave in new ways. Pronouncements without action are hopes, not goals. Furthermore, stretch goals must be goals, not mission statements. They must set specific targets rather than offer vague expressions or beliefs. A perfect example of a stretch goal is U.S. President John F. Kennedy's assertion in 1961 that the country would land a man on the moon before the end of the decade. Notice he did not say, "We need to do something to strengthen the space program," or "We believe in the potential of space." He established a BHAG that included a specific target.

"We believe in high levels of learning for all students" is not a stretch goal. "We will ensure all students demonstrate proficiency on the district or provincial assessment,"

"We will eliminate achievement gaps based on socioeconomic status," and "We will ensure the academic success of every student in every grade level" are examples of stretch goals because they are stated as targets.

If schools and districts limit themselves to the pursuit of attainable goals, they run the risk of never moving outside their comfort zones. Organizations are unlikely to experience dramatic improvement if they are content with creeping incrementalism— slowly inching forward over time. If the only goals educators pursue are easily attainable, the focus shifts to how good do we have to be rather than how good can we be.

On the other hand, if the only goals educators pursue are stretch goals, teachers and principals are prone to give up in hopelessness. If educators perceive goals as unrealistic to the point of being unattainable, and there are no successes to celebrate, they will be discouraged from taking action to achieve those goals.

If schools and districts limit themselves to the pursuit of attainable goals, they run the risk of never moving outside their comfort zones. . . On the other hand, if the only goals educators pursue are stretch goals, teachers and principals are prone to give up in hopelessness.

We have found that in the early stages of building a PLC, celebrating small wins is key to sustaining the effort, and attainable goals are an essential element of results-oriented small wins. Therefore, we strongly recommend that goals established by collaborative teams should be attainable and include short-term goals that serve as benchmarks of progress. Teams should feel reasonably confident they have the capacity to achieve their goals. They should be able to say, "If we seek and implement best practices, we have reason to believe we will achieve our team goal."

Furthermore, frequent feedback and intermittent reinforcement are two factors that help sustain the effort essential to achieving goals. A team that establishes a goal of improving student performance on a provincial or territorial test receives neither feedback nor reinforcement for almost a year unless it establishes some short-term goals. For example, consider the team that analyzes the results from the common formative assessments its members administered in the first unit of the previous school year. Its members determine that 64 percent of students were able to meet the established essential outcome for writing proficiency by the end of October. That team sets a goal that at least 75 percent of students will meet that essential outcome by the same date this year. In this instance, short-term goals can inform the team of progress and create a basis for celebration prior to the end of the school year.

District goals, however, should be clearly linked to the purpose of learning for all students, should establish challenging targets, and should require innovation and long-term commitment if they are to be achieved. District goals should be so bold that they require the development of new capacities. A few district goals such as those listed in this chapter are long-term stretch goals representing a life's work rather than a short-term project. Therefore, the district leadership should commit to these goals year after year until they are achieved. New hot topics will be touted on the professional development circuit, political leaders will come and go, and special interest groups will demand schools pay more attention to their cause. Rather than reacting to each shift in the wind by placing more initiatives on their schools, the central office staff must help buffer them from the constant turbulence so educators can stay the course.

A blank "SMART Goal Worksheet" appears on page 87. The "SMART Goal Worksheet" reproducibles (pages 88–94) provide examples of how different district and school goals might be translated into SMART goals for collaborative teams. Note that when this process is in place, a team that accomplishes its SMART goal contributes to the ongoing improvement of its school and its district.

SMART Goal Worksheet

School:

Team Members:

District Goals:

School Goals:

Team Name:

Team Leader:

Team SMART Goal	Strategies and Action Steps	Who Is Responsible	Target Date or Timeline	Evidence of Effectiveness

SMART Goal Worksheet: Third-Grade Team

School: Sir John A. MacDonald Elementary School **Team Name:** Third Grade **Team Leader:** Theresa Smith

Team Members: Ken Thomas, Joe Ramirez, Cathy Armstrong, Amy Wu

District Goal:

- We will increase student achievement and close the achievement gap in all areas using a variety of indicators to document improved learning on the part of our students.

School Goal:

- We will improve student achievement in language arts as measured by local, district, province or territory, and national indicators.

Team SMART Goal	Strategies and Action Steps	Who Is Responsible	Target Date or Timeline	Evidence of Effectiveness
Our Current Reality: Last year, 85 percent of our students met or exceeded the target score of 3 on our province or territory's writing prompt in May. **Our SMART Goal:** This year, at least 90 percent of our students will meet or exceed the target score of 3 on our province or territory's writing prompt in May.	**Curriculum** 1. Clarify and pace essential student learning in writing using essentil outcomes documents, curriculum guides, assessment blueprints and data, and the wish list of skills from the fourth-grade team.	All members of our team	October 15	Lists of essential student learning outcomes and pacing guide Increased results for all students on team, district, provincial or territorial, and national indicators

page 2 of 3

Team SMART Goal	Strategies and Action Steps	Who Is Responsible	Target Date or Timeline	Evidence of Effectiveness
	Assessments 2. Develop, implement, and collaboratively score grade-level formative writing prompts to: a. Frequently monitor each student's learning of essential writing outcomes b. Provide students with multiple opportunities to demonstrate progress in meeting and exceeding learning targets in writing c. Learn with and from each other better ways to help students become proficient writers	All members of our team	October–May Checkpoints at midpoint of each grading period District benchmark assessments at end of each semester	Common writing prompts Common writing rubric Increased results for all students on team, district, provincial tor territorial, and national indicators
	3. Provide students with writing assignments in all subject areas, and utilize a variety of instructional strategies to help students learn all essential writing skills.	All members of our team Principal Resource staff Volunteers	Daily, September–May	Intervention or enrichment schedule Student learning results
	4. Initiate individual and small-group sessions to provide additional intervention and enrichment focused on writing.	All members of our team	Daily, September–May	Intervention or enrichment schedule Student learning results

Team SMART Goal	Strategies and Action Steps	Who Is Responsible	Target Date or Timeline	Evidence of Effectiveness
	5. Provide parents with resources and strategies to help their children succeed as writers.	All members of our team	First semester workshop: October 20 Second semester workshop: January 19 Newsletters End-of-grading-period conferences	Number of parents in attendance Study guides and newsletters
	Staff Development 6. Develop, implement, and evaluate our team action research project in writing to improve our individual and collective ability to help our students learn to write at high levels. Use information from our common formative assessments to identify staff development needs and engage in ongoing, job-embedded staff development in the area of writing.	All members of our team	Weekly collaborative team meetings Staff development days Faculty meeting sessions Additional professional learning time by request	Common assessments Quarterly reviews Midyear progress reports End-of-year team evaluations Increased results for all students on team, district, province or territory, and national indicators

page 3 of 3

SMART Goal Worksheet: Eighth-Grade Mathematics

School: John Cabot Middle School **Team Name:** Eighth-Grade Mathematics **Team Leader:** Chris Rauch

Team Members: Chris Carter, Dolores Layco, Mary Fischer

District Goal:

- We will increase student achievement and close the achievement gap in all areas using a variety of indicators to document improved learning on the part of our students.

School Goal: We will—

1. Reduce the failure rate in our school.

2. Increase the percentage of students scoring at or above the established proficiency essential outcome on the province or territory assessment in all areas.

Team SMART Goal	Strategies and Action Steps	Who Is Responsible	Target Date or Timeline	Evidence of Effectiveness
Our Current Reality: Last year, 24 percent of our students failed one or more semesters of mathematics, and 31 percent of our students were unable to meet the province or territory proficiency essential outcome in mathematics.	We will align each unit of our mathematics program with province or territory essential outcomes, study the results of the last province or territory assessment, identify problem areas, and develop specific strategies to address those areas in our course.	Entire team	We will complete the analysis on the teacher workday prior to the start of the year. We will review our findings prior to the start of each new unit.	Written analysis of province or territory assessment and strategies to address weaknesses
Our SMART Goal: This year, we will reduce the percentage of failing grades to 10 percent or less and the percentage of students unable to meet province or territory essential outcomes to no more than 15 percent.	We will develop common formative assessments and administer them every three weeks. These assessments will provide repeated opportunities for students to become familiar with the format used on the province or territory assessment.	Entire team	Formative assessments will be created prior to the start of each unit of instruction throughout the year. They will be administered on a day designated by the team.	Student performance on team-endorsed common assessments

Team SMART Goal	Strategies and Action Steps	Who Is Responsible	Target Date or Timeline	Evidence of Effectiveness
	After each common assessment, we will identify any student who does not meet the established proficiency essential outcomes and will work with the counselor to have those students reassigned from study hall to the mathematics tutoring centre.	Members of entire team will request tutoring as their supervisory responsibility; team leader will work with the counselor after each assessment.	Assessments will be administered every three weeks. Students will be assigned to the tutoring centre within one week of assessment.	Daily list of students receiving tutoring in mathematics
	We will replace failing grades from our common assessments with the higher grade earned by students who are able to demonstrate proficiency in key skills on subsequent forms of the assessment after completing tutoring.	Entire team will create multiple forms of each assessment. Tutors will administer the assessment after a student has completed the required tutoring.	Multiple forms of an assessment will be created prior to the start of each unit of instruction. Tutors will administer the second assessment within two weeks of a student's assignment to the tutoring centre.	Compilation of results from subsequent assessments
	We will examine the results of each common assessment to determine which member of the team is getting the best results on each skill, and then share ideas, methods, and materials for teaching those skills more effectively.	Each member of the team	Ongoing throughout the year each time a common assessment is administered	Analysis of findings after each common assessment is administered Decrease in the failure rate Increase in percentage of students proficient on province or territory assessment

page 2 of 2

SMART Goal Worksheet: Canadian Government

School: A. B. Lucas High School **Team Name:** Canadian History and Government **Team Leader:** Tom Botimer

Team Members: Dan Hahn, Andy Bradford, Nick Larsen, Helen Harvey

District Goals:

1. We will increase student achievement and close the achievement gap in all areas using a variety of indicators to document improved learning on the part of our students.

2. We will provide more students with access to our most rigorous curriculum in each subject area and grade level.

School Goals: We will increase by at least 10 percent the number of students earning credit in—

1. Advanced placement (AP) courses

2. Capstone courses in a departmental sequence

Team SMART Goal	Strategies and Action Steps	Who Is Responsible	Target Date or Timeline	Evidence of Effectiveness
Our Current Reality: All students must complete a semester of Canadian history and government as a graduation requirement. Last year only 10 percent of the graduating class fulfilled that requirement by enrolling in AP Canadian history and government.	We will make a presentation in each section of Canadian history, encouraging students to enroll in AP Canadian history and government and listing the advantages for doing so.	Team leader will coordinate the schedule for these presentations with the team leader for Canadian history. Each member of the team will assist in making these presentations and will distribute a written list of advantages created by the team.	Complete presentations by the end of January prior to students registering for their courses for next year.	The presentation has been made in every Canadian history class.

Team SMART Goal	Strategies and Action Steps	Who Is Responsible	Target Date or Timeline	Evidence of Effectiveness
Our SMART Goal: At least 20 percent of the current junior class will enroll in and earn a score of 3, 4, or 5 on the AP Canadian history and government exam by the end of next school year.	We will coordinate with the guidance department to ensure that when counselors register students for classes, they encourage any student who receives an A at the end of the first semester of history to enroll in AP Canadian history and government.	Team leader will attend the counselors' team meeting to enlist their support, explain advantages of the AP program, and share the team's strategies for supporting students in Canadian history and government.	End of first semester	Minutes of meeting
	We will advise parents of the benefits of AP Canadian history and government.	The team will draft a letter to parents of students who earn an A in history at the end of the semester. The letter will list the advantages of completing this course while in high school for any student planning on attending college. It will also include the team's strategy to provide students with additional support. The team will also create a flyer on the benefits of the AP program to be distributed during parent open house.	The flyer will be created for distribution at the open house in early October. The letter will be sent at the end of the first semester.	Completed documents
	We will create study groups to review material prior to the comprehensive assessments we administer every six weeks.	The team will create the common comprehensive assessments. Each member will be responsible for conducting one study group to help students review for these tests. Study groups will be held on three evenings in the week prior to the test.	Ongoing throughout the semester	Completion of common assessments and student performance on common assessments

The number of students earning honour grades on the AP exam in Canadian history and government will double over last year's total. |

page 2 of 2

Focusing on Results, Not Activities

Once again, a school that defines its purpose as "High levels of learning for all students" will insist that teams include the language of learning in their goals. This is contrary to the traditional approach of writing goals that focus on evidence of what teachers will do rather than on evidence of what students will learn. Statements such as, "We will integrate technology into our course," "We will align our curriculum with the newly adopted textbook," "We will increase the use of cooperative learning activities," or "We will solicit more parent involvement" may describe worthwhile initiatives, but they do not represent goals. If the purpose of these initiatives is to increase student learning, that purpose should be explicitly stated in a goal. Effective team goals will help answer the question, "How will we know if our strategies are resulting in gains in student learning?" The goals will focus on the intended outcome rather than on the strategies to achieve the outcome.

Leaders must find a balance between the attainable goals teams feel they can achieve in the short term and stretch goals—goals so ambitious they could not possibly be achieved unless practices within the organization change significantly.

Part Three

Here's Why

Why should educators abandon traditional strategic planning and focus instead on ensuring that each collaborative team in every school is working toward SMART goals that are specifically linked to a few school and district goals? Most simply, because there is no evidence that formal strategic planning leads to improved results. In his study of "great" organizations, Jim Collins (2001) was unable to discover any link between formal planning and organizational effectiveness. Jeffrey Pfeffer and Robert Sutton (2000) are even more emphatic in their conclusion, "Existing research on the effectiveness of formal planning efforts is clear: Planning is essentially unrelated to organizational performance" (p. 42). In his study of strategic planning in education, Doug Reeves (2009) actually found a negative correlation between district-led formal strategic planning and improved student achievement.

There is no evidence that formal strategic planning leads to improved results.

Whereas effective leaders are skillful in making the complex simple, strategic planning almost inevitably makes the simple complex. The one thing most strategic plans for school districts have in common is their girth. Voluminous tomes place far too many initiatives on schools and obscure rather than clarify priorities. The ambiguity and interchangeable use of terms adds to the confusion. How many people can assert with confidence that they can specify the differences between a strategic goal, a key objective, and a performance outcome? Furthermore, strategic plans often serve as a barrier to the relentless action orientation of effective organizations (Pfeffer & Sutton, 2000). Far too many school districts confuse developing or possessing a plan with taking meaningful action to ensure that something actually happens. Michael Fullan (2010) offers succinct advice to those hoping to improve their schools and districts: "Beware of fat plans" (p. 24).

The biggest factor in the ineffectiveness of formal strategic planning rests on its faulty underlying assumption: some people in organizations (the leaders) are responsible for thinking and planning, while others (the workers) are responsible for carrying out those plans. This separation of thought and action is the antithesis of a learning community, which requires widely dispersed leadership and strategic thinkers throughout the organization (Fullan, 2005). Asking employees to follow a five-year strategic plan chartered by others does little to generate a focus on or commitment to improved results. Engaging those employees in a process of ongoing continuous improvement in which they establish their own short-term goals, develop their own plans to achieve them, act on those plans, and make frequent adjustments based on their analysis of evidence is much more likely to instill a results orientation throughout the organization.

Not only do collaborative teams represent the optimum setting for the pursuit of meaningful SMART goals, but SMART goals also represent an essential tool in developing powerful collaborative teams. Teams benefit when they have a few key goals that clarify the results they seek and how each member can contribute to achieving those results (Lencioni, 2005; Schaffer & Thomson, 1992). They are more effective when they see how their goals and their efforts are linked to the larger organization (Druskat & Wolff, 2001). They are strengthened from the accomplishment and celebration of short-term wins (Collins, 2001; Katzenbach & Smith, 1993; Kotter, 2012; Kouzes & Posner, 1987). They are more committed, empowered, and motivated when they set their own targets and create their own plans to achieve them (Amabile & Kramer, 2011; Axelrod, 2002; Pink, 2011).

*There is **nothing** more important in determining the effectiveness of a team than each member's understanding of and commitment to the achievement of results-oriented goals to which the group holds itself mutually accountable.*

In short, there is *nothing* more important in determining the effectiveness of a team than each member's understanding of and commitment to the achievement of results-oriented goals to which the group holds itself mutually accountable. Helping teams translate long-term purpose into specific, measurable short-term SMART goals, and then helping members develop the skills to achieve those goals, is one of the most important steps leaders can take in building the capacity of a group to function as a high-performing collaborative team (Katzenbach & Smith, 1993). Furthermore, as teams achieve their short-term goals, it creates the opportunity to celebrate progress and builds commitment to the PLC process. We provide you with a small sample of the research showing the importance of team-developed goals (see the reproducible, "Why Do We Need SMART Goals?").

Why Do We Need SMART Goals?

"According to research, goal setting is the single most powerful motivational tool in a leader's toolkit. Why? Because goal setting operates in ways that provide purpose, challenge, and meaning. Goals are the guideposts along the road that make a compelling vision come alive. Goals energize people. Specific, clear, challenging goals lead to greater effort and achievement than easy or vague goals do" (Blanchard, 2007, p. 150).

"Goal setting is one of the simplest and most effective organizational interventions that can be used to increase employee performance" (O'Hora & Maglieri, 2006, p. 132).

"[Schools with teachers who learn and students who achieve] use clear, agreed-upon student achievement goals to focus and shape teacher learning" (WestEd, 2000, p. 12).

"Collegial support and professional development in schools are unlikely to have any effect on improvement of practice and performance if they are not connected to a coherent set of goals that give direction and meaning to learning and collegiality" (Elmore, 2003, p. 60).

California elementary schools that outperformed schools with similar student populations assigned a high priority to student achievement, set measurable goals for improved student achievement, and had a well-defined plan to improve achievement (Williams et al., 2005).

"Consistently higher performing high schools set explicit academic goals that are aligned with and often exceed state standards" (Dolejs, 2006, p. 1).

"Our investigations suggest it is critical to define and publish a protocol that articulates specific inquiry functions: jointly and recursively identifying appropriate and worthwhile goals for student learning; finding or developing appropriate means to assess student progress toward those goals; bringing to the table the expertise of colleagues and others who can assist in accomplishing these goals; planning, preparing, and delivering lessons; using evidence from the classroom to evaluate instruction; and, finally, reflecting on the process to determine next steps" (Gallimore et al., 2009, pp. 548–549).

"One of the greatest challenges to team success is the inattention to results. . . . But there is no getting around the fact that the only measure of a great team—or a great organization—is whether it accomplishes what it sets out to accomplish. . . . When it comes to how a cohesive team measures its performance, one criterion sets it apart from noncohesive ones: its goals are shared across the entire team" (Lencioni, 2012, pp. 65–66).

Schools that have the greatest impact on student learning establish clear and measurable goals focused on improving overall student achievement at the school level. "Data are analyzed, interpreted, and used to regularly monitor progress toward student achievement goals" (Marzano, Warrick, & Simms, 2014, p. 57).

"The problem is not the absence of goals in districts and schools today but the presence of too many that are ad hoc, unconnected, and ever-changing. . . . [They are too often fragmented and so] people see them as discrete demands with little or no connection to . . . their daily work. . . . The solution lies in developing limited goals, persisting, and avoiding distractors. . . . These leaders . . . [use goals] to establish continuous focused direction" (Fullan & Quinn, 2016, pp. 20–21).

Part Four

Assessing Your Place on the PLC Journey

It is important to help your staff build shared knowledge regarding your school's current status in addressing the critical step on the PLC journey of creating a results orientation. We have created a tool to assist you in that effort. "The Professional Learning Communities at Work® Continuum: Using School Improvement Goals to Drive Team Goals" is available at **go.SolutionTree.com/ca/PLCbooks** as a free reproducible. Once your staff have established greater clarity regarding the current status of your collaborative teams, we urge you to turn your attention to the "Where Do We Go From Here?" worksheet that accompanies the continuum (also available for free to download at **go.SolutionTree.com/ca/PLCbooks**). It will prompt you to take the action necessary to close the knowing-doing gap.

Part Five

Tips for Moving Forward: Using Goals to Focus on Results

1   **Remember less is more:** Limit the number of district and school initiatives, and make certain the initiatives reflect the priority of high levels of learning for all students.

2   **Tie all goals to district goals:** Assuming the district has created learning-focused goals, require each school to pursue a few schoolwide goals and each collaborative team within the school to establish a limited (two or three) number of SMART goals that are specifically aligned with school and district goals.

3   **Provide templates for goal setting for every team:** The templates should reinforce the premise that the team must (1) focus on improved results rather than implementing activities and (2) clarify how the achievement of the goal will be attained, monitored, and measured.

4   **Make certain goals are team goals rather than individual goals:** Remember that an effective goal will require team members to work interdependently in order to achieve it. Members should be able to clarify both individual and collective responsibilities.

5   **Ensure team goals are established by teams rather than for teams:** Teams should be expected to create goals that align with school and district goals, to write goals that represent continuous improvement, and are consistent with specified parameters. However, each team should enjoy considerable autonomy in articulating its goals.

6 **Monitor work toward a goal by requiring teams to create specific products that are directly related to achieving the goal:** Typical products include collective commitments or norms, aligned curriculum, common assessments, collective analysis of results, improvement plans, and so on.

7 **Celebrate progress:** Plan for, seek out, and celebrate small wins.

8 **Consider affective goals as well as academic goals:** The high levels of learning a school or team seeks for its students need not be limited to academic areas. Affective areas aligned to essential social and academic behaviours (for example, responsibility, empathy, self-efficacy, independence, and so on) are perfectly legitimate areas for establishing goals. Because these behaviours should be demonstrated schoolwide, these goals should usually be written by and include the entire faculty. There is a tendency when establishing such goals, however, to be content with the implementation of new programs or the nobleness of the cause. Neither the completion of projects nor the unassailability of good intentions should substitute for results-oriented goals. Teams must discipline themselves to address the question, "How will we know our students are achieving this goal?" for every goal they establish.

9 **Include stretch goals in direct goals:** These goals will be so challenging that people throughout the organization will be called on to build new capacities in order to achieve them.

10 **Be wary of the complacency that can set in when a stretch goal has been achieved:** It is easy for an organization to drift into the "we have arrived" mode when it has been successful in the pursuit of a challenging goal (Collins & Porras, 1994). Combat that tendency and promote continuous improvement by celebrating the accomplishment and then creating a new stretch goal.

Part Six

Questions to Guide the Work of Your Professional Learning Community

To promote the commitment to a results orientation in your school or district, ask:

1. What evidence do we have that district goals are directly impacting the work of schools and collaborative teams within the school?

2. Does every collaborative team have a goal that aligns with district and school goals?

3. Are team goals SMART: strategic and specific, measurable, attainable, results oriented, and time bound?

4. Is there a plan in place to monitor each team's progress? Does the plan include monitoring the team's products as it works toward its goals?

5. Are teams provided with relevant and timely feedback regarding their progress? Remember that goals are effective motivators, but only if teams receive feedback.

6. Is a plan in place to identify, acknowledge, and celebrate small wins as teams make progress toward their goals?

7. Do district goals include stretch goals?

Part Seven

Dangerous Detours and Seductive Shortcuts

Beware of goals that are so narrow that they can be accomplished even if students learn less. For example, a team that establishes a SMART goal of improving student performance in the skill of capitalization could achieve that goal even if the proficiency of their students actually declines in reading comprehension or writing. Be certain to establish goals that focus on the knowledge and skills that are most essential in the given content or grade level.

Beware of morally impeccable goals that are impossible to monitor. A team that announces its goal is to help its students become lifelong learners has certainly established a noble goal, but unless it can identify the specific indicators it will monitor to assess students' progress as lifelong learners, they have not yet established a SMART goal.

Finally, beware of goals that do not require students to learn at higher levels. Once again, educators are accustomed to focusing on what they will do rather than the knowledge and skills that students will demonstrate. If the goal can be accomplished without students learning at higher levels (for example, "Our team will create four new common assessments"), it is not a SMART goal.

If the goal can be accomplished without students learning at higher levels (for example, "Our team will create four new common assessments"), it is not a SMART goal.

Final Thoughts

The way in which a school or district structures its planning and goal-setting process can help or hinder the adoption of the PLC process. When a school has organized its faculty into meaningful teams, provided them with time to collaborate, helped each team clarify its commitments to its members, and established SMART goals that require them to work interdependently and demonstrate mutual accountability, the teams are well positioned to begin their collective inquiry into the critical questions that will drive their work. We turn our attention to the first of those questions—What do we want our students to learn?—in the next chapter.

CHAPTER 5
Establishing a Focus on Learning

Part One

The Case Study: What Do We Want Our Students to Learn?

When Karen Power became superintendent of School District 2 in New Brunswick, she knew that she wanted to bring the PLC process to all thirty-eight schools in the district. She had been successful implementing the PLC process as a principal and knew that it would make a difference if she could get all district schools to understand and implement the work.

She invited her district leaders and several principals to attend a PLC at Work Institute. At the conference, one thing became very evident to Superintendent Power and her team: in order to authentically do this work, the district had to help the schools become very clear on answering the first PLC question, "What do we want students to know and be able to do?"

As is the case in most provinces, curriculum outcomes are decided at the provincial level. In New Brunswick, the number of outcomes for each content level was vastly outnumbering the time that teachers had to ensure mastery of them. Teachers were overwhelmed by the requirements, and Superintendent Power and her team knew that they were not meeting the needs of students when they could not provide a guaranteed and viable curriculum. They set out to change this.

Assistant Superintendent Gregg Ingersoll organized a professional development day for all teachers in the district. Much planning went into the day, with Superintendent Ingersoll ensuring that ninety facilitators were trained to lead small groups of teachers, meeting together by grade and content level. He developed key messages to share with all teachers explaining the *why* and importance of establishing clarity on *what* they wanted students to know and be able to do. The teachers worked collaboratively to determine what they saw as essential learnings and started clarifying what they knew that they had to ensure students mastered from the curriculum outcomes. They were able to talk about the *need to knows* versus the *nice to knows*. The day was so successful that most teacher groups continued to meet across the district, formally and informally, throughout the year to complete their list of essentials.

After a few weeks, the provincial education department came to meet with the superintendents. Members expressed concerns that the district was asking teachers to eliminate outcomes and not complying with provincial direction. They stated that students from the district would not be successful on provincial assessments because all outcomes were not being taught. Some teachers were also nervous that they were eliminating content that was required. The representatives from the teacher professional organization also expressed their doubts about the process as they saw this as more work for their members.

The superintendents knew that this was the right work, but as time passed, it was evident that they were always going to have resistance. They continued to support the work of determining the essentials and expected collaborative teams to plan from these outcomes, but as time passed, it became a *loose* rather than a *tight* expectation.

Reflection

Consider superintendents Power and Ingersoll's efforts to engage their teachers in clarifying the essential outcomes. If you were called on to consult in this district, what advice would you offer?

Part Two

Here's How

The superintendents in this case study confronted a common dilemma: there were certain important tasks in which they hoped to engage the staff in order to further their agreed-on commitment to learning for all students; however, they wanted the staff to be a part of the process and to feel empowered as the district moved forward.

- Should they insist that the teachers develop common outcomes for their courses, or should they abandon a process vital to a PLC because of the objections raised by the staff?

- Is the district better served by a culture of control that demands adherence to certain practices or a culture of freedom that encourages individual or departmental autonomy?

In their study of high-performing organizations, Collins and Porras (1994) discovered ineffective organizations succumbed to the "Tyranny of Or"—"the rational view that cannot easily accept paradox, that cannot live with two seemingly contradictory forces at the same time. We must be A or B, but not both" (p. 44). High-performing organizations, however, rejected this false dichotomy and embraced the "Genius of And" by demonstrating the ability to honour both extremes at the same time. Collins and Porras (1994) clarified that the Genius of And "is not just a question of 'balance' because balance implies going to the midpoint—fifty-fifty. A visionary company does not seek the gray of balance, but seeks to be distinctly both 'A' and 'B' at the same time" (p. 45).

If Superintendent Power and her teachers were to apply these findings to their situation they would create a district culture that was simultaneously loose and tight as we described in chapter 1 (page 9). Schools and districts need not choose between demanding adherence to certain core principles and practices or empowering the staff. Certain critical issues must be addressed, and certain important tasks must be accomplished in a PLC. The school or district is tight in those areas, demanding faithfulness to specific principles and practices.

At the same time, however, individuals and teams can benefit from considerable autonomy and freedom in terms of how things get done on a day-to-day basis because the school or district is loose about much of the implementation. Members of the school have the benefit of clear parameters that provide direction and coherence to the improvement process; however, they are also given the freedom and tools to make their own contribution to that process. This autonomy allows the school community to benefit from the insights and expertise of those who are called on to do the actual work.

The question "Learn what?" is one of the most significant questions the members of a PLC will consider. In fact, the entire PLC process is predicated on a deep understanding on the part of all educators of what all students must know and be able to do as a result of every unit of instruction. Therefore, one of the "tight" expectations the school must establish is that every teacher will be called on to work collaboratively with colleagues to clarify the question, "What is it we want our students to learn?"

The question "Learn what?" is one of the most significant questions the members of a PLC will consider.

By the same token, if Superintendent Power intends to hold collaborative teams accountable for establishing a guaranteed and viable curriculum, she has a responsibility to provide them with the clarity, parameters, resources, support, and rationale to help them succeed in what they are being asked to accomplish. Let's consider how she might work with school and team leaders to address those questions.

If teams are going to be asked to create a guaranteed and viable curriculum, members must be clear regarding what the term represents. Members of the collaborative teams should understand that a "guaranteed and viable curriculum" (1) gives students access to the same essential learning outcomes regardless of who is teaching the class and (2) can be taught in the time allotted (Marzano, 2003). It does not mean that teachers must adhere to lockstep pacing by which members are teaching from the same page on the same day. It does not mean that all teachers must use the same instructional strategies or same materials. It does mean that during a unit presented within a specific window of time established by the team (for example, three weeks), each team member will work to ensure every student acquires the knowledge and skills the team has agreed are most essential for that unit.

In many schools and districts, educators settle for creating the illusion of a guaranteed curriculum by proving all teachers with a copy of provincial, territorial, or district essential outcomes and pretend that the mere distribution of the same curriculum document ensures a guaranteed curriculum. In a PLC, the first step educators take when making decisions is to *learn together*. As we argue in *Concise Answers to Frequently Asked Questions About Professional Learning Communities at Work*:

In a PLC, the first step educators take when making decisions is to learn together.

Merely providing teachers with a copy of the state standards [or essential outcomes] for their grade level does not ensure all students will have access to a guaranteed curriculum that can be taught in the amount of time available for teaching. Teachers may ignore the [outcomes or] standards, assign different priorities to the standards, vary dramatically in how much time they devote to the standards, have huge discrepancies in terms of what the standard looks like in terms of student work, and have significant differences in their ability to teach the standards. (Mattos et al., 2016, p. 17)

There are no shortcuts; establishing a guaranteed and viable curriculum requires that teachers engage in a process of collective inquiry.

There are no short cuts; establishing a guaranteed and viable curriculum requires that teachers engage in a process of collective inquiry. Superintendent Power and her educators should embrace a process that includes the following six steps.

1. Collectively study the outcomes using a variety of internal and external resources.

2. Reach consensus on the highest priority outcomes by differentiating those that are "nice to know" from those that all students "must know."

3. Clarify how the highest outcomes (or essential learnings) are translated into the specific knowledge, skills, and dispositions that all students must demonstrate.

4. Establish what proficiency for each outcome or essential learning looks like.

5. Establish common pacing guides and agreed-on assessment schedules.

6. Commit to one another that they will actually teach that agreed-on curriculum.

In order to support the task of creating a guaranteed and viable curriculum, Superintendent Power should provide all staff members with the pertinent resources to help them address the question of "Learn what?" Some of the resources she should provide to assist teacher teams in creating a guaranteed and viable curriculum include:

- Copies of current provincial, territorial, or curriculum expectations or outcomes

- Recommended outcomes from professional organizations (for example, from the National Council of Teachers of Mathematics)

- District curriculum guides

- A list of prerequisite skills that colleagues at the next course or grade level have established as essential for success at that level

- Assessment frameworks (how students will be assessed on provincial, territorial, national, and district assessments)

- Data on student performance on past assessments

- Examples of student work and of specific criteria that could be used in judging the quality of student work

- Recommendations and essential outcomes for workplace skills

- Recommendations on curriculum design from authors such as Doug Reeves, Heidi Hayes Jacobs, Robert Marzano, Grant Wiggins, and Jay McTighe

When developing a guaranteed and viable curriculum, teachers continually refine and clarify their understanding of what all students should know and be able to do as they move from prioritizing and unwrapping essential outcomes, to identifying specific learning targets, to creating "I can" statements for students.

Prioritizing Expected Outcomes

Essential outcomes refer to the general knowledge, skills, and dispositions that students are expected to acquire as a result of the teaching and learning process. Typically developed by content specialists (at provincial, territorial, or district level) external to the school, outcomes can be complex and densely worded statements that describe global outcomes for each content area.

Developing a guaranteed and viable curriculum requires prioritization of these expected outcomes and a recognition of the fact that while all outcomes are important, some are more essential than others. In this U.S. example (using standards instead of outcomes), Sharon Kramer (2015) writes:

> Although they are more targeted, the Common Core standards and other new or revised state standards are far too many to learn in a school year. Teams must collaborate to determine which of the standards are essential from those that are nice to know or peripheral. Essential standards do not represent all that teachers teach. They represent the minimum a student must learn to reach high levels of learning. They serve to establish the focus for assessing student learning and implementing interventions when students do not learn. Teachers are not creating a list but building shared knowledge of what the most important skills, concepts, and understandings are that will result in higher levels of achievement. This is about focus, focus, focus. (p. 21)

For schools, the question is not whether teachers should determine their essential outcomes. For years individual teachers have made decisions about what they will teach and what they will skip. The question confronting schools is whether principals will engage teachers in a rational, focused, and collaborative process designed to identify the most essential expectations, the ones that all students must learn, or will the critical task of prioritizing the learning outcomes be relegated to an informal process based on the personal preferences of individual educators?

When developing a guaranteed and viable curriculum, teachers continually refine and clarify their understanding of what all students should know and be able to do.

Larry Ainsworth (2015a) offers a helpful process to guide educators in establishing the essential outcomes (priority standards). He recommends that teachers working in grade-level or course-specific teams apply a four-part test to each of the outcomes proposed by their province, territory, or district.

1. **Does the outcome have endurance?** Are students expected to retain the knowledge and skill beyond the unit and the course?

2. **Does the outcome have leverage?** Will the student be able to apply the standard in more than one subject area?

3. **Does the outcome prepare students for success at the next level?** Has this outcome been identified as an essential prerequisite skill in the next course or grade level?

4. **Will the outcome prepare students for success on high stakes external exams?** Is this a concept or skill that students are most likely to encounter on provincial or territorial exams, college entrance exams, or occupational competency exams?

Collaborative team members must go beyond the mere study of the outcomes for their course or grade level.

It should be evident that in order to answer these questions, collaborative team members must go beyond the mere study of essential outcomes for their course or grade level. They must also engage in vertical articulation with their colleagues above and below their course or grade level to clarify prerequisite skills. They must also become students of the high-stakes external exams to become familiar with the content and format of those exams.

As collaborative teams consider each expected outcome, Larry Ainsworth (2015b) recommends that they underline the teachable concepts (important nouns and noun phrases) and capitalize the skills (verbs) students are to demonstrate. He offers the following examples:

> RI.6.6: DETERMINE an <u>author's point of view or purpose</u> in a text and EXPLAIN <u>how it is conveyed</u> in the text. (Adapted from NGA & CCSSO, 2010a)

The following is an example of an "unwrapped" second-grade mathematics essential outcome in the domain of Number and Operations in Base Ten:

> 2.NBT.9: EXPLAIN WHY addition and subtraction strategies work, USING place value and the properties of operations. (Adapted from NGA & CCSSO, 2010b)

When considering whether to place a higher priority on one particular outcome over another, Ainsworth (2015b) also recommends that teachers use Webb's Depth of Knowledge (DOK) as the framework to help decide which outcome is the more *comprehensive* or *rigorous*—not the more foundational. Here again, the study of external high-stakes exams can help educators come to a better understanding of the rigor their students will encounter on those exams and thus guide their decisions regarding the rigor they pursue in their instruction and team-developed assessments.

We recommend that teams consider a fifth question during their review of essential learnings.

5. **What content do we currently teach that we can eliminate from the curriculum because it is not essential?**

Superintendents Power and Ingersoll could help foster a new mindset in their district if they asked each team to identify content it was removing from the curriculum each time a team planned a unit of instruction.

Creating a Process for Identifying Nonessential Curriculum

When Tom Many works with schools, he uses a simple process called "Keep, Drop, Create" to engage teachers in dialogue regarding a guaranteed and viable curriculum. At least once a quarter, teachers devote a grade level or departmental meeting to analysis of the intended versus the implemented curriculum. Each team member brings his or her lesson plan books and a copy of the essential curriculum. Three pieces of butcher paper are posted on the wall of the meeting room and labeled with one of the three categories: Keep, Drop, or Create. Each team member is then given sticky notes in three colours—yellow for Keep, pink for Drop, and green for Create—and is asked to reflect honestly on his or her teaching.

Teams begin their analysis using their lesson plans (either digital or hard copies) as the record of what was actually taught (the implemented curriculum) and copies of provincial or district curriculum guides to review the intended curriculum. Topics identified in the essential curriculum documents and included in each teacher's lesson plans are recorded on the Keep page. Topics identified as essential but not addressed in a teacher's lesson plans (either because the topics have not yet been taught or because they have been omitted) are listed on the Create page. Finally, topics included in a teacher's lesson plans but not reflected in the essential curriculum documents are put on the Drop page.

This process not only assists in discovering curriculum gaps and topics that must be addressed in upcoming units, but it also helps teams create a stop-doing list of topics that are not essential. As teachers engage in this activity over time, they become more clear, more consistent, and more confident in their response to the question, "What must our students know and be able to do as a result of this unit we are about to teach?"

Visit the website of Kildeer Countryside Community Consolidated School District 96 (www.kcsd96.org/curriculum/curriculum-frameworks.cfm) to review the guaranteed and viable curriculum of a district that has used this approach. Although this is a U.S. example, it highlights the important work needed in our Canadian schools and districts to ensure we have a protocol or process in place to formally identify what are essential learnings. A scan of Canadian provincial and territorial departments of education provides evidence that curriculum is established at that level and teachers are provided with broad essential outcomes. In some cases, there are many and some have just a few. Engaging teachers in the discussion of *what* they absolutely want students to be proficient in is critical work whether there are many or a few outcomes that the jurisdiction defines.

The process of prioritizing the essential outcomes has significant benefits. It creates greater clarity about what teachers will teach which in turn, promotes more efficient planning and sharing of resources. Perhaps the greatest benefit is that it encourages teachers to embrace more in-depth instruction by reducing the pressure to simply cover the material.

Identifying the Learning Targets

Once teams have established the essential outcome, they should create learning targets to clarify the desired outcome of an individual lesson or series of lessons. As our colleague Nicole Dimich Vagle (2015) points out, "Learning goals [targets] tightly align to the standards [essential outcomes], representing the learning students need to reflect the essence of the standards [essential outcomes]" (p. 27).

It is through the simple, yet powerful process of unwrapping targets that teams come to understand what each essential outcome requires that teachers should teach and students should learn. A single outcome typically includes multiple learning targets. Thus, it is virtually impossible for teams to determine if a curriculum is viable—meaning a curriculum that can be taught in the amount of time that is available to teach—unless teachers first develop a deep, rich understanding of how many learning targets each outcome contains. Once again, the goal of unwrapping is not to create another list of mini outcomes (teachers have enough lists!), it is to get at what Vagle (2015) refers to as the "essence" of each learning expectation.

Creating "I Can" Statements

Rick Stiggins (2004) encourages teachers to translate learning targets into student-friendly statements called "I can" statements, which help students understand their progress toward mastery of the outcome. Developing "I can" statements serves a number of important purposes. They clarify for students what students are learning—what they should know and be able to do—in language students can understand. They enable students to monitor and assume major responsibility for their own learning, a practice associated with a 32 percentile point gain in student achievement (Marzano, 2010).

Developing "I can" statements also helps teachers sharpen both their own understanding of what students are expected to do in order to demonstrate their learning and the level of rigor necessary to demonstrate proficiency. They help teams develop appropriate formats for formative and summative assessments and enhance specificity regarding the kind of support that will benefit students who are experiencing difficulty.

"I can" statements can also be a valuable resource for parents, providing them with a clear explanation of what their child is expected to be able to know and do. These statements can assist parents in their support of their own child's learning. Consider the following essential outcomes and the example of team developed "I can" statements for grade 3. These statements can be used to keep parents informed about their child's learning and students can also use the statements to self-monitor and improve their own learning. For example, students can keep "I can" statements as part of their portfolio, and after formative assessments, students fill out forms, such as in the chart that follows, to track the skills they have mastered as well as those requiring additional work.

Essential Outcomes

Grade 3 reading: Determine the main idea of a text; recount the key details and explain how they support the main idea.

Grade 3 writing: Write informative or explanatory texts to examine a topic and convey ideas and information clearly.

Grade 3 speech and language: Determine the main ideas and supporting details of a text read aloud or information presented in diverse media and formats, including visually, quantitatively, and orally. (Adapted from NGA & CCSSO, 2010a).

Target	Not Yet (1)	Starting To (2)	Yes! (3)
I can identify the main topic of the text.			
I can identify main ideas about a topic.			
I can identify details that support main ideas.			
I can determine which details are important (key) and which are less important.			
I can explain why details I identified are key details that support the main idea.			
I can listen to text to determine topic, main ideas, and details.			
I can read about a topic of interest and organize my thinking using topic, main ideas, and details.			
I can organize and clearly communicate my thinking about a topic orally.			
I can plan my informational writing using a topic, main ideas, and details.			
I can organize and clearly communicate my thinking about a topic in writing.			

Clarifying What Proficient Student Work Will Look Like

Once a team has agreed that a particular outcome is essential, its members must also clarify what represents proficient student work. Superintendents Power and Ingersoll can engage teachers in a process to clarify essential outcomes by asking them to address the question, "What would this outcome, if mastered, *look like* in terms of student work?" This strategy of clarifying essential learnings through the lens of student work leads teams through a natural progression of questions.

Once a team has agreed that a particular outcome is essential, its members must also clarify what represents proficient student work.

- What is it we want our students to learn?

- What is the evidence we expect students to generate in order to demonstrate proficiency?

- What will proficient student work look like?

- What will our assessments look like in order to gather the appropriate evidence?

One of the most important lessons team members must learn in working together is that it is impossible to establish a guaranteed and viable curriculum unless and until they have agreed on what constitutes proficient work. As John Hattie (2012) concludes in his book *Visible Learning for Teachers: Maximizing Impact on Learning*, a synthesis of the research on factors that impact student learning:

> One of the major messages from *Visible Learning* is the power of teachers learning from and talking to each other about planning— learning intentions, success criteria, what is valuable learning, progression, what it means to be "good at" a subject. . . . Only by having some common understanding of what it means to be "good at" something can the resulting debates about forms of evidence, quality of teaching, and student outcomes make sense. . . . Sharing a common understanding of progression is the most critical success factor in any school; as without it, individualism, personal opinions, and "anything goes" dominate. (p. 60)

Collaborative teacher teams must avoid the trap of thinking that "proficiency" is the ultimate expectation that all students should reach.

Determining Proficiency and Beyond

Collaborative teacher teams must avoid the trap of thinking that "proficiency" is the ultimate expectation that all students should reach. It is incumbent that teacher teams also determine what "beyond proficiency" looks like. Marzano Resources offers proficiency scales tied to critical concepts to assist teams with this challenge. Visit Marzano Resources (www.marzanoresources.com/educational-services/critical-concepts) to learn the process for identifying and articulating critical concepts in English language art, mathematics, and science.

Pacing the Guaranteed and Viable Curriculum

After teams have prioritized and unwrapped essential outcomes, translated learning targets into "I can" statements, and reached consensus on what proficiency looks like, they turn their attention to pacing. Grant Wiggins (2012) observes that the pacing of curriculum is (1) a dynamic, not static process that (2) should concern itself first and foremost with the pace of the learner, not the teacher. His observations align perfectly with our belief that the fundamental purpose of school is learning, not teaching.

The pacing of a guaranteed and viable curriculum concentrates on designing an instructional sequence for the highest essential outcomes as identified earlier in the process. It also requires that teams focus on teaching, as opposed to simply covering, the curriculum.

Pacing is another topic for the crucial conversations teams must engage in; it simply cannot be delegated to external consultants, textbook publishers, or even district-level administrators. Many districts publish district-level pacing guides that serve as good starting places for team discussions, but pacing guides that mandate the strict adherence to rigid schedules and timelines promote covering the curriculum as opposed to teaching the curriculum.

We believe teams must have the autonomy to adjust pacing based on students' needs. According to Jane David (2008), "The best pacing guides emphasize curricular guidance instead of prescriptive pacing" (p. 88). She continues, "Constructive pacing guides assume differences in teachers, students, and school contexts. They adjust expectations through frequent revisions based on *input from teachers*" (p. 88, emphasis added).

Teams must have the autonomy to adjust pacing based on students' needs.

The best way for teachers to provide input into pacing of the curriculum is by using the results of their common formative assessments. Once a team has established an assessment schedule for the unit, they may decide that proficiency is demonstrated when 80 percent of the students achieve 80 percent mastery on a common assessment. If only 55 percent of the students demonstrate 80 percent mastery, the team should consider slowing down and exploring new ways to teach the skills.

Committing to Each Other and the Curriculum

The "Learn what?" question is simply too vital to the PLC process to be left either to individual teachers or those outside of the school. It was really important for Superintendents Power and Ingersoll to involve their educators in this process. The constant collective inquiry into this question is a professional responsibility of every faculty member in a PLC. Thus, the challenge of developing and implementing a guaranteed and viable curriculum is *both* a top-down *and* bottom-up process (Eaker & Keating, 2012).

On the one hand, district- and school-level leaders must provide guidelines, resources, training, examples, and feedback to assist teachers in sharpening their understanding of what is essential that their students be able to do and know (from the top down). On the other hand, the actual development and implementation of a guaranteed and viable curriculum must be grounded in the work of collaborative teacher teams who bring their collective expertise to the task (from the bottom up).

Opportunity to learn is a powerful factor in student learning. This concept rests on the logical proposition that students are most likely to learn what they are taught and will have a difficult time learning things that they are not taught (Marzano et al., 2014). Leaving the "Learn what?" question to individual teachers deprives students of an equal opportunity to learn and results in an inequitable educational lottery in which the knowledge and skills a student acquires depend on the teacher to whom that student has been assigned. As our colleague Tim Brown asserts in his work at PLC at Work Institutes, a guaranteed and viable curriculum represents more than a list of

Developing and implementing a guaranteed and viable curriculum is the essential cornerstone for making the cultural shift from a focus on teaching content to a focus on the deep, rich, rigorous learning of each student.

intended outcomes. It is the promises we as educators make to our students about what we will ensure that they learn.

In summary, developing and implementing a guaranteed and viable curriculum is the essential cornerstone for making the cultural shift from a focus on teaching content to a focus on the deep, rich, rigorous learning of each student. Implementing a guaranteed and viable curriculum is a process, not an event. Effective teams realize that the actual implementation of a guaranteed and viable curriculum is an ongoing process of examination and sharpening the focus on what students should know and what the learning should look like in student work.

Part Three

Here's Why

Reciprocal accountability requires leaders not only to help educators understand how to address a task but also to make the case for why the task is essential.

Reciprocal accountability requires leaders not only to help educators understand how to address a task but also to make the case for why the task is essential. Schools are most effective when the people throughout the organization are clear regarding their fundamental purpose. Educators can play a role in the success of their organizations when they know not only how to perform their specific tasks but also when they understand why they do them—how their work contributes to a larger purpose (DuFour & Fullan, 2013). This clarity of purpose directs their day-to-day actions and decisions. As Jim Collins (2001) notes, "Great organizations simplify a complex world into a single organizing idea, a basic principle or concept that unifies and guides everything" (p. 91).

In chapter 2 (page 25), we argued that the fundamental purpose—the single organizing idea—that unifies and guides the work of a PLC is ensuring high levels of learning for all students. No school or district can accomplish that purpose unless it can answer the question, "Exactly what is it each student is expected to learn?" School districts are most effective when these questions are addressed in a systematic way by the professionals most responsible for ensuring learning: classroom teachers.

The premise that every teacher must know what he or she must teach and what students must learn is found in virtually every credible school improvement model (see page 116, "Why Should We Ensure Students Have Access to a Guaranteed and Viable Curriculum?"). It only makes sense that teachers are most effective in helping all students learn when they are clear regarding exactly what their students must know and be able to do as a result of the course, grade level, and each unit of instruction.

This finding presents schools and districts with an important question: "What is the best way to ensure each teacher knows what students must learn?" One approach is to provide each teacher with a copy of the outcomes that have been established for their subject area or grade level as well as a provincial, territorial, and district curriculum guides for addressing those essential learnings. The assumption behind this practice is that if the right documents are distributed to individual teachers, each will teach the same curriculum as his or her colleagues. This assumption lingers despite decades of evidence that it is erroneous. Almost every veteran educator would agree with the research that there is a huge discrepancy between the intended curriculum and the implemented curriculum (Marzano, 2003). The former specifies what teachers are called on to teach; the latter reflects what is actually taught. The idea that all students within the same school have access to the same curriculum has been described as a "gravely misleading myth" (Hirsch, 1996, p. 26), and district curriculum guides have been characterized as "well intended, but fundamentally fictional accounts" of what students are actually learning (Jacobs, 2001, p. 20).

To ensure all students have an opportunity to master the same essential learning, school and district leaders must do more than deliver curriculum documents to teachers. They must engage every teacher in a collaborative process to study, to clarify, and most importantly, to commit to teaching the curriculum. All teachers should be expected to clarify essential learning with their colleagues—even in provinces with delineated outcomes and in districts with highly developed curriculum guides. They should do so because of the following five reasons.

1. **Collaborative study of essential learning promotes clarity:** Even if individual teachers take the time to review provincial, territorial, and district curriculum expectations, it is unlikely they will interpret those outcomes consistently. Dialogue clarifying what the outcomes mean and what they look like in the classroom helps promote a more consistent curriculum.

2. **Collaborative study of essential learning promotes consistent priorities:** Just because teachers interpret a learning outcome consistently does not guarantee that they will assign the same priority to the learning. One teacher may conclude a particular outcome is very significant and devote weeks to teaching it, while another teacher may choose to spend only a day on the same outcome.

3. **Collaborative study of essential learning is crucial to the common pacing required for common formative assessments:** If teachers have not agreed on the meaning and significance of what they are being asked to teach, they will not be able to establish common pacing in their courses and grade levels. Common pacing is a prerequisite for common formative assessments, which, as we will demonstrate in the next chapter, are among the most powerful tools for improvement available to a school.

4. **Collaborative study of essential learning can help establish a curriculum that is viable:** One of the most significant barriers to clarity regarding essential learning for students is curriculum overload (Consortium on Productivity in the Schools, 1995; Reeves, 2004). In the United States, for example, one analysis concludes it would take up to twenty-three years to cover adequately all the outcomes (standards) that have been established at the state and national levels (Marzano, 2003). As a result, individual teachers are constantly making decisions regarding what content to omit in their classrooms, making it difficult for subsequent teachers to know what has been taught and what has not (Stevenson & Stigler, 1992). This is true in Canadian schools as well. If teachers work together to make these decisions,

To ensure all students have an opportunity to master the same essential learning, school and district leaders . . . must engage every teacher in a collaborative process to study, to clarify, and most importantly, to commit to teaching the curriculum.

Why Should We Ensure Students Have Access to a Guaranteed and Viable Curriculum?

To improve student achievement, educators must determine the *power standards*—essential outcomes that are most essential because they possess the qualities of endurance, leverage, and readiness for success at the next level; "the first and most important practical implication of power standards is that leaders must make time for teachers to collaborate within and among grade levels to identify the power standards" (Reeves, 2002, p. 54).

"The staff in the effective school accepts responsibility for the students' learning of the *essential curricular goals*" (Lezotte, 2002, p. 4, emphasis added).

Professional learning communities are characterized by an academic focus that begins with a set of practices that bring clarity, coherence, and precision to every teacher's classroom work. Teachers work collaboratively to provide a rigorous curriculum that is crystal clear and includes a compact list of learning expectations for each grade or course and tangible exemplars of student proficiency for each learning expectation (Saphier, 2005).

The first step in curriculum development is to "identify desired results. What should students know, understand, and be able to do? What content is worthy of understanding? What 'enduring' understandings are desired? What essential questions will be explored? [This step] calls for clarity about priorities" (Tomlinson & McTighe, 2006, pp. 27–28).

One of the keys to improving schools is to ensure teachers "know the learning intentions and success criteria of their lessons, know how well they are attaining these criteria for all students, and know where to go next in light of the gap between students' current knowledge and understanding and the success criteria"; this can be maximized in a safe and collaborative environment where teachers talk to each other about teaching (Hattie, 2009, p. 239).

"Implementing a strategy of common, rigorous standards with differentiated resources and instruction can create excellence and equity for all students" (Childress, Doyle, & Thomas, 2009, p. 133).

A high-reliability school provides students with a guaranteed and viable curriculum focused on enhancing student learning. The curriculum is focused enough that it can be adequately addressed in the time available to teachers. All students have the opportunity to learn the critical content of the curriculum. Individual teachers do not have the option to disregard or replace content that has been designated as essential (Marzano et al., 2014).

"The only way the curriculum in a school can truly be guaranteed is if the teachers themselves, those who are called upon to deliver the curriculum, have worked collaboratively to do the following:

- Study the intended curriculum.
- Agree on priorities within the curriculum.
- Clarify how the curriculum translates into student knowledge and skills.
- Establish general pacing guidelines for delivering the curriculum.
- Commit to one another that they will, in fact, teach the agreed-upon curriculum" (DuFour & Marzano, 2011, p. 91).

"If we want to mobilize concerted action and a deep shift in practice then governments, districts, and schools need to develop clarity of outcomes and build shared understanding of these by educators, students, and parents" (Fullan & Quinn, 2016, p. 83).

they can establish a curriculum that can be taught in the allotted time, and they can clarify the scope and sequence of the curriculum with colleagues who teach in the preceding and subsequent courses or grade levels.

5. **Collaborative study of essential learning creates ownership of the curriculum among those who are called on to teach it:** Attempts to create a guaranteed curriculum for every student throughout a province, territory, or district often create a uniform intended curriculum but do little to address the *implemented* curriculum. Teachers throughout Canada often feel neither ownership of nor accountability for the content they are being asked to teach. They were not meaningfully involved in the process of creating that content, and they often critique the decisions of those who were: provincial departments of education, district committees, central office curriculum coordinators, and so on. Others do not debate the merits of the curriculum; they simply ignore it. A guaranteed curriculum exists in theory but not in fact.

Certainly teacher ownership of and commitment to the curriculum their students will be expected to master play an important role in the quality of student learning. Successful implementation of any course of study requires people who care about intended outcomes and have a determination to achieve them. Teachers need to be convinced of the value of the skills they are teaching. As the Organisation for Economic Co-operation and Development (2009) advises, "Involving teachers themselves and drawing on their expertise . . . is a first step towards ensuring their commitment to [the skills they are teaching] as well as being essential for tapping into their knowledge and experience" (pp. 16–17).

Successful implementation of any course of study requires people who care about intended outcomes and have a determination to achieve them.

Collaborative Study of Essential Learning . . .

- Promotes clarity
- Promotes consistent priorities
- Is crucial to the common pacing required for formative assessments
- Can help establish a curriculum that is viable
- Creates ownership of the curriculum among those who are asked to teach it

Ownership and commitment are directly linked to the extent to which people are engaged in the decision-making process (Axelrod, 2002). Stephen Covey (1989) was emphatic on this point, writing, "Without involvement there is no commitment. Mark it down, asterisk it, circle it, underline it. *No involvement, no commitment*" (p. 143). As a result, there is a direct correlation between participation and improved results (Wheatley, 1999). An attempt to bring about significant change in a school without first engaging those who will be called on to do the work in meaningful dialogue creates a context for failure.

So what is the best way to engage staff in an improvement process? The greatest ownership and strongest levels of commitment flow to the smallest part of the organization to which each member belongs because that is where people's engagement levels are highest. Teachers are de facto members of their provincial or territorial systems of education, but they feel greater allegiance to their local district than they do to the province or territory. Most teachers, however, feel greater loyalty to their individual schools than to their districts. Teachers are likely to feel even greater allegiance to their departments than to their schools. If their departments have been organized into teams, they probably feel greater loyalty to their teammates than to the department as a whole. It is at the team level that teachers have the greatest opportunity for engagement, dialogue, and decision making. When teachers have collaboratively studied the question, "What must our students learn?" when they have created common formative assessments as a team to monitor student learning on a timely basis, and when they have promised each other to teach essential content and prepare students for the assessments, they have exponentially increased the likelihood that the agreed-on curriculum will actually be taught.

We are not advocating that a teacher team should be free to disregard provincial, territorial, or district guidelines and pursue its own interests. We are instead contending that one of the most powerful ways to bring the guidelines to life is to create processes to ensure every teacher becomes a true student of them.

When school leaders establish clear expectations and parameters like those we list earlier in this chapter, they create a process that promotes consistency and engages teachers in ways that encourage ownership and commitment. Those guidelines also demand accountability because a team must be able to demonstrate that its decisions have led to more students achieving at higher levels as measured by multiple indicators. Furthermore, the team format itself promotes accountability. Teachers recognize that failure to address agreed-on content will have an adverse impact on their students when they take common assessments and will prevent the team from achieving its goals. Few teachers will be cavalier about letting down their students and their teammates, particularly when evidence of their failure to honour commitments is readily available with each common assessment.

For too long, administrators have settled for the illusion of uniformity across the entire district.

For too long, administrators have settled for the illusion of uniformity across the entire district: they dictated curriculum to schools while teachers provided students in the same course or grade level with vastly different experiences. Effective leaders will view engagement with the question, "What do we want our students to know and be able to do?" as a professional obligation incumbent on every teacher, and they will create the processes and parameters to promote far greater consistency in the implemented curriculum.

Part Four

Assessing Your Place on the PLC Journey

It is important to help your staff build shared knowledge regarding your school's current status in addressing the critical step on the PLC journey of creating a focus on learning. We have created a tool to assist you in that effort. "The Professional Learning Communities at Work® Continuum: Clarifying What Students Must Learn" is available at **go.SolutionTree.com/ca/PLCbooks** as a free reproducible. Once your staff have established greater clarity regarding the current status of your collaborative teams, we urge you to turn your attention to the "Where Do We Go From Here?" worksheet that accompanies the continuum (also available for free to download at **go.SolutionTree.com/ca/PLCbooks**). It will prompt you to take the action necessary to close the knowing-doing gap.

Part Five

Tips for Moving Forward: Clarifying and Monitoring Essential Learning

1 **Remember less is more:** Remember that the main problem with curricula in North America is not that we do not do enough, but rather that we attempt to do too much. As Doug Reeves (2005) writes, "While academic standards vary widely in their specificity and clarity, they almost all have one thing in common: there are too many of them" (p. 48). We recommend that teams start by identifying the eight to ten most essential outcomes students will be expected to achieve in their course or subject area for that semester. There is nothing sacred about that total; it is merely meant to serve as a guideline for team dialogue.

2 **Focus on proficiency in key skills—not coverage:** Teachers throughout Canada are confronted with a multitude of outcomes and expectations for learning, and they fear that any one of them may be addressed on district, provincial, territorial, and international tests. Therefore, they focus on covering the content rather than ensuring students become proficient in the most essential skills. But not all outcomes are of equal importance. Some are vital to a student's success, and others are simply nice to know. By focusing on essential skills, teachers prepare students for 80 to 90 percent of the content that will be addressed on provincial or territorial tests and provide them with the reading, writing, and reasoning skills to address any question that could appear (Reeves, 2002).

Part Six

Questions to Guide the Work of Your Professional Learning Community

To clarify essential learning, ask:

1. What is it we want all students to know and be able to do as a result of this course, grade level, or unit of instruction?

2. How can we be sure each student has access to the same knowledge and skills regardless of who is teaching the course?

3. What knowledge and which skills in our curriculum pass the four-part test: endurance, leverage, necessity for success at the next level, and likely to be assessed on high-stakes external tests?

4. What material can we eliminate from our curriculum?

5. How should we pace the curriculum to ensure that all students have the opportunity to master the essential learning?

6. Have we agreed on what proficient student work looks like? Can we consistently apply our agreed-on criteria for student work to ensure students receive reliable feedback?

Part Seven

Dangerous Detours and Seductive Shortcuts

It is the process of team members collaboratively building shared knowledge and collectively making decisions about curriculum and assessment that results in adult learning and improved professional practice. Beware of any action that removes teachers from the process or minimizes their role because in every instance the impact of the process will be diminished. Examples of shortcuts that are frequently used to circumvent this critical collaborative team dialogue include:

- Distributing provincial, territorial, and district guidelines to individual teachers as a substitute for team dialogue

- Assigning a committee of teachers to establish the curriculum and present it to their colleagues

- Purchasing the curriculum

- Allowing the textbook to determine the curriculum

Teachers and administrators both may argue that teachers are too busy to clarify curriculum or create assessments. They may assert that having someone else do the work provides teachers with an important service. Some may argue that teachers lack the knowledge and skills to do the work well. It is certainly true that school leaders will need to provide collaborative teams of teachers with time, resources, and training to assist them in this important work. Once again, however, the critical question, "What must our students learn?" must be addressed in a systematic way by the professionals most responsible for ensuring learning—classroom teachers. It is by engaging the process that teachers learn, so do not remove them from the process.

It is the process of team members collaboratively building shared knowledge and collectively making decisions about curriculum and assessment that results in adult learning and improved professional practice.

Final Thoughts

When teachers work together to establish clarity regarding the knowledge, skills, and dispositions all students are to acquire as a result of each course, grade level, and unit of instruction, schools take a significant step forward on their PLC journey. When those same teachers establish frequent common formative assessments that provide timely feedback on each student's proficiency, their schools advance even further, because these assessments help identify students who are experiencing difficulty in their learning. We turn our attention to common formative assessments in the next chapter.

CHAPTER 6
Creating Team-Developed Common Formative Assessments

Part One

The Case Study: How Do We Know if They Have Learned It?

As the coordinators of learning for North East School Division in Saskatchewan, the leadership team—Katie White, Reanne Usselman, and Stephanie Rutley—knew the value of common formative assessments. From their research, they understood that if they wanted to meet the needs of students through timely and targeted interventions and extensions then their teachers had to have ongoing evidence of learning through their formative practices. They also understood that if the teachers met together to plan their assessments and collectively reviewed student data, their instructional practices would improve as well.

To begin their common formative assessment journey as a division, they purchased a common formative reading assessment (RAD) for grades 1–9. The division leaders believed that the product was strong and structured collaborative professional learning experiences to ensure the RAD tool was being used effectively. There were opportunities for teachers to build collective understanding of the importance of reading comprehension, for data to be stored and shared, and a scope and sequence was developed so that teachers could measure skills from grade level to grade level. Principals were brought together to share growth opportunities and discuss next steps. In other words, the team did all that it could to ensure that the RAD assessment was useful in informing instruction, nurturing effective strategy use, and documenting student growth.

Despite all of these efforts, several teachers continued to see this as a top-down implementation, and they consistently expressed concern over being judged based on student results. And, when teachers scored the student responses on their own, the results varied widely and did not reflect other assessment results that they were seeing in daily reading comprehension work. The teachers also expressed their disappointment that the reading selections were not always reflective of what students in Saskatchewan could relate to and the teachers became more and more dissatisfied with the wording of the questions on the assessments. As time passed, the teachers recognized that the rubrics provided did not help them truly clarify the expectations. And, lastly, they only were assessing twice a year and recognized that if they wanted to measure growth and respond immediately to student needs, then they had to assess more frequently.

After many years of trying to make a prepackaged product work as an authentic formative assessment, the division abandoned the RAD tool. Eventually the teachers asked to create their own assessments. It was time to revisit the purpose of common formative assessments and how to do the work.

Reflection

The teachers of North East School Division had not objected to the idea of common formative assessments and had worked hard to implement the RAD tool. As they moved to teacher-created assessments, what were their next steps? How would they ensure that they could meet the needs of their students using the evidence from their collective efforts?

Part Two

Here's How

Because clarity precedes competence, the teachers of North East School Division will struggle in their attempt to develop and implement a common formative assessment process until they establish a shared understanding of what that process entails. Using a common assessment means students who are in the same curriculum and are expected to acquire the same knowledge, skills, and disposition will be assessed using the same instrument or process, at the same time, or within a very narrow window of time. If the assessment is a pencil-and-paper test, it will be the same pencil-and-paper test. If the assessment is performance based, the assessment will focus on the same performance and teachers will use the same criteria in judging the quality of student work.

Provincial assessments, territorial assessments, district benchmark assessments, advanced placement exams, and universal screening instruments are examples of common assessments. But these tests are rarely perfectly aligned to the essential outcomes that a teacher team identified for a specific unit of study. Therefore, in the PLC process, the team develops one or more common assessments for each unit of instruction.

In the PLC process, the team develops one or more common assessments for each unit of instruction.

The proposal to use common assessments often leads to the question, "But what about students who have been identified as having special needs?" The answer to this question is found in the student's individualized education plan (IEP) or personalized education plan (PEP). If that plan indicates the student's condition is *so profound* that the student is not expected to achieve the intended outcomes of the grade level or course, but instead is pursuing entirely different goals or learning outcomes, there would be no need to administer the common assessment to that student. His or her assessment would be based on the learning outcomes established in the IEP. Considering that less than 3.2 percent of students in Canada have learning disabilities, denying a student access to grade-level common assessments should be a rare occurrence at most schools (Learning Disabilities Association of Canada, 2017). Typically, however, a student with special needs should be expected to acquire the same knowledge and skills as the other students in the class but will need additional support services in order to do so. In that case, the student would take the common assessment but, once again, the IEP or PEP would specify accommodations or modifications that should be applied. If, for example, the IEP or PEP stipulates a student should have extended time to take the test or that the test should be read to the student, those accommodations would apply.

Formative Assessments

The use of the formative assessment process is typically contrasted with the use of summative assessments. Rick Stiggins (2005) distinguishes between the two by saying that a summative assessment is an assessment *of* learning while a formative assessment is an assessment *for* learning. As he explains, educators use the formative assessment process when they use assessment to help students understand the following three items.

1. The achievement target they are aspiring to

2. Where they are now in relation to that expectation

3. How to close the gap between the two

The Organisation for Economic Co-operation and Development (as cited in Looney, 2005) defines formative assessment as "frequent, interactive assessments of students' progress and understanding to identify learning needs and adjust teaching appropriately" (p. 21). Dylan Wiliam (2011) advises that an assessment is formative "to the extent that teachers, learners, or their peers elicit evidence about student achievement to make decisions about the next steps in instruction that are likely to be better, or better founded, than the decisions they would have taken in the absence of that evidence" (p. 43).

We think the following helps clarify the difference between summative and formative assessments. A summative assessment gives the student the opportunity to *prove* what he or she has learned by a certain deadline and results in a dichotomy—pass or fail, proficient or not proficient. A formative assessment gives the student the opportunity to *improve* on his or her learning because it informs both the teacher and student as to appropriate next steps in the learning process. Canadian assessment expert Katie White (2017b) writes:

> Here's the truth as I now know it: Assessment *is* instruction. It is all those moments, big and small, when we make the time and space to notice learning as it unfolds and to make decisions that redirect, reinforce, celebrate, and imagine learning in relation to goals. It is not separate from instruction; it cannot be separate. Without it, we render ourselves incapable of precision, flexibility,

A summative assessment gives the student the opportunity to prove what he or she has learned. . . . A formative assessment gives the student the opportunity to improve on his or her learning.

and engagement. We need assessment as a *process*, through which we equip ourselves to respond to learner needs and to invite students into our thinking and planning.

This statement clearly articulates the benefits of formative assessment.

There are several misunderstandings about formative assessment. Often educators think of formative assessment as an event or a test rather than an ongoing process. Effective teachers, as White (2017b) describes, use formative assessment during instruction almost minute by minute to check for student understanding so they know where to go next with instruction. Formative assessments that give both the teacher and students insights as to what should come next in the teaching and learning process occur when teachers:

- Randomly direct purposeful questions to students and have others in the class respond to the answer

- Ask students to write their answers in their notes as the teacher circulates the room to determine student responses

- Have students use clickers, whiteboards, and exit slips to gain insight into student thinking

- Create signals for students to indicate their level of understanding

The team members then use the evidence of student learning from their common formative assessments to inform their individual and collective practice in four ways.

In high-performing PLCs, the assessment process also must include team-developed common formative assessments as team members attempt to answer the second critical question of PLCs: "How do we know our students are learning?" The team members then use the evidence of student learning from their common formative assessments to inform their individual and collective practice in four ways:

1. To inform each teacher of individual students who need intervention because they are struggling to learn or who need enrichment because they are already proficient

2. To inform students of the next steps they must take in their learning

3. To inform each member of the team of his or her individual strengths and weaknesses in teaching particular skills so each member can provide or solicit help from colleagues on the team

4. To inform the team of areas where many students are struggling so that the team can develop and implement better strategies for teaching those areas (DuFour & DuFour, 2012, p. 41)

Another misunderstanding about common formative assessments is that the content of an assessment or when the assessment takes place determines whether or not it is formative. A short quiz that is given to students early in a unit can be summative if it is used only to assign a grade. A comprehensive exam at the end of a unit can be formative if it is used to identify students who are struggling to demonstrate proficiency in a particular skill or concept, if those students are required to keep working on the skill or concept through the school's systematic plan for intervention until they become proficient, and if they are given another opportunity to demonstrate that they have learned. In this scenario, a student who fails an assessment after three weeks of instruction but is able to demonstrate proficiency in the fourth week after engaging in systematic interventions would be assigned a grade that reflects proficiency. In this scenario, the end-of-unit assessment is part of the formative process. Thus, it is how the results are used, or what happens *after* the assessment, that determines whether or not it is part of a formative process.

Finally, in too many schools, team-developed common formative assessments are viewed as tools to determine which students need interventions but not as powerful tools for informing and improving teacher practice. All of the steps in the PLC process are intended to provide a teacher team with transparent evidence of student learning so team members can determine which instructional strategies are working and which are not. This collective analysis of the evidence enables team members to make informed adjustments to their teaching. So we want to stress that unless collaborative teams are using evidence of student learning to inform and improve their individual and collective professional practice, the school is not fully engaged in the PLC process.

Protocols and Tools to Guide the Work of Collaborative Teams

By providing teachers with protocols to guide their work, the North East School Division's leadership team can help their teachers make the analysis of evidence of student learning in the service of improved student and adult learning part of the school's organizational routine. Protocols ensure all voices are heard on the critical issue at hand, help members look closely at evidence of student learning, examine success as well as failure, and help all participants become skillful in facilitating dialogue on the right work (McDonald, Mohr, Dichter, & McDonald, 2007). Put more simply, "A protocol creates the structure that makes it safe for teachers to ask challenging questions of each other" (Quate, n.d.).

Most protocols consist of a structured format that includes a tentative time frame and specific guidelines for communication among team members. All protocols do two things: "They provide a structure for conversation—a series of steps that a group follows in a fixed order—and specify the roles different people in the group will play" (Larner, 2007, p. 104).

One example of a protocol adapted from the Collaborative Assessment Conference is Harvard's Project Zero (cited in McDonald et al., 2007), which includes the following six steps.

1. Team members examine evidence of student learning or examples of student work in silence and take notes on their observations.

2. The team leader asks, "What did you see?" Members are asked to make factual, nonevaluative statements.

All of the steps in the PLC process are intended to provide a teacher team with transparent evidence of student learning so team members can determine which instructional strategies are working and which are not.

3. The team leader asks, "What questions does this evidence of student learning raise for you?" Members speculate about students' thought processes and gaps in their understanding.

4. Members discuss implications for their teaching.

5. Members establish action plans to act on their learning.

6. Members share their reactions to and assessment of the meeting.

Teams can also use protocols to create a safe environment for an individual teacher to pose a problem and seek the help of his or her colleagues. Remember back to our U.S. example of an exemplary PLC school, Adlai Stevenson High School. At this school, teams use a six-step tuning protocol called Descriptive Review as a way to support one another (Blythe, Allen, & Powell, 1999).

1. **Introduction:** A team member presents the results of an assessment or examples of student work to teammates (five minutes).

2. **Teacher presentation:** Team members review the presented work as the presenting member explains his or her concerns or questions. No interruptions or questions are allowed during this presentation (ten minutes).

3. **Clarifying questions:** Participants may ask clarifying questions, but again no discussion is allowed at this point (five minutes).

4. **Feedback:** The team discusses the work together, giving three kinds of feedback each in separate intervals. The presenting teacher listens and takes notes while his or her colleagues talk (ten minutes).

   The feedback must directly relate to the assessment or examples of student work at hand. The three kinds of feedback include the following.

   a. *Warm feedback*—Positive points associated with the work

   b. *Cool feedback*—Questions, doubts, or possible gaps in the work

   c. *Hard feedback*—Challenges related to the work

5. **Reflection:** The presenting teacher responds to team members' feedback, highlighting new insights, seeking clarifications, and identifying changes to be made (ten minutes).

6. **Debrief:** The team leader solicits feedback regarding the team's perceptions of the process (five minutes).

There are also excellent tools to help teams focus on the right work that are less formulaic than protocols.

Teams should also return to the results of their analysis when they prepare to teach the same unit in the next school year. They should examine where students experienced difficulty on the assessment, their theories as to why students struggled, and the corrective actions they took to improve their ability to teach that skill or concept more effectively. They would then set a short-term SMART goal for the unit to improve on the student achievement levels in the previous year. An example of that tool is on page 87. This ongoing effort to use evidence of past students' learning to get better results in the present is the essence of the continuous improvement process that drives the work of collaborative teams in a PLC. The most helpful resource we have seen for protocols and tools to guide the work of collaborative teams is *Common Formative Assessment: A Toolkit for Professional Learning Communities at Work* by Kim Bailey and Chris Jakicic (2012). We highly recommend it.

Deeper Learning

There is general consensus among policymakers and educators alike that assessments of student learning must focus less on recall of information, become more rigorous, and call on students to demonstrate deeper learning:

> Being able to recall scientific concepts, identify historical events, or memorize mathematics facts and algorithms, while acutely impressive, is no longer sufficient to prepare students for the changing world they will face. Identifying characters, theme, and symbolism used to be the focus of education, and it was enough. In the past, learners would occasionally have opportunities to collaborate, communicate, critically think, and creatively problem solve, but that was the *means*, not the *end*. After engaging in dialogue, problem solving, or analysis, learners would typically take a multiple-choice test or an essay prompt would ask them to recall details or themes discussed in class. As critical competencies shift to be the *end* rather than the *means*, recalling facts is not nearly as important as being able to find the content, critically evaluate its value and credibility, apply it appropriately in different contexts, or put new ideas together to generate something interesting and original. Content is not obsolete; rather, the memorization (and recall) of it is. More than ever it is essential for educators to provide more meaningful tasks so learners tap into rich content while demonstrating the critical competencies through application. (Erkens, Schimmer, & Vagle, 2019, pp. 6–7)

The American National Research Council's Committee on Defining Deeper Learning stipulates that *deeper learning* is "the process through which an individual becomes capable of taking what was learned in one situation and applying it to new situations (i.e., transfer) . . . by developing cognitive, interpersonal, and intrapersonal competencies" (as cited in Pellegrino & Hilton, 2012, p. 5). The Hewlett Foundation defines deeper learning as preparing students to "master core academic content, think critically and solve complex problems, work collaboratively, communicate effectively, and learn how to learn" (for example, self-directed learning; as cited in Vander Ark & Schneider, 2012, p. 9).

Norman Webb has classified Depth of Knowledge (DOK) criteria into the following four levels, with levels three and four representing deeper learning (Herman & Linn, 2013). The levels are as follows.

DOK 1: Recall of a fact, term, concept, or procedure—basic comprehension

DOK 2: Application of concepts or procedures involving some mental processing

DOK 3: Applications requiring abstract thinking, reasoning, or more complex inferences

DOK 4: Extended analysis or investigation that requires synthesis and analysis across multiple contexts and nonroutine applications

If educators are to help students acquire deeper knowledge and skills, they must create assessments that provide timely information on each student's proficiency.

If educators are to help students acquire deeper knowledge and skills, they must create assessments that provide timely information on each student's proficiency in these key areas of learning. The first step in the process in creating these assessments is the first step in every aspect of the PLC process—educators must *learn together*. They must engage in collective inquiry regarding how to monitor deeper learning for their students. They must become students of assessments that are intended to provide insights into a student's ability to apply his or her knowledge and skills.

The North East School Division leadership team can help the teams in this collective inquiry by providing them with clear parameters and guidelines for creating assessments that will call on students to demonstrate deeper learning. Such guidelines might call on teams to:

- Create a specific minimum number of common assessments to use in their course or grade level during the semester to ensure student learning is monitored on a timely basis

- Include multiple levels of knowledge questions on each assessment

- Demonstrate how each item on the assessment is aligned to an essential outcome of the course or grade level

- Specify the proficiency essential outcome for each skill or concept so that teachers and students alike are able to identify, with precision, where the student needs help

- Clarify the conditions for administering the test consistently

- Ensure that demonstration of proficiency on the team assessment will be highly correlated to success on high-stakes testing at the district, provincial, territorial, or national level

- Assess a few key concepts frequently rather than many concepts infrequently

Once again, if the leadership team in our case study calls on teachers to create new common formative assessments, reciprocal accountability demands that they must support the teachers' efforts by providing them with time to address the task and resources to help them build quality assessments. Such resources might include:

- Provincial or territorial assessment frameworks to make sure staff are familiar with the format and rigor of the provincial or territorial test

- Data on student performance on past indicators of achievement

- Examples of rubrics for performance-based assessments

- Recommendations from assessment experts such as Rick Stiggins, W. James Popham, Dylan Wiliam, and Larry Ainsworth, as well as Canadians Katie White, Tom Schimmer, and Ken O'Connor

- Tests that individual team members developed

One of the most powerful tools that the North East School Division leadership team can provide teams is ready access to websites that support educators in developing more rigorous assessments. Team members should work together to become students of more rigorous assessments to learn about both their format and content. The following are examples of such websites.

- OECD's Programme for International Student Assessment (www.oecd.org/pisa)

- Canadian Assessment for Learning Network (www.caflnforum.ca)

- Canadians for 21st Century Learning and Innovation (www.c21canada.org)

- Council of Ministers of Education, Canada (www.cmec.ca)

- Partnership for Assessment of Readiness for College and Careers (PARCC; www.parcconline.org/samples/item-task-prototypes)

- Smarter Balanced Assessment Consortium (www.smarterbalanced.org)

Assessment experts agree that the best way for educators to build their capacity to create quality assessments is to address the challenge as collaborative team members rather than as individuals. The collaborative team structure is described as essential in any effort to build the assessment literacy of educators (Stiggins, 1999), the best way to support teachers in learning how to use powerful classroom assessments (Wiliam, 2007), and "the best way to accomplish a schoolwide implementation of formative assessment" (Popham, 2008, p. 119). Teams should have the autonomy to develop the kind of assessments they believe will result in valid and authentic measures of the learning of their students. They should have autonomy in designating the proficiency targets for each skill; however, they should also be called on to demonstrate that student success on their assessments is strongly correlated to success on other indicators of achievement the school is monitoring.

Team members should work together to become students of more rigorous assessments to learn about both their format and content.

Assessment experts agree that the best way for educators to build their capacity to create quality assessments is to address the challenge as collaborative team members rather than as individuals.

Common Mistakes

The North East School Division leadership team must resist any effort to exempt teachers from working together to create the frequent common formative assessments that enable a team to verify the proficiency of each student in each essential skill. Frequent monitoring of each student's learning is a critical element of effective teaching, and no teacher should be absolved from that task or allowed to assign responsibility for it to provincial or territorial test-makers, central office coordinators, or textbook publishers.

Finally, it is critical that the division's leadership team make commitments to the staff that common assessment data will not be used in a punitive way to formally or informally evaluate teacher performance. When teachers compare results on a common assessment, invariably one teacher is going to have the lowest scores. This delineation should not be interpreted as the teaching is inferior but instead that the instructional practices used did not best meet students' learning needs. If teachers fear that common assessment data will be used to negatively evaluate or publicly humiliate them, then they have every right to resist engaging in the process.

Part Three

Here's Why

One of the most powerful, high-leverage strategies for improving student learning available to schools is the creation of frequent, high-quality common formative assessments by teachers who are working collaboratively to help a group of students acquire agreed-on knowledge and skills. Such assessments serve a distinctly different purpose than the provincial, territorial, national (PCAP), and international (PISA) tests that have become the norm in Canada. These tests typically serve as summative assessments: attempts to determine if students have met intended outcomes by a specified deadline. They are assessments of learning, typically measuring many things infrequently. They can provide helpful information regarding the strengths and weaknesses of curricula and programs in a country, district, school, or department, and they often serve as a means of promoting institutional accountability and establishing benchmarks for understanding the performance of overall systems. The infrequency of these end-of-process measurements, however, limits their effectiveness in providing the timely feedback that guides teacher practice and student learning (Stiggins & DuFour, 2009).

In Canada, the benefits of formative assessment practices are increasingly understood and researched. For example, the Canadian Assessment for Learning Network (CAfLN) promoted the theme, "Moving Assessment Forward in Strong and Wise Ways" at their May 2019 conference. This theme focuses on the processes of change and how assessment for learning can move us closer to achieving quality and equity education for all learners. The change in question may be small in scope, such as a teacher who designs learning where students serve as resources for one another, or a cross-grade group of teachers who use clear criteria to help students learn. However, it may be large in scope, such as with a system that has moved from sorting to learning by using assessment for learning principles (CAfLN, 2019).

In its report, "Education Accountability With a Human Face," the Canadian Teachers' Federation (CFT, 2004) states:

> Accountability systems based on test scores and school rankings that result in rewards and sanctions for students, teachers and schools essentially treat accountability as punishment. The teaching profession is strongly opposed to this coercive approach because it undermines equity and the quality of education—in other words, it simply doesn't work. At the same time, teachers are cognizant of the fact that public accountability is a fundamental principle underlying public education and firmly believe there is a better way to achieving it. There may be reason for cautious optimism on the testing front. There are indications of growing public support for teacher-led assessment. According to the CTF 2002 National Issues in Education Poll, which surveyed nearly 2,300 people across the country, Canadians place a high value on classroom assessment. By a significant margin of two to one, Canadians said that teacher evaluations of student work—not standardized large-scale tests—are the best way to measure student achievement and school performance. The poll also found that test scores are a relatively minor factor in how the public evaluates schools in their community. Canadians would give much greater consideration to such factors as interactions between teachers and parents, the nature of the curriculum, the size of classes in the school, and student fluency in the language of instruction. In response to the question, "Why measure students' progress?", Canadians are unequivocal—by a factor of eight to one (with even stronger support among public school parents), they said that the most important reason to assess student progress is to evaluate how well students are learning, not to rank or compare students and schools.

Formative assessments are part of an ongoing process to monitor each student's learning on a continuous basis. Formative assessments typically measure a few things frequently and are intended to inform teachers regarding the effectiveness of their practice and to inform students of their next steps on the scaffolding of learning. When done well, formative assessment advances and motivates, rather than merely reports on, student learning. The clearly defined goals and descriptive feedback to students provide them with specific insights regarding how to improve, and the growth they experience helps build their confidence as learners (Stiggins & DuFour, 2009).

The case for formative assessment is compelling (see page 134, "Why Should We Use Formative Assessments?"). The case for team-developed common formative assessments as a powerful tool for school improvement is also compelling (see page 135, "Why Should We Use Common Assessments?").

Why Should We Use Formative Assessments?

"There is strong and rigorous evidence that improving formative assessment can raise standards of pupils' performance. There have been few initiatives in education with such a strong body of evidence to support a claim to raise standards" (Black & Wiliam, 1998, p. 20).

"Studies have demonstrated assessment for learning rivals one-on-one tutoring in its effectiveness and that the use of assessment particularly benefits low-achieving students" (Stiggins, 2004, p. 27).

"Assessment for learning . . . when done well, this is one of the most powerful, high-leverage strategies for improving student learning that we know of. Educators collectively at the district and school levels become more skilled and focused at assessing, disaggregating, and using student achievement as a tool for ongoing improvement" (Fullan, 2005, p. 71).

"[Formative assessments are] 'one of the most powerful weapons in a teacher's arsenal.' An effective standards-based, formative assessment program can help to dramatically enhance student achievement throughout the K–12 system" (Marzano, 2006, back cover).

Effective use of formative assessment, developed through teacher learning communities, promises not only the largest potential gains in student achievement but also a process for affordable teacher professional development (Wiliam & Thompson, 2007).

"Deeper learning is enhanced when formative assessment is used to: (1) make learning goals clear to students; (2) continuously monitor, provide feedback, and respond to students' learning progress; and (3) involve students in self- and peer assessment" (Pellegrino & Hilton, 2012, p. 166).

"Formative assessment works. That's right: Ample research evidence is now at hand to indicate emphatically that when the formative-assessment process is used, students learn better—lots better. It's really not surprising that formative assessment works so well. What is surprising is how few U.S. teachers use the process" (Popham, 2013, p. 29).

"Teachers are reluctant to persist in implementing new practices in the absence of evidence that what they're doing makes a positive difference. Therefore, it's important to build some mechanism into the implementation process to show teachers that these new practices are working. . . . Because teachers have the most confidence in evidence they gather themselves, results from classroom formative assessments provide an ideal feedback source" (Guskey, 2014).

"One characteristic that separates good teaching from masterful teaching is the teacher's routine use of formative assessment techniques that are embedded in every lesson" (Ferlazzo, 2014).

The major purpose of assessment in schools should be to provide interpretative information to teachers and school leaders about their impact on students, so that these educators have the best information possible about what steps to take with instruction and how they need to change and adapt. Using assessments as feedback for teachers is powerful. And this power is truly maximized when the assessments are timely, informative, and related to what teachers are actually teaching (Hattie, 2015c).

Why Should We Use Common Assessments?

Reviews of accountability data from hundreds of schools reveal the schools with the greatest gains in achievement consistently employ common assessments, nonfiction writing, and collaborative scoring by faculty (Reeves, 2004).

Powerful, proven structures for improved results are at hand. "It starts when a group of teachers meet regularly as a team to identify essential and valued student learning, develop common formative assessments, analyze current levels of achievement, set achievement goals, and then share and create lessons and strategies to improve upon those levels" (Schmoker, 2004b, p. 48).

The schools and districts that doubled student achievement added another layer of testing—common formative or benchmark assessments. These assessments were designed to provide detailed and concrete information on what students know and do not know with respect to specific learning targets (Odden & Archibald, 2009).

The key to improved student achievement was moving beyond an individual teacher looking at his or her classroom data. Instead, it took getting same-grade teacher teams to meet, analyze the results of each interim assessment to understand what concepts in the curriculum were posing difficulty for students, share ideas, figure out the best interventions, and actually follow up in their classrooms (Christman et al., 2009).

In schools that help students burdened by poverty achieve remarkable success, teachers work in collaborative teams to build common formative assessments and use the data to identify which students need help and which need greater challenges. But they also use data to inform teachers' practice, to discuss why one teacher is having success in teaching a concept and others are not, and what the more successful teacher can teach his or her colleagues (Chenoweth, 2009).

"High-growth schools and districts use frequent, common short-cycle assessments—at least every three to six weeks. Teachers create formative assessments before developing their lessons for a unit and clarify success criteria. The importance of focusing the attention of teachers on formative assessment practices and developing and using short-cycle common assessments was one of the most consistent findings of the study" (Battelle for Kids, 2015).

One of the most effective ways educators can use formative assessments is by collaboratively creating common formative assessments with grade-level or course-level colleagues . . . to assess student understanding of the particular learning intentions and success criteria currently in focus within a curricular unit of study. Common formative assessments afford teacher teams a clear lens through which to see their instructional impact on student learning (Ainsworth, 2014).

We argue that the benefits of using team-developed common assessments for formative purposes are so powerful that no teacher team should be allowed to opt out of creating them.

We argue that the benefits using team-developed common assessments for formative purposes are so powerful that no teacher team should be allowed to opt out of creating them. We are not suggesting that they take the place of the ongoing checks for understanding that should occur in an individual teacher's classroom each day. Furthermore, schools should certainly use a variety of assessments: those that individual teachers develop, a provincial or territorial test, district tests, national tests, tests that accompany textbooks, and so on. But school leaders should never allow the presence of these other assessments to be an excuse for ignoring the need for common, team-made formative assessments for the following seven reasons.

1. **Common assessments promote efficiency for teachers:** If all students are expected to demonstrate the same knowledge and skills regardless of the teacher to whom they are assigned, it only makes sense that teachers would work together to assess student learning. For example, suppose four third-grade teachers will assess their students on four reading skills during a unit. It would be more efficient for each teacher to develop activities or questions for one skill and present them to teammates for review, feedback, and, ultimately, agreement about inclusion on the common assessment than for each teacher to work separately creating items on all four skills, thereby duplicating the effort of his or her colleagues. It is ineffective and inefficient for teachers to operate as independent subcontractors who are stationed in proximity to others, yet work in isolation. Those who are called on to complete the same task benefit by pooling their efforts.

2. **Common assessments promote equity for students:** When schools utilize common assessments, they are more likely to—

   • Ensure that students have access to the same essential curriculum

   • Use common pacing

   • Assess the quality of student work according to the same criteria

   It is ironic that schools and districts often pride themselves in the fair and consistent application of rules and policies while at the same time ignoring the tremendous inequities in the opportunities students are given to learn and the criteria by which their learning is assessed. Schools will continue to have difficulty helping all students achieve high outcomes if the teachers within them cannot develop the capacity to define an essential outcome with specificity and assess it with consistency.

3. **Common assessments represent a powerful strategy for determining whether the guaranteed curriculum is being taught and, more importantly, learned:** Doug Reeves (2004) refers to common, teacher-made formative assessments as the "best practice in assessment" (p. 71) and the "gold standard in educational accountability" (p. 114) because they promote consistency in expectations and provide timely, accurate, and specific feedback to both students and teachers. Furthermore, as teachers work together to study the elements of effective assessment and critique one another's ideas for assessment, they improve their assessment literacy. Perhaps most importantly, teachers' active engagement in the development of the assessment leads them to accept greater responsibility for the results.

4. **Common assessments inform the practice of individual teachers:** Individual teacher's tests generate plenty of data (mean, mode, median, percentage of failing students, and so on), but they do little to inform the teacher's practice by identifying strengths and weaknesses in his or her teaching. Common assessments provide teachers with a basis of comparison as they learn, skill by skill, how the performance of their students is similar to and different from the other students who took the same assessment. With this information, a teacher can seek assistance from teammates on areas of concern and can share strategies and ideas on skills in which his or her students excelled. For generations, teachers have been told that effective teaching is preceded by planning and followed by reflection. But the single greatest determinant of how a teacher will teach is not reflection, but rather how he or she has taught in the past (Elmore, 2010). One of the most comprehensive studies ever conducted of factors that impact student achievement concludes that reflection enhances student learning only when it is collective—a team of teachers reflecting rather than an individual—and based on actual evidence of student learning rather than an appraisal of particular teaching strategies (Hattie, 2009). Team-developed common assessments are ideally suited to this collective reflection based on evidence.

Common assessments provide teachers with a basis of comparison as they learn, skill by skill, how the performance of their students is similar to and different from the other students who took the same assessment.

5. **Common assessments build a team's capacity to achieve its goals:** When collaborative teams of teachers have the opportunity to examine achievement indicators of all students in their course or grade level and track those indicators over time, they are able to identify and address problem areas in their program. Their collective analysis can lead to new curriculum, pacing, materials, and instructional strategies designed to strengthen the academic program they offer. A longitudinal study of schools engaged in reform efforts found that for two years those schools showed no gains despite the fact that teachers were meeting in teams. It wasn't until the collaborative teams of teachers looked at evidence of student learning from common assessments, identified the consistent problems students were experiencing, and then developed specific action plans to resolve those problems that students experienced dramatic gains in their learning (Gallimore et al., 2009).

6. **Common assessments facilitate a systematic, collective response to students who are experiencing difficulty:** Common assessments help identify a group of students who need additional time and support to ensure their learning. Because the students are identified at the same time and because they need help with the same specific skills that have been addressed on the common assessment, the team and school are in a position to create timely, directive, and systematic interventions. We will address this topic in detail in the next chapter.

7. **Common formative assessments are one of the most powerful tools for changing the professional practice of educators:** The main challenge in any substantive improvement initiative is getting people to change their behaviour, that is, to change what they have traditionally done (Kotter & Cohen, 2002). But what might persuade veteran educators to change their traditional practice?

Learning new instructional strategies at workshops won't change teacher practice unless participants return to a culture where they have an opportunity for practice, feedback, and coaching.

Learning new instructional strategies at workshops won't change teacher practice unless participants return to a culture where they have an opportunity for practice, feedback, and coaching. In a survey, however, only one in ten teachers report that they have frequent opportunities for practicing new skills (New Teacher Project, 2015). It is expected that a similar pattern would be seen in Canada.

Poor student performance on assessments does not persuade teachers to explore new practices. A survey of educators reveals that 84 percent of teachers feel "very confident" that they have the knowledge and skills necessary to enable their students to succeed academically and the remaining 16 percent were "somewhat confident." The same survey also reveals that only 36 percent of teachers believe all of their students have the ability to succeed (Markow & Pieters, 2010). In another survey, more than 80 percent of teachers rated their teaching as a four or five on a five-point scale (New Teacher Project, 2015). Thus, from the perspective of the majority of teachers, poor student performance on a test clearly reflects deficiencies in students rather than the need for educators to explore new strategies.

Principals are being urged to devote more time to being *instructional leaders* by observing teachers in classrooms so they can supervise and evaluate teachers into better instructional practices. There is, however, overwhelming evidence that this strategy has little impact on either teacher practice or student achievement. A three-year study of more than one hundred principals concludes, "We find no relationship between [a principal's] overall time spent on instructional activities and either school effectiveness or improvement" (Grissom, Loeb, & Master, 2013, p. 15). The same study finds that the common practice of principals conducting brief walkthroughs of classrooms actually had a negative impact on student achievement.

A survey of teachers in the United States reveals that three out of four teachers feel they receive absolutely no benefit from the teacher-evaluation process in their school (Duffett, Farkas, Rotherham, & Silva, 2008). Another study concludes that most teacher evaluation does not recognize good teaching, leaves poor teaching unaddressed, and "does not inform decision-making in any meaningful way" (Weisberg, Sexton, Mulhem, & Keeling, 2009, p. 1). In Canada, teacher evaluation practices vary from province and territory and are often established within collective bargaining agreements. The quality and effectiveness of teacher evaluation in Canada is clearly dependent on the spirit and manner in which it has been developed and implemented.

A longitudinal study of effective school leadership describes the premise of instructional leadership as "an idea that refuses to go away." As that study concludes:

> Policy makers and practitioners should avoid promoting, endorsing, or being unduly influenced by conceptions of instructional leadership which adopt an excessively narrow focus on classroom instruction. Classroom practices occur within larger organizational systems which can vary enormously in the extent to which they support, reward, and nurture good instruction. School leaders who ignore or neglect the state of this larger context can easily find their direct efforts to improve instruction substantially frustrated. (Louis, Leithwood, Wahlstrom, & Anderson, 2010, p. 76)

Robert Marzano (2009), a leading researcher on effective teaching, agrees that focusing on the instructional practices of teachers is ineffective because none of those practices is guaranteed to work in all situations. He contends the checklist approach to providing teachers with feedback that is often used in teacher evaluation "probably doesn't enhance instructional expertise [and] in fact, such practice is antithetical to true reflective practice" (Marzano, 2009, p. 37).

A joint study from the National Commission on Teaching and America's Future and WestEd warns that using evaluation and compensation systems in an attempt to improve schools by improving individual teachers would not result in effective schools (Fulton & Britton, 2011). As that study concludes, "Performance appraisal, compensation, and incentive systems that focus on individual teacher efforts at the expense of collaborative professional capacity building could seriously undermine our ability to prepare today's students for 21st century college and career success" (Fulton & Britton, 2011, p. 4).

Michael Fullan (2014) predicts that this individualistic strategy of improving schools one teacher at a time through supervising their instruction will be a "bloody disaster" (p. 84), and W. James Popham (2009) considers the attempt to improve schools by focusing on instruction as one of the biggest mistakes in education in the past fifty years. We concur. It should be evident that a secondary principal lacks the content expertise to provide meaningful feedback to teachers in all of the various disciplines taught in the school. As Rick and Mike write:

> As former social studies teachers, we were not prepared to help a Spanish teacher improve when we couldn't understand what he or she was saying. We were ill-equipped to enhance the pedagogy of an industrial arts teacher when we were mechanically inept. Because we frequently were unable to determine the appropriateness of either the content or the level of its rigor, we had to resort to generic observations about teaching and apply what we knew about effective questioning strategies, student engagement, classroom management, and so on. . . . If principals want to improve student achievement in their school, rather than focus on the individual inspection of *teaching*, they must focus on the collective analysis of evidence of student *learning*. (DuFour & Mattos, 2013, pp. 36–37)

So we return to the question, "What might persuade veteran educators to change their practice?" There are two powerful levers to bring about this change. The first is concrete evidence of irrefutably better results. If a teacher discovers that students in the next room are consistently demonstrating higher levels of learning on a skill or concept that the teacher has agreed is essential and on an assessment that the teacher helped to create and agreed it was a valid assessment of student learning, at some point, the teacher will become curious as to how his or her colleague is consistently getting better results. In a study of how to influence people to change their behaviour, Kerry Patterson and colleagues (2008) conclude that "the great persuader is personal experience . . . the mother of all cognitive map changes. . . . Nothing changes the mind like the hard cold world hitting it with actual real-life data" (p. 51). Richard Elmore (2003) came to a similar conclusion, writing "Teachers have to believe there is some compelling reason for them to change practice, with the best direct evidence being that students learn better" (p. 38). Additionally, Elmore (2010) writes, "Adult beliefs about what children can learn are changed by watching students do things that the adults didn't believe that they—the students—could do" (p. 8). Concrete evidence of irrefutably better results is a powerful persuader.

When people work interdependently to achieve a common goal for which all members are mutually accountable, the performance of each individual directly impacts the ability of the team to achieve its goal.

Another powerful lever for changing behaviour is the positive peer pressure and support that comes with being a team member. When people work in isolation, their success or failure has little or no direct and immediate bearing on others. When people work interdependently to achieve a common goal for which all members are mutually accountable, the performance of each individual directly impacts the ability of the team to achieve its goal. This interdependence and reluctance to let colleagues down can be an effective catalyst for changing behaviour (Blanchard, 2007; Fullan, 2008; Lencioni, 2005; Patterson et al., 2008).

Once again, the collective analysis of evidence of student learning from multiple common assessments is ideally suited to utilize the power of positive peer pressure and support. Transparent results make it very difficult for people to hide from their students or teammates or to duck their responsibility (Chenoweth, 2009; Kanter, 2004). An educator who can feign compliance or find excuses for poor results in a hierarchical system will find it increasingly problematic to remain disengaged or ignore results when the achievement of his or her students routinely prevents the team from accomplishing its goal. Transparency of results and openness about practice create a peer-based accountability system that becomes part of the culture (Fullan, 2011).

Consider This Series of Assertions

1. The key to the ability of schools to impact student learning is the collective expertise of the educators within a school or district.

2. Improved student learning will require improved professional practice.

3. Improved professional practice will require educators to change many of their traditional practices.

4. Two of the most powerful motivators for persuading educators to change their practice are (1) concrete evidence of irrefutably better results and (2) the positive peer pressure and support inherent in working interdependently with others to achieve a common goal.

5. The best strategy for utilizing these motivators and improving professional practice is engaging collaborative team members in the individual and collective analysis of team-developed common formative assessments on a regular basis as part of the teaching and learning process.

The reason that PLCs improve teaching is, paradoxically, because they focus on learning. Educators in a PLC work together collaboratively in constant, deep collective inquiry into the questions, "What is it our students must learn?" and "How will we know when they have learned it?" The dialogue generated from these questions results in the academic focus, collective commitments, and productive professional relationships that enhance learning for teachers and students alike. School leaders cannot waffle on this issue. Working with colleagues on these questions is an ongoing professional responsibility from which no teacher should be exempt.

Common Formative Assessments . . .

- Promote efficiency for teachers
- Promote equity for students
- Provide an effective strategy for determining whether the guaranteed curriculum is being taught and, more importantly, learned
- Inform the practice of individual teachers
- Build a team's capacity to improve its program
- Facilitate a systematic, collective response to students who are experiencing difficulty
- Offer the most powerful tool for changing adult behaviour and practice

Part Four

Assessing Your Place on the PLC Journey

It is important to help your staff build shared knowledge regarding your school's current status in addressing the critical step on the PLC journey of creating common formative assessments. We have created tools to assist you in that effort. "The Professional Learning Communities at Work® Continuum: Turning Data Into Information" and "The Professional Learning Communities at Work® Continuum: Monitoring Each Student's Learning" are available at **go.SolutionTree.com/ca/PLCbooks** as free reproducibles. Once your staff have established greater clarity regarding the current status of your collaborative teams, we urge you to turn your attention to the "Where Do We Go From Here?" worksheets that accompany the continuums (also available for free to download at **go.SolutionTree.com/ca/PLCbooks**). It will prompt you to take the action necessary to close the knowing-doing gap.

Part Five

Tips for Moving Forward: Using Common Formative Assessments

 Recognize that common assessments might create teacher anxiety: Common assessments are likely to create anxiety among teachers who are concerned that the results from these assessments could be used to expose weaknesses in their instruction. The inner voice of teachers may very well say, "But what if I am the weakest teacher on my team? My teammates will lose respect for me. The principal may use the results in my evaluation. If the results become public, parents may demand that their children be removed from my class. I don't want to participate in a process that can be used to humiliate or punish me. I would rather work in blissful ignorance than become aware that I may be ineffective."

These very real and understandable human emotions should be acknowledged but should not be allowed to derail the effort to create a common curriculum and common assessments. For example, principals can promise teachers that the results will not leave the building, appear in board of education reports, or show up in district newsletters.

Principals can and should assure staff that student performance on common assessments will not be used as a factor in teacher evaluation. The process to assess student learning should be distinct from the process to evaluate teachers. In fact, common formative assessments are an ineffective tool for evaluating teachers. If a team with four members administers a common assessment, it is inevitable that one member will be fourth in terms of results. This inevitability does not speak to the teacher's effectiveness. The team could have four outstanding teachers. Conversely, if a team with four inept teachers gives a common assessment, one member will have the best of the terrible results. Common assessments are worthless in terms of ranking and rating teachers but they are powerful in terms of giving each teacher the feedback and information necessary to improve.

Certainly a teacher's failure to contribute to the team process or unwillingness to change practices to improve results when students are not being successful can be addressed in the teacher's evaluation; however, scores from common assessments should not be.

2   **Remember that common formative assessments are only one element of an effective and balanced assessment process for monitoring student learning:** That process will continue to rely on individual teachers' assessments within the classroom on a day-by-day basis, assessments individual teachers create for their own students, occasional district benchmark assessments, summative assessments that the team or district creates, or the provincial or territorial assessments. All can play a role in improving schools.

3   **Remember districts can play a role:** Districts make a mistake when they create common assessments as a substitute for teacher-developed assessments at the team level. Districts can create their own assessments to monitor student learning throughout the entire district, but these assessments should supplement rather than replace team-level assessments and should be administered much less frequently (for example, two or three times each year). Districts can also create test-item banks as a resource for teachers, but teams should be expected to engage in the process of developing their own tools to answer the question, "How do we know our students are learning?"

4   **Create shared understanding of the term *common formative assessment*:** Once again, we have discovered that people who use the same terms do not necessarily assign them the same meaning. For example, a team of teachers that agrees to use the quiz provided at the end of each chapter of the textbook could claim they are using common assessments, but they would not experience the benefits we have outlined. Common assessments in the PLC context "are developed *collaboratively* in grade-level and departmental teams and incorporate each team's collective wisdom (professional knowledge and experience) in determining the selection, design, and administration of those assessments" (Ainsworth & Viegut, 2006, p. 13). Effective team-developed common assessments provide three forms of feedback: (1) "information about important learning targets that are clear to students and teacher teams," (2) "timely information for both students and teacher teams," and (3) "information that tells students and teacher teams what to do next" (Bailey & Jakicic, 2012, p. 49).

5   **Embrace the regular and routine use of protocols and team tools:** When teacher teams use protocols and tools to help structure their conversations about student learning, they sharpen their pedagogy and deepen their content knowledge. According to the National Turning Points Center (NTPC, 2001), teachers who use protocols have a more complete and comprehensive understanding of what students know and are able to do. The regular use of protocols also helps teachers develop a shared language for assessing student work and promotes the creation of a common understanding of what quality student work looks like.

Initially, many teachers may feel protocols are a waste of time, but effective principals encourage teachers to try them anyway. Initially, many teachers may feel protocols are a waste of time, but effective principals encourage teachers to try them anyway. "Schools or colleges mired in norms of private practice and used to ignoring the actual impact of the practice on students' learning may not take easily to learning with protocols. . . . however, . . . pressed to see them all the way through, even reluctant participants may find them refreshing" (McDonald et al., 2007, p. 1).

 Use assessments as a means rather than an end: In too many Canadian schools, administrators and educators have become preoccupied with the pursuit of higher test scores. Test scores should be an indicator of our effectiveness in helping all students learn rather than the primary focus of the institution. They should be viewed as a means rather than an end. Doug Reeves (2004) does a wonderful job of providing schools with fail-safe strategies to improve test scores: increase the dropout rate, assign higher percentages of students to special education, warehouse low-performing students in one school, create magnet programs to attract enough high-performing students to a low-performing school to raise its average, eliminate electives to devote more time to areas of the curriculum that are tested, and so on. Sadly, these strategies are still routinely being used in schools that are attempting to increase scores without improving learning.

Educators will not be driven to extraordinary effort and relentless commitment to achieve the goal of increasing student performance, for example, on PISA, PCAP, or provincial or territorial tests by five points. Most entered the profession because they felt they could make a significant difference in students' lives, and school leaders are more effective in marshalling and motivating faculty efforts when they appeal to that moral purpose.

Test scores will take care of themselves when schools and the people within them are passionately committed to helping each student develop the knowledge, skills, and dispositions essential to his or her success.

Part Six

Questions to Guide the Work of Your Professional Learning Community

To clarify the importance of creating common formative assessments, ask:

1. How will we monitor each student's learning of each essential skill on a timely basis?

2. Have we agreed on what proficient student work looks like?

3. What are the criteria we will use in judging the quality of student work?

4. What evidence do we have that suggests we apply the criteria consistently?

5. What evidence do we have that suggests we are using the results of common assessments to identify students who require additional time and support for learning?

6. What evidence do we have that suggests we are using the results of common assessments to extend the learning for students who demonstrate they are highly proficient?

7. What evidence do we have that suggests we are using the results from common assessments to identify strengths and weaknesses in our individual teaching?

8. What evidence do we have that suggests we are using common assessment results as part of a continuous improvement process that is helping our team get better results?

9. Does student performance on our team assessments correlate with their achievement on other assessments at the district, provincial, territorial, or national level?

10. Does student performance on our assessments correlate with the grades students are earning in my course or grade level? Do our assessment practices encourage or discourage learning on the part of our students?

Part Seven

Dangerous Detours and Seductive Shortcuts

It is the *process* of team members collaboratively building shared knowledge and collectively making decisions about assessment that results in adult learning and improved professional practice. Beware of any action that removes teachers from the process because doing so minimizes their role, limits their learning, and diminishes the impact of common formative assessments. Do not substitute district benchmark assessments, textbook assessments, or commercially prepared assessments for team-developed common formative assessments.

Remember that common assessments are formative only if educators use the results to better meet individual students' needs through intervention and enrichment *and* if educators use the results of the assessments to inform and improve their individual and collective instructional practice.

It is the **process** *of team members collaboratively building shared knowledge and collectively making decisions about assessment that results in adult learning and improved professional practice.*

Final Thoughts

The question, "How do we know our students are learning?" is the cornerstone of the PLC process. Before a team can answer that question, members must reach agreement on what knowledge, skills, and dispositions their students should acquire as a result of the unit they are about to teach. After the assessment is administered, teams will face the challenge of how can we intervene for students who need additional time and support and extend the learning for students who are highly proficient? The results from common formative assessments provide teams with the information and feedback they need to improve their professional practice. So the critical questions of the PLC process flow up and down from common formative assessments. If, however, the school does nothing to assist individual students who struggle to demonstrate proficiency on the assessments, little has been accomplished. The next chapter explores the critical questions, "How will we respond when some students don't learn?" and "How do we extend the learning for highly proficient students?"

CHAPTER 7

Responding When Some Students Don't Learn

Part One

The Case Study: Systematic Interventions Versus an Educational Lottery

When Harold Freiter started his tenure as principal of St. Andrews School in St. Andrews, Manitoba, he faced a situation common in many Canadian schools. At quick glance, the school was being successful meeting the needs of its students. For example, a high percentage (77 percent in this case) of students were reading at grade level. Principal Freiter, however, had attended an RTI at Work Institute and knew, just knew, that there would still be work to do!

As the new principal, he wanted to "go slow to go fast" (slow down to assess the situation and get a full view to move forward). He didn't want to change things just for the sake of changing things; he knew many things must have been working well already. He was able to review a perception survey that that the staff completed the previous spring. From the survey, he learned that there was a desire to collaborate. Principal Freiter knew that this was great news as he recognized that having a staff willing to collaborate would be critically important in order to meet all students' needs.

The only intervention in place seemed to be a pull-out program that had the lowest-performing students sent off to work with paraprofessionals. He heard from many teachers that the pull-out program was the traditional way of doing business at the school. Many were quick to say they knew the program wasn't working for all students, but they didn't know how to fix it. The teachers knew that they were not targeting specific root causes, for example, fluency or phonics, as they were just addressing the very general "he or she cannot read" scenario. There was a feeling of isolation, and it was up to individual teachers and the resource team to figure out what was needed and then determine which paraprofessional was going to work with the particular group of students.

As Principal Freiter spent more time observing and having conversations with staff members, they all noticed that few students successfully returned to the classroom from their pull-out program. Once they were assigned to pull-out, they seemed to be there for a long time. And, most disturbing to the principal and other staff, was the feeling that the school had created a system that was an educational lottery: whether or not a student's needs were being met depended on the pull-out program to which he or she was assigned. It was very apparent to Principal Freiter that the staff, teachers, and paraprofessionals were working very hard and wanted only the best for their students. He knew that the problem wasn't a lack of willingness, but rather, there was a need for an overall more effective plan of action.

Principal Freiter and his staff realized that this traditional system of pull-out was common to many Canadian schools as the way of responding to student needs. They were determined, however, to change this. What they wanted and needed was an intervention system that would meet the needs of all students. Principal Freiter knew that he had to develop a vision, plan, and timeline. He knew that he had to work with the staff to take action to address the inequities.

Reflection

Consider the dilemma presented in this case study—leaving the question of how to respond when students don't learn to each teacher's discretion or to a traditional, generic pull-out program inevitably results in profound inequities. How closely does this story simulate conditions in your school or district? Assuming that Principal Freiter has no additional resources to hire additional intervention staff, and no way to lengthen the school day to offer extra help, how can he best address this problem?

Part Two

Here's How

Principal Freiter and his school are confronting the third and fourth critical questions of the professional learning community process.

- How will we respond when our students don't learn?

- How do we respond when our students do learn?

Up to this point, each teacher has been left to resolve these questions on his or her own, based on his or her own assumptions, educational philosophies, and availability. The result is that students who experience difficulty in learning are subject to very different experiences. Any school dedicated to a mission of learning for all students would acknowledge the inherent limitations to this individualistic approach, and would instead take collective responsibility for each student's success and create a schoolwide, systematic process for interventions and extensions.

To address the issue, Principal Freiter and the school's guiding coalition should present their current reality to the staff and ask them to assess the situation in terms of its effectiveness, efficiency, and equity. Most importantly, they should question whether these practices are aligned to the school's mission of ensuring every student's success. An honest evaluation of the facts would lead the staff to the following conclusions and desired outcomes.

- We know that all students do not learn the same way, enter school with the same prior knowledge, or have the same academic supports at home. Subsequently, some students will need additional time and support to learn at high levels. Unless we create a more effective process to intervene when students struggle, there is no way we can achieve our school's mission.

- A single teacher cannot meet the diverse needs of all his or her students, so we must create a systematic intervention process to ensure that struggling students receive additional time and support for learning that goes beyond what an individual classroom teacher can provide. Achieving this goal will require staff members to work collaboratively and take collective responsibility for each student's success.

- Every student who demonstrates the need, regardless of the teacher to whom the student is assigned, must receive extra support. This will require us to create a timely, systematic process to identify students who need extra support.

- Students cannot miss new essential instruction to get extra help. Interventions must be in addition to core instruction, not in place of it. This will require us to embed dedicated intervention time into our school's master schedule.

- Some students cannot come to school early or stay late, so we must provide help during the school day, when students are required to be at school and all staff members are available to assist.

- Some students will struggle in school because they lack necessary academic and social behaviours. In addition to providing students extra support in learning essential academic skills and knowledge, we must also provide support for students who need additional help learning and consistently demonstrating essential behaviours.

- Some students will not voluntarily take advantage of additional support. Because our mission is to *ensure* that all students succeed, students will not be given the option of failing. Interventions will be directive. Students will be required, not invited, to attend.

- Additional time and support will not come at the expense of students who have already mastered essential grade-level curriculum. We will provide these students with additional time and support to extend their learning and master more rigorous curriculum.

Once the staff confronts the "brutal facts" of their current situation and identifies the preferred outcomes required to achieve their mission, Principal Freiter and the staff would engage in collective inquiry—they would learn together about how to create an effective system of interventions and extensions. A task force—comprised of teachers, support staff, and administration—could be formed to dig deeply into the topic and report back to the staff with recommendations. The task force would study current research on creating an effective system of interventions, as well as contact and visit similar schools that are successfully providing systematic interventions during the school day.

After sharing this learning with the faculty to build shared knowledge on the topic, Principal Freiter would lead the staff through an analysis of this research and evidence, with the goal of identifying immediate action steps that the school can pilot to begin creating a multitiered intervention system that is timely, directive, systematic, and provided within the school day. As they clarify specific steps, staff members would also identify the collective commitments they would need to make that are essential to the success of their new intervention system. They would set specific, results-oriented student-achievement goals to help monitor the effectiveness of the system. Finally, they would begin implementing that system, monitor its impact, and make adjustments and improvements based on their results.

We want to stress that it is not just students who benefit from this systematic support. In traditional schools, if a student is experiencing difficulty, the only professional who knows it and the only person who has responsibility for resolving the problem is the individual classroom teacher. In a PLC with a strong system of interventions, many adults support the classroom teacher in helping students to succeed. The teacher is not alone. As Canadian schools continue to embrace a more inclusive education system, teacher collaboration around what a student needs to be successful has never been more important.

In *Raising the Bar and Closing the Gap: Whatever It Takes* (DuFour, DuFour, Eaker, & Karhanek, 2010), we describe nine very different schools and three very different districts that have created systematic interventions to ensure their students receive additional time and support for learning. In each case, the schools and districts created their systems using their existing resources. In each case, however, it was imperative that the staff agreed to modify the schedule and assume new roles and responsibilities. We can offer this observation gleaned from our work with schools and districts throughout Canada and the United States. Faculties that are truly committed to ensuring that *every* student learns at high levels will work through the scheduling and resource obstacles and create a systematic process that ensures students will receive extra time and support for learning in a timely, directive, and systematic way. Conversely, faculties that place a higher value on protecting their traditional culture, structures, and schedules will find every excuse why systematic interventions are impossible to achieve at their school.

Faculties that are truly committed to ensuring that every student learns at high levels will work through the scheduling and resource obstacles and create a systematic process that ensures students will receive extra time and support for learning in a timely, directive, and systematic way.

Creating a Common Understanding of Systematic Intervention

Principal Freiter and the faculty must understand that the school does not have a system of interventions in place until staff can make the following promise to every parent whose child attends the school: *it doesn't matter which teachers your student is assigned to—if your child needs additional time and support to learn at high levels, we guarantee he or she will receive it until he or she succeeds* (Buffum, Mattos, & Weber, 2012). To achieve this outcome, the school must create a fail-safe process to identify every student who needs interventions or extensions, and then ensure that each student receives the appropriate help in a timely manner. While this systematic identification process will likely look slightly different from school to school, there are a few essential characteristics that must be present for the process to be effective.

First, every faculty member must participate. The people best positioned to identify students in need of additional help at school are the adults who work with them every day—teachers and support staff. Because teacher teams in the PLC process take primary responsibility in determining essential outcomes for each unit of study, teaching the curriculum, and assessing student progress, they are in the best position to identify, by student and by outcome, who needs additional help. Equally important, teachers and support staff get to know the student behind the assessment score, and can glean the subjective information also needed to identify students in need of help in the areas of behaviour, attendance, and social skills. So, just as every school has a clearly defined and mandatory processes for teachers to submit student progress information for report cards, each school should use a similar approach to creating a timely, mandatory process to have staff members identify students for interventions. If a single teacher is allowed to opt out of this process, then the school is allowing the educational lottery to persist.

Second, the identification process must be timely. Our experience is that schools often use report card grades, district benchmark testing, universal screeners, and provincial, territorial, national, or international assessment data to identify students who are at risk and in need of extra help. Unfortunately, these assessments usually happen every five to six weeks at the minimum, which allows students to fail too long before receiving help. We recommend that a school reassess which students are in need of interventions and extensions at least every three weeks. Furthermore, the process cannot be unfairly laborious for the staff. We find that when teachers have a voice in creating the process, it will be fair and respectful of teacher time.

After identifying students in need of additional help, the school must also guarantee that each student can actually receive the targeted help matched to each student's needs. We have worked with schools that have an effective way of identifying students who need additional help, but then face the following types of obstacles.

- A student needs to attend the after-school homework help club, but he or she rides a bus and can't stay.

- A student needs intensive reading support, but the reading specialist is paid for with categorical funds, and the student does not meet the funding criteria.

- A student could benefit from services provided by the special education staff, but the student does not have a disability.

In each of these cases, the school cannot call their intervention systemic, because the school can't guarantee every student who needs each intervention actually receives the intervention.

After identifying students in need of additional help, the school must also guarantee that each student can actually receive the targeted help matched to each student's needs.

Creating a Multitiered System of Intervention

A multitiered system of interventions is designed to address four essential outcomes needed to ensure all students learn at high levels.

1. If the ultimate goal of a learning-focused school is to ensure that every student ends each year having acquired the essential skills, knowledge, and behaviours required for success at the next grade level, then all students must have access to grade-level essential curriculum as part of their core instruction.

2. At the end of every unit of study, some students will need some additional time and support to master this essential grade-level curriculum.

3. Some students will enter each school year lacking essential foundational skills that should have been mastered in prior years—skills such as foundational reading, writing, number sense, and English language. These students will require intensive interventions in these areas to succeed.

4. Some students will require all three of these outcomes to learn at high levels.

A multitiered system of interventions, also commonly referred to as a multitiered system of support (MTSS) or response to intervention (RTI), is designed to address these four realities. Often captured visually with the shape of a pyramid, the base of the pyramid represents the school's core instruction program. The purpose of this tier—Tier 1—is to provide *all* students access to essential grade-level curriculum and effective initial teaching. When the core is taught well, most students should succeed most of the time without the need for additional help.

There will be a point in every unit of study when most students have demonstrated mastery of the unit's essential learning outcomes, and the teacher will need to proceed to the next topic. But because some students may not master the essential curriculum by the end of the unit, the school must dedicate time to provide these students additional support to master this essential grade-level curriculum without missing critical new core instruction. This supplemental help to master grade-level curriculum is the second tier—Tier 2—in an MTSS. Because this support is focused on very specific essential outcomes and learning targets, placement into Tier 2 interventions must be timely, targeted, flexible, and fluid.

And for students who need intensive remediation in foundational skills, the school must have a plan to provide this level of assistance, too. Intensive remediation is the purpose of the third tier of interventions—Tier 3. Students can only develop these skills over time, so schools must provide intensive interventions for targeted students as part of their instructional day and by highly trained staff in the student's targeted area of need.

This approach is called a multitiered system of interventions because students are not moved from tier to tier; instead, the tiers are cumulative. All students need effective initial teaching on grade-level essential outcomes at Tier 1. In addition to Tier 1, some students will need additional time and support in meeting grade-level essential outcomes at Tier 2. And in addition to Tier 1 and Tier 2, some students will need intensive help in learning essential outcomes from previous years. Creating this level of support cannot be done effectively by an individual teacher in his or her own classroom. Instead, it requires a schoolwide collective effort, utilizing the specialized training and unique talents of each staff member. This collaborative approach to ensure learning for all is essential to the PLC process.

Crafting a Schedule That Supports Intervention

If the existing schedule restricts a school's ability to provide supplemental and intensive interventions during the school day, then revise the master schedule! At Tier 2, schools should dedicate a block of time at least twice a week—but preferably more frequently—for students to receive additional time and support to master essential grade-level curriculum. As a general rule, each session should be at least thirty minutes. This time should be flexible and fluid, meaning students should be able to move into and out of these interventions based on demonstrated mastery of the targeted learning outcomes.

Because Tier 3 addresses significant gaps in foundational skills, schools should provide these interventions daily by embedding them into a student's individualized daily instructional program. At the elementary level, this is usually accomplished by extra support "pushing into" classrooms during guided or independent practice activities or "pulling" students during those times when new direct instruction on essential outcomes is not occurring. At the secondary level, intensive interventions are most commonly provided through designed courses. Again, the key is that schools must provide these services *in addition to* a student's access to essential grade-level curriculum, not as a replacement.

Many schools respond to these straightforward recommendations with the refrain, "But we can't change our schedule." This is a baffling claim. Many schools regularly change their master schedule—for sports games, guest speakers, awards assemblies, testing schedules, parent conferences, fine-arts events, fundraisers, and, in Canada, often for inclement weather. In almost every case, these situations and events did not require district approval, a teacher professional organization vote, or a change to provincial or territorial policy. If the average high school can shorten classes to recognize their fall sports teams at an all-school assembly, then what is stopping them from using the same modified schedule to provide targeted instruction to improve student achievement?

Schools must come to regard time as a tool rather than a limitation. For too long, learning has been a prisoner of time, with clock and calendar holding students and teachers captive (Goldberg & Cross, 2005). Of course, schools could lengthen the school day or the school year to create more time, but faculties typically are not in a position to do so unilaterally and are understandably unwilling to do so unless they are compensated accordingly. Faculties can, however, examine the way they are using the existing time available to them to create more opportunities for students to learn. The answer to the scheduling challenge lies within the school.

Schools must come to regard time as a tool rather than a limitation.

To see examples of master schedules that provide time for intervention from model PLCs, visit the AllThingsPLC website. One Canadian school, Pollard Meadows School in Edmonton, shares its intervention master schedule (AllThingsPLC, n.d.a). South Kamloops Secondary High School also shares its successful reduction of its failure rate in all departments through a change to its intervention practices (AllThingsPLC, n.d.c). Other great examples can be found on the AllThingsPLC website:

- Highland Elementary master schedule (www.allthingsplc.info/files/uploads /schedule_examples_elementary.pdf)

- Middle and High School intervention examples (www.allthingsplc.info/files /uploads/middle_high_intervention_examples.pdf)

- See the Evidence database (www.allthingsplc.info/evidence)

Considering the Key Criteria for Targeting Interventions

First, a school must target interventions **by student, by outcome.**

To target interventions effectively, we recommend a school consider two criteria. First, a school must target interventions *by student, by outcome.* Students in the same intervention should need assistance on the exact same essential outcome, learning target, or behaviour. This level of intervention specificity is why identifying essential outcomes is so vital to effective interventions. Unless a school has clearly identified the essential learnings that every student must master—unit by unit—it would be nearly impossible to have the curricular focus and specific assessment data necessary to target interventions to this level.

The second targeting criteria is **by kid, by cause.**

The second targeting criteria is *by kid, by cause.* We must address the cause of a student's struggles, not merely the symptoms. Failing grades, low test scores, disruptive behaviour, or poor attendance are all symptoms that demonstrate the student is struggling, but there are often multiple reasons why the student is demonstrating these outcomes. The more important questions are: Why is this student failing a class? Why did this student fail the exam? Why is this student demonstrating disruptive behaviour? Why is this student chronically absent? If a school staff can eliminate the cause of a student's struggles, they will solve the problem. In 2013, the province of New Brunswick (Government of New Brunswick, 2013) led inclusionary practices in Canada with its establishment of Policy 322, requiring all schools to be inclusive. Included in the policy statement are these goals for inclusive public education:

- Recognizes that every student can learn

- Is universal—the provincial curriculum is provided equitably to all students and this is done in an inclusive, common learning environment shared among age-appropriate peers in their neighbourhood school

- Is individualized—the educational program achieves success by focusing on the student's strengths and needs, and is based on the individual's best interest

- ▪ Requires the school personnel to be flexible and responsive to change

- ▪ Is respectful of student and staff diversity in regard to their race, colour, religion, national origin, ancestry, place of origin, age, disability, marital status, real or perceived sexual orientation or gender identity, sex, social condition, or political belief or activity

- ▪ Is delivered in an accessible physical environment where all students and school personnel feel welcome, safe, and valued

To achieve this outcome, school leaders are expected to "ensure that school-wide academic and behaviour interventions are based on data analysis and evidence-based practices, and used systemically to respond to varied student needs" (Government of New Brunswick, 2013). In New Brunswick and other provinces that have followed this lead, the key to identifying needs and responding with a timely intervention plan is critical. We contend that the only way to accomplish the goals established in Policy 322 is with an effective system of intervention.

Requiring, Not Inviting, Students to Participate in Systems of Intervention

Interventions must be directive. When interventions are optional, the students most likely to take advantage of the offer are the ones already succeeding, while the students least likely are those most in need of help. If a school is dedicated to ensuring the success of every student, then allowing a student to take the misguided path of choosing failure is unacceptable.

Making interventions mandatory should not be too difficult if a school places the same priority on requiring students to attend interventions as it does on requiring students to attend core instruction. For regular classroom instruction, virtually every school has a schoolwide attendance process that requires students to be in specific places throughout the day. This process includes steps to monitor student attendance, recognize positive attendance, and systematically respond when students fail to meet these expectations. If a school would apply these same attendance procedures to intervention attendance, the vast majority of students would be where they need to be most of the time.

Addressing Extension as Well as Intervention

We believe there is an important difference between enrichment and extension. We define *enrichment* as students having access to the subjects traditionally taught by specials or electives teachers, such as music, art, drama, applied technology, and physical education. We strongly believe that this curriculum is essential. These subjects often teach essential core curriculum through different modalities. Also, students usually view these subjects as the fun part of school. When students are pulled from enrichment to receive extra help in core curriculum, interventions turn into a punishment. Subsequently, a student's motivation and attitude can suffer. Finally, it is an equity issue. More often than not, the students who need interventions come from economically disadvantaged homes. The only way these students will learn a musical instrument or use advanced technology is at school. For these reasons, students should not be denied access to enrichment because they need additional time and support in core subjects.

Extension is when students are stretched beyond essential grade-level curriculum or levels of proficiency. This outcome can be achieved in multiple ways, including:

- Students can be asked to demonstrate mastery of essential outcomes at a level beyond what is deemed grade-level proficient. For example, many schools applying a four-point rubric to a grade-level writing prompt will deem a score of three as grade-level proficient. Stretching students beyond to a score of four would be an example of extended learning. For specific examples of this extended learning on a four-point scale for different subject areas, visit Marzano Resources' Critical Concepts (www.MarzanoResources.com /educational-services/critical-concepts).

- Students can have access to more of the required grade-level curriculum that is deemed important, but not essential.

- Students can be taught above grade-level curriculum. An example might be AP classes.

If a school is going to embed flexible time into its master schedule to provide targeted students additional time and support in learning essential grade-level outcomes, then there is no reason why this time could not also be used to extend students that have already learned these outcomes.

This outcome is easier to achieve if teacher teams consider extension opportunities when answering PLC critical question one, "What is it we want students to know and be able to do?" As teams determine the essential learning outcomes within a particular unit of study, they should expect that some students might have already learned the outcomes, while others will learn it during first initial instruction. So even before the unit starts, the team can discuss and identify what they can do to extend learning for the students, then use the school's dedicated intervention time to extend these students.

Using Your Existing Resources

A school improvement initiative that requires significant increases in expenditures is unlikely to be given serious consideration in most districts.

A school improvement initiative that requires significant increases in expenditures is unlikely to be given serious consideration in most districts. While extra resources are helpful, creating an effective system of interventions does not require increased funding, additional staffing, or a longer school day. Instead, it requires schools to use their existing resources differently and more effectively. The schools with exemplary intervention systems that we featured in *Raising the Bar and Closing the Gap: Whatever It Takes* (DuFour et al., 2010) were not flush with resources. For example, Lakeridge Junior High School is in Orem, Utah, and Utah ranks last among the fifty states in per-pupil expenditure. Yet this school was recognized as the best school in Utah for two consecutive years because, as Principal Garrick Peterson advises, "We realized we were in control of time in our school" (personal communication, May 1, 2008).

Specifically, schools like Lakeridge addressed their limited resource concerns in three ways by:

1. **Repurposing existing intervention resources**—Many schools have implemented the same interventions for years: interventions that often don't work, have never worked, and predictably won't work in the future. A school should assess the effectiveness of all their current site interventions, including special education, their use of instruction aides, push-in support, and remedial classes. For each intervention, ask this question: "Are a vast majority of students excelling in this intervention?" If the answer is "No," then stop the intervention and repurpose those resources toward better solutions.

2. **Targeting students by need, not by label**—If there were no labels on students at your school—such as *regular ed, special ed EL, honours,* and *gifted*—how would you target students for interventions? Wouldn't you group students together who have the same learning need? For example, students who need additional help mastering single-digit subtraction would be grouped together for reteaching. Within any elementary school, it is likely there will be students from different grade levels, and with different labels, who need help with this foundational mathematics skill. Unfortunately, many schools group students for interventions by their label, which likely means the same skill might be taught multiple times—in one group for the special education students, in another for first graders who need help with the skill, and again for the second graders. Obviously, this is not very efficient. When possible, schools should group students by need.

3. **Staying focused**—A school can't intervene on everything; there is just too much curriculum. Effective interventions and resource allocation begins with identifying a limited, realistic number of absolutely essential academic skills and behaviours that all students *must* learn. These outcomes are not all that your school will teach, but the minimum that all students must learn in a particular unit, term, grade level or course. When the targeted outcomes are reasonable and achievable, securing sufficient time and resources becomes possible.

Part Three

Here's Why

We have known for more than thirty-five years that effective schools create a climate of high expectations for student learning; that is, such schools are driven by the assumption that all students are able to achieve the essential learning of their course or grade level (Cotton, 2000; Georgiades, Fuentes, & Snyder, 1983; Good & Brophy, 2002; Lezotte, 1991; Newmann & Wehlage, 1996; Purkey & Smith, 1983). One of the most authentic ways to assess the degree to which a school is characterized by "high expectations" is to examine how the organization responds "when some students do not learn" (Lezotte, 1991, p. 2).

We have known for more than thirty-five years that effective schools create a climate of high expectations for student learning.

Key to an effective response for students who struggle is the provision of additional time and support for learning. Benjamin Bloom's research on mastery learning in the 1960s establishes that if all students were to learn, some students would need additional time and support for learning. Bob Marzano's (2003) meta-analysis of research on school-level factors that impact student learning reveals that the schools that have a profound impact on student achievement "provide interventions that are designed to overcome student background characteristics" (p. 8). Doug Reeves (2006), in his studies of high-poverty, high-minority, high-achieving schools, finds that those schools implement a plan for "immediate and decisive intervention" when students don't learn (p. 87). In their study of school districts that were able to double student achievement, Allan Odden and Sarah Archibald (2009) find that those districts extended learning time for struggling students. A decade of research by the Southern Regional Education Board (2000) into "things that matter most in student achievement" concludes that "extra help and time are important if they are designed to help students meet the standards of higher-level academic courses" (p. 8). Schools that improved most required students to get extra help when they performed poorly on tests. The message is clear: some students will require a greater opportunity to learn—they will need more time and support than others—and the most effective schools ensure that they receive it. (See the reproducible, "Why Should We Implement Systematic Interventions?" for expert commentary on this issue.)

John Hattie's (2012) comprehensive study of what most impacts student learning finds that education's powerful leverage points hinge on features *within* the school, rather than outside factors like home and environmental and economic conditions. Specially, he found that creating an effective MTSS has an exceptional yearly impact rate of 1.07 standard deviation growth. In comparison, the average yearly impact of an individual teacher's instruction is 0.30.

Another reason to create a timely, multitiered system of intervention for any student who experiences difficulty is because that is exactly what the Canadian Human Rights Act expects. "The Canadian Human Rights Act prohibits discrimination against persons with disabilities and the Equality Rights Section of the Canadian Charter of Rights and Freedoms guarantees people with disabilities equal benefit and protection before and under the law" (Council of Canadians With Disabilities, 2013).

Schools in Canada are expected to respond to the needs of students in a timely manner when asked to implement a systematic RTI. This is similar to what is expected in the United States, "to integrate assessment and intervention within a multi-level prevention system to maximize student achievement and reduce behavior problems" (National Center on Response to Intervention, 2008). In short, RTI aligns perfectly with the timely, directive, systematic process to provide students with additional time and support for learning that constitutes such a vital element of a PLC (Buffum, Mattos, & Weber, 2009).

But most importantly, schools must create a highly effective system of interventions because failure in the K–12 system is arguably a death knell in a student's chances to live a successful adult life. We began this book with the compelling statistics of what happens to students who don't succeed in school. It is naïve and profoundly unprofessional to expect individual teachers, working in isolation, to provide each of their students with the time and support needed to succeed.

Why Should We Implement Systematic Interventions?

Characteristics of high-performing schools include setting high expectations for all students, using assessment data to support student success, and employing systems for identifying intervention (Ragland, Clubine, Constable, & Smith, 2002).

"Reforms must move the system toward early identification and swift intervention, using scientifically based instruction and teaching methods" (President's Commission on Excellence in Special Education, 2002, p. 8).

"A criterion for schools that have made great strides in achievement and equity is immediate and decisive intervention. . . . Successful schools do not give a second thought to providing preventive assistance for students in need" (Reeves, 2006, p. 87).

"The most significant factor in providing appropriate interventions for students was the development of layers of support. Systems of support specifically addressed the needs of students who were 'stretching' to take more rigorous coursework" (Dolejs, 2006, p. 3).

"High-performing schools and school systems set high expectations for what each and every child should achieve, and then monitor performance against the expectations, intervening whenever they are not met. . . . The very best systems intervene at the level of the individual student, developing processes and structures within schools that are able to identify whenever a student is starting to fall behind, and then intervening to improve that child's performance" (Barber & Mourshed, 2007, p. 34).

In order to raise student achievement, schools must use diagnostic assessments to measure students' knowledge and skills at the beginning of each curriculum unit, on-the-spot assessments to check for understanding during instruction, and end-of-unit assessments and interim assessments to see how well students learned. "All of these enable teachers to make mid-course corrections and to get students into intervention earlier" (Odden & Archibald, 2009, p. 23).

In higher-performing school systems "Teachers identify struggling students as early as possible, and direct them towards a variety of proven intervention strategies, developed at both the school and district level, that assist all students in mastering grade-level academic objectives" (National Center for Educational Achievement, 2009, p. 34).

"One of the most productive ways for districts to facilitate continual improvement is to develop teachers' capacity to use formative assessments of student progress aligned with district expectations for student learning, and to use formative data in devising and implementing interventions during the school year" (Louis et al., 2010, p. 214).

"If a school can make both teaching and time variables . . . and target them to meet each student's individual learning and developmental needs, the school is more likely to achieve high levels of learning for every student" (Mattos & Buffum, 2015, p. 2).

There is nothing that is counterintuitive in what we are proposing regarding systematic intervention, and it represents nothing less than what educators would want for their own children.

There is nothing that is counterintuitive in what we are proposing regarding systematic intervention, and it represents nothing less than what educators would want for their own children. Whenever a school makes time and support for learning a fixed constant, the variable will always be student learning. Some students, probably most students, will learn the intended skill or concept in the given time and with the given support. Some students will not. PLCs make a conscious and sustained effort to reverse this equation. They advise students that learning is the constant—"All of you will learn this essential skill"—and then recognize that if they are to keep that commitment, they must create processes to ensure that students who need additional time and support for learning will receive them.

"Opportunity to learn" has been recognized as a powerful variable in student achievement for more than thirty years (Lezotte, 2005). In fact, Marzano (2003) concludes that "opportunity to learn has the strongest relationship with student achievement of all school level factors" (p. 22). Research on the topic has typically focused on whether or not the intended curriculum was actually implemented in the classroom; that is, were the essential skills actually taught? We are arguing that opportunity to learn must move beyond the question, "Was it taught?" to the far more important question, "Was it learned?" If the answer is "No" for some students, then the school must be prepared to provide additional opportunities to learn during the regular school day in ways that students perceive as helpful rather than punitive.

In the previous chapter, we made the case for the use of team-developed common formative assessments as a powerful tool for school improvement. These assessments help collaborative teams of teachers answer the question, "How do we know if our students are learning?" It is pointless to raise this question, however, if the school is not prepared to intervene when it discovers that some students are not learning. The lack of a systematic response to ensure that students receive additional opportunities for learning reduces the assessment to yet another summative test administered solely to assign a grade. Once again, the response that occurs *after* the test has been given will truly determine whether or not it is being used as a formative assessment. If it is used to ensure students who experience difficulty are given additional time and support as well as additional opportunities to demonstrate their learning, it is formative; if additional support is not forthcoming, it is summative. Canadian author Katie White (2017b) writes, "Summative assessment should be a snapshot in time; it should not mean finished and forgotten." She explains, "Summative assessment is the way we verify learning and determine proficiency. It is an essential part of the learning cycle" (White, 2017a, p. 153).

Many teachers have come to the conclusion that their job is not just difficult—it is impossible. If schools continue to operate according to traditional assumptions and practices, we would concur with that conclusion. Individual teachers working in isolation as they attempt to help all of their students achieve at high levels will eventually be overwhelmed by the tension between covering the content and responding to the diverse needs of their students in a fixed amount of time with virtually no external support. As Canadian schools continue to implement inclusive education practices, it is critically important that teachers collaborate to meet the needs of their students. Identifying these needs collectively in a timely fashion, and being well supported and trained in how to systematically respond, will decrease the feeling that it is an impossible task.

We cannot make this point emphatically enough: it is disingenuous for any school to claim its purpose is to help all students learn at high levels and then fail to create a system of intervention to give struggling learners additional time and support for learning. If time and support remain constant in schools, learning will always be the variable.

Furthermore, we cannot meet our students' needs unless we assume collective responsibility for their well-being. Seymour Sarason (1996) described schools as a "culture of individuals, not a group . . . [with] each concerned about himself or herself" (p. 367), a place in which "each teacher dealt alone with his or her problems" (p. 321), an environment in which teachers "are only interested in what they do and are confronted within their encapsulated classrooms" (p. 329). The idea so frequently heard in schools—"These are *my* students, *my* room, and *my* materials"—must give way to a new paradigm of "These are *our* students, and we cannot help all of them learn what they must learn without a collective effort." As the president of the National Commission on Teaching and America's Future notes:

> The idea that a single teacher, working alone, can know and do everything to meet the diverse learning needs of 30 students every day throughout the school year has rarely worked, and it certainly won't meet the needs of learners in years to come. (Carroll, 2009, p. 13)

Jon Saphier (2005) was exactly correct when he said, "The success of our students is our joint responsibility, and when they succeed, it is to our joint credit and cumulative accomplishment" (p. 28).

Part Four

Assessing Your Place on the PLC Journey

It is important to help your staff build shared knowledge regarding your school's current status in addressing the critical step on the PLC journey of creating systematic interventions. We have created a tool to assist you in that effort. "The Professional Learning Communities at Work® Continuum: Providing Students With Systematic Interventions and Extensions" is available at **go.SolutionTree.com/ca/PLCbooks** as a free reproducible. Once your staff have established greater clarity regarding the current status of your collaborative teams, we urge you to turn your attention to the "Where Do We Go From Here?" worksheet that accompanies the continuum (also available for free to download at **go.SolutionTree.com/ca/PLCbooks**). It will prompt you to take the action necessary to close the knowing-doing gap.

It is disingenuous for any school to claim its purpose is to help all students learn at high levels and then fail to create a system of interventions.

Part Five

Tips for Moving Forward: Creating Systematic Interventions and Extensions to Ensure Students Receive Additional Time and Support for Learning

Start with PLC critical questions one and two: Most schools don't have a scheduling problem; they have a targeting problem. This reality is captured best when we hear educators say, "We would like to revise our schedule and provide students additional time to learn, but we can't because we have too much to cover." This claim demonstrates that the school still embraces a mission of teaching, not learning. The goal of a learning-focused school is not to cover curriculum, but to ensure students actually learn the skills, content, and behaviours that are critical to their future success. The four critical questions of the PLC process not only focus the collaboration of a team, but they also provide a logical sequence to the work. When teams skip the first two questions, ("Learn what?" and "How will we know?"), then responding effectively when students don't learn is impossible.

Beware of appeals to mindless precedent: Appeals to mindless precedent include the phrases, "But we have always done it this way," "We have never done it that way," and the ever-popular, "The schedule won't let us." These appeals pose a formidable barrier to the creation of a PLC.

We have carefully perused both the Old and New Testaments and can find no evidence that any school schedule was carved into stone tablets and brought down from Mount Sinai. Yet in schools throughout Canada, the schedule is regarded as an unalterable, sacrosanct part of the school not to be tampered with in any way. The reverence afforded the schedule is puzzling. Mere mortals created it, and educators should regard it as a tool to further priorities rather than as an impediment to change.

An advocate for a schedule that provides additional time and support for student learning might present the following argument.

- We contend that our fundamental purpose and most vital priority is to ensure all students learn at high levels.

- Research, as well as our own experience and intuition, make it clear that it is impossible for all students to learn at high levels if some do not receive additional time and support for learning.

Even the most ardent advocates of the premise that all students can learn acknowledge that they will not learn at the same rate and with the same support.

* If the only time we offer this service is before or after school, some of our students cannot or will not utilize the services. It will be difficult for us to require those students to do what is necessary to be successful if our only access to them is beyond the school day.

* Therefore, the priority in designing our schedule should be ensuring we have access to students for intervention during the school day in ways that do not deprive them of new direct instruction in their classroom.

3   **Acknowledge that traditional special education is not the answer:** For most of the past half-century, the only systematic intervention process that was mandated for every school to provide was special education. Objective analysis of the results would conclude that special education has not only failed to close student achievements gaps, but has actually been detrimental to achieving this outcome. We are not suggesting that special education services should be discontinued altogether, or that educators should disregard student IEPs. What we are suggesting is that provinces and territories continue to support collaborative efforts and educator training to ensure that schools can provide much more flexibility to meet all students' needs. But taking advantage of this power requires schools to rethink the way regular and special education have worked for years.

4   **Focus on what you can control:** We find many schools, when planning interventions for struggling students, spend an inordinate amount of time identifying and discussing factors that they cannot directly change. These topics include a student's home environment, a lack of district support, the pressure of preparing students for high-stakes provincial or territorial assessments, and ill-conceived provincial or territorial and federal educational policies. While these concerns are real, and might be impacting both the student and the site educators, they are rarely the primary reason why a student has not learned a specific essential learning outcome. Instead of spending precious intervention planning time focusing on factors that cannot immediately change, a school staff should focus on what lies within their sphere of influence, like providing students with time and targeted instruction during the school day to master essential outcomes. In the end, schools have a significant amount of control over the instructional decisions made on behalf of their students every day.

5   **Ensure an intervention plan recognizes the unique context of the school:** Faculties should create their own plans rather than merely adopting the program of another school. In *Raising the Bar and Closing the Gap* (DuFour et al., 2010), we offer specific and detailed explanations and examples of how intervention plans operate in elementary, middle, and high schools. It is important that faculties realize, however, that eventually they are called on to create their own systems of intervention within the context of their own schools. Once again, engaging staff in the process of exploring and resolving the question, "What will we do when students do not learn in our school?" creates far more ownership in and commitment to the resulting plan than the adoption of someone else's plan.

 Remember more of the same is not effective intervention: Effective intervention will be characterized by differentiation and precision. Intervention will offer a setting and strategies that are different from those that have already proven to be ineffective for the student. A student who failed to grasp a concept that was taught in a large-group setting by a teacher using a particular strategy is not likely to learn the concept if the intervention takes place in another large-group setting and replicates the same instructional strategy. Effective intervention will require diverse formats for delivery and truly differentiated instruction. Furthermore, an intervention system that merely reports a student is failing mathematics will not be as effective as a system that can identify the precise skill or skills that are causing the student difficulty.

 Align your school's grading practices to promote, celebrate, and reward students for effort, improvement, and learning: Many school intervention programs are undermined by traditional grading practices designed to rank student achievement, punish students for initial failure, deny students opportunities to fix mistakes, value promptness over learning, and demotivate struggling students. Examples include the following—

- Establishing a "no late work accepted" policy where once a deadline has passed there is no reason for the struggling student to complete the assignment

- Giving half credit for late work, which guarantees the student will fail the assignment whether he or she makes it up or not

- Averaging grades so that first attempts will always weigh into a grade, regardless of how much the student improves

- Not giving make-up tests, so once a student is assessed at the end of a unit, there is no way to improve the grade even if the student attends interventions

- Grading on a curve, so a student's grade is not based on if he or she met the outcome, but instead on how students do in comparison to each other

All these traditional grading policies, which are prevalent in most schools, discourage students from fixing mistakes or deny them the opportunity to improve. Canadians Ken O'Connor, Damian Cooper, and Tom Schimmer are excellent resources for more effective grading practices.

8 **Celebrate with students *how* they overcame their initial struggles:** The goal of any intervention is not only to have students learn a specific academic outcome but also to teach students how to learn. We want students to develop what Carol Dweck (2006) refers to as a *growth mindset*—that one's abilities are not based on innate talents, but can be developed through a one's dedication and effort. We can foster this attitude when we have students reflect on how they ultimately succeeded—by getting a little extra help, giving a little extra effort, and sticking with it until they learned the concept. Helping students to adopt a growth mindset will improve their self-efficacy and ultimately teach them to self-advocate once they enter more sink-or-swim environments.

9 **Realize that no support system will compensate for ineffective teaching:** A school characterized by weak and ineffective teaching will not solve its problems by creating a system of timely intervention for students. Eventually, that system will be crushed by the weight of the mass of students it is attempting to support. At the same time the school is creating its system of intervention, it must also take steps to build the capacity of every teacher in the school to become more effective in meeting students' needs. The battle to help all students learn must be fought on both fronts: support for students and support for the professional staff. To focus on one and exclude the other will never result in victory. In the province of New Brunswick, with the implementation of Policy 322 (Council of Canadians With Disabilities, 2013), educators recognized the importance of inclusive education as defined and established in this policy. As implementation continued, however, it became more and more evident that it had to be coupled with a professional development plan for teachers. Implementation of Policy 322 in New Brunswick included mandatory training about the PLC process, differentiated instruction, and formative assessment practices in all districts. Principals and teachers must engage in a process of continuous improvement, constantly examining their practices and expanding their repertoire of skills. But no matter how skillful the professional, at the end of each unit of instruction, it is likely some students will not master the intended learning. At that point, the system of intervention comes to the aid of both students and teachers. Schools need both skillful teachers and effective, schoolwide interventions.

Additional Resources on Intervention

To dig deeper into the topic of interventions, a number of outstanding books have been written on the topic of how to leverage the PLC process to effectively respond when students need interventions and extension.

- DuFour, R., DuFour, R., Eaker, R., & Karhanek, G. (2010). *Raising the bar and closing the gap: Whatever it takes.* Bloomington, IN: Solution Tree Press.

- Buffum, A., Mattos, M., & Weber, C. (2009). *Pyramid response to intervention: RTI, professional learning communities, and how to respond when kids don't learn.* Bloomington, IN: Solution Tree Press.

- Buffum, A., Mattos, M., & Weber, C. (2012). *Simplifying response to intervention: Four essential guiding principles.* Bloomington, IN: Solution Tree Press.

- Buffum, A., & Mattos, M. (Eds.). (2015). *It's about time: Planning interventions and extensions in elementary school.* Bloomington, IN: Solution Tree Press.

- Mattos, M., & Buffum, A. (Eds.). (2015). *It's about time: Planning interventions and extensions in secondary school.* Bloomington, IN: Solution Tree Press.

- Buffum, A., Mattos, M., & Weber, C., & Hierck, T. (2015). *Uniting academic and behavior interventions: Solving the skill or will dilemma.* Bloomington, IN: Solution Tree Press.

- Buffum, A., Mattos, M., & Malone, J. (2018). *Taking action: A handbook for RTI at Work.* Bloomington, IN: Solution Tree Press.

The DVD *Through New Eyes: Examining the Culture of Your School* (DuFour, 2003) provides an excellent, compelling representation of the difference between how traditional schools respond when students do no learn compared to PLCs. It clearly demonstrates how two different schools respond to the same student who is unwilling to do what is necessary to succeed in his classes.

Part Six

Questions to Guide the Work of Your Professional Learning Community

To develop systematic interventions that ensure students receive additional time and support for learning on a timely and directive basis, ask:

1. Which areas of student need should we address first?

2. How will we identify students who need additional time and support so that no student will slip through the cracks?

3. How often will we identify students so that they do not drop too far behind before receiving assistance?

4. How proactive are we? What steps do we take to identify the students who will need us most before they come to our school?

5. How will we determine which staff members will take the lead for each intervention?

6. How will we schedule time for each intervention so that identified students will not miss new essential instruction?

7. How will we ensure that targeted students attend their assigned intervention?

8. How will we monitor student progress and the effectiveness of our efforts?

9. How fluid is our system of intervention? Are students assigned to intervention for a fixed period of time, or can they move in and out of intervention based on evidence of their proficiency?

10. How can we use flexible time and targeted instruction to provide students with assistance in extending their learning?

Part Seven

Dangerous Detours and Seductive Shortcuts

Beware of pseudo plans of intervention. For example, an after-school tutoring program for students who elect to seek help is not systematic intervention. The students who need help most are typically the least likely to seek it. Furthermore, it is difficult for educators to insist that students remain after school given busing, family requirements, jobs, and so on that make it impossible for some students to remain after school. An intervention plan that is directive will occur during the school day when educators serve in loco parentis.

If the time scheduled for intervention is so infrequent that the school must attempt to support every student who needs assistance during a narrow window of opportunity, the effectiveness of intervention is diminished. A high school of two thousand students that attempts to support all students who are struggling during the same single thirty-minute period twice a week will not be as effective as a school that builds time for intervention for small groups of students throughout the entire day, every day.

Resist the temptation to purchase a "silver bullet" intervention program—a program that claims to remediate every struggling reader, or software that will identify and target the mathematics needs of each student. There are some effective intervention programs available, but they should not replace the ongoing processes described in this chapter. No program can or should replace a systematic process of intervention.

Beware of attempts to use intervention to further exonerate educators from responsibility for student learning. In the wrong school culture, a system of interventions could be viewed as yet another reason the teacher is not responsible for student learning: "I taught it, they didn't get it, so let the intervention people deal with it." To be effective, the program must be just one part of an explicit schoolwide commitment to help all students learn by providing those who struggle with additional time and support at the same time that the school establishes a process to inform and improve the professional practice of every teacher and every team.

But perhaps most importantly, we must stop judging a student's ability to learn at high levels based on their demographic characteristics. We know that a student's ethnicity, native language, and economic status do not reduce the student's innate capacity to learn. Yet, many schools are making assumptions on what they *think* students are capable of learning based on these demographic factors. Any school dedicated to ensuring all students learn at high levels must stop debating what they *think* students can or can't do, and instead change the question to this: *How will we get every student there?* It is unlikely an intervention will be effective when educators begin with the assumption that some students can't do it in the first place.

Any school dedicated to ensuring all students learn at high levels must stop debating what they think students can or can't do, and instead change the question to this: **How will we get every student there?**

Final Thoughts

One of the major obstacles to creating an effective system of interventions is the long-standing assumption that it is the teacher's job to teach and the student's job to learn. Educators who operate under this assumption assert that students who do not put forth sufficient effort to learn should suffer the logical consequence of their decision: failure. To provide these students with additional time and support, the educators argue, is to ensure their learning simply enables them and does not prepare them for the harsh realities of the real world. If this assumption prevails in the 21st century, schools can anticipate the same results that they experienced throughout the 20th century: high levels of failure, particularly among the most disadvantaged students. As we have stressed, however, the consequences of student failure today are much more dire than they have been in the past. Educators must not ignore those consequences.

We return to the first and biggest of the big ideas that drive the PLC process: *the fundamental purpose of the school is to ensure that all students learn at high levels (grade level or higher)*. Variations on this assertion dominate school mission statements throughout Canada. Educators who align their behaviour with this mission will create multitiered systems of interventions because without those systems it is impossible to help all students learn at high levels. Those who continue to insist that they have fulfilled their responsibility by merely teaching a lesson should feel compelled to amend their mission statements to reflect their beliefs and practices.

A common concern from schools is that just as their teams are starting to function well, new members come on board and disrupt the forward momentum the team has created. We address the challenge of selecting, training, and retaining staff in the next chapter.

CHAPTER 8
Hiring, Orienting, and Retaining New Staff

Part One

The Case Study: The Disruption of Adding New Staff

When Yvonne Careen became directrice générale, superintendent of the Commission scolaire francophone des TNO in the Northwest Territories, she knew that she wanted to ensure that her schools implemented the PLC process. She worked diligently with her staff to create deep understanding of what it meant to be student centred in a collaborative culture focused on results.

Over the years, collaborative teams engaged in learning sequences based on the four PLC critical questions. Teachers understood that their collaborative work should lead to an increase in student achievement and that this was the expectation and focus of their time together. It is all about the students in this district.

Superintendent Careen recognized that the geography of her district created challenges. For example, her two schools are five hours apart. She knew that in order to develop a deeply embedded PLC culture she would need to create common language and make sure that everyone had the same PLC training. Superintendent Careen worked with a consultant to ensure that the learning continued from year to year.

As we all know, there are always a few detours on the road to success. One road block Superintendent Careen stumbled on was what happened when she hired new staff members. She recognized that every time she had to hire someone new, she had to start again with the learning and training. She really felt the pressure and stress of this when she had to hire two teachers in April, with three months left in the school year. These two teachers, teaching different grade levels, joined a school functioning as a PLC. They were joining existing collaborative teams that understood the work and had a rhythm and process to their focus. Even if Superintendent Careen and her team had made sure their interview questions were focused on the PLC process and she felt certain the principal and teachers on site could support the new teachers, she knew it was not guaranteed that the new teachers would understand the work and not disrupt the flow of the collaborative processes at each school.

> ## Reflection
>
> Superintendent Careen understands the PLC process and has ensured that deep implementation is ongoing in her district. She is, however, correct to worry about the times when she has to add new staff to her schools. It doesn't matter if it is a large, urban district or a small, rural district, the stress of ensuring that implementation is not disrupted is real. What are the factors that influence how you hire and how you ensure continuous effective PLC practices in your school when you are faced with new hires?

Part Two

Here's How

Let's begin with the assumption that the teaching candidates do not want to disrupt the flow of the collaborative processes at the school. If that is true, the problem of the disconnect between what candidates understand about the work and their subsequent actions as employees is most likely the result of the following factors.

The Need for an Expanded Selection Process

The goal of the hiring process in a PLC is not to complete the process quickly but to ensure that the candidate will be an asset to the school because he or she is a good fit for the culture. Rather than hiring capable people and attempting to persuade them to embrace the culture, effective leaders "hire people who already have a predisposition to your core values and hang onto them" (Collins, 2009, p. 159).

It is certainly a mistake for schools or districts to delay the hiring process until a few weeks or days before the school year begins.

It is certainly a mistake for schools or districts to delay the hiring process until a few weeks or days before the school year begins. Too often this approach results in a sense of urgency that leads to "any warm body will do" syndrome. Superintendent Careen was correct in ensuring the effectiveness of the hiring process by bringing the right people into the district and schools and not putting too much emphasis on completing the process quickly. She was clear on what will be expected of them.

One way to improve the process is if Superintendent Careen had contacted the principal of a candidate's former school (or a cooperating teacher if the candidate has not had a previous position) to ask for a candid assessment of past performance. Reviewing written references serves a purpose, but directing pointed questions to knowledgeable people about a candidate's effectiveness in the past is a step that should never be skipped in the hiring process. As former principal and author Kim Marshall (2015) admits:

> My biggest regret from my years as a principal was when I rushed
> to make a last-minute hiring decision rather than persisting until
> we found the right person—and when I cut corners on calling ref-
> erences or didn't push previous employers to give the full story.
> (p. 37)

Superintendent Careen could also improve the hiring process by giving teams a role to play in selecting their new colleagues. For example, the principal and assistant principal or the principal and department chair could complete an initial round of interviews and reference checks and narrow the choices to two or three candidates. Teams could then interview each finalist during which time members could ensure each candidate becomes well versed on the teams' norms, protocols, essential outcomes, and common assessments.

The hiring process should also include having finalists demonstrate their skill in the classroom. Superintendent Careen could have asked the candidates to prepare and present a lesson on an appropriate essential outcome while she and team members observed. As the final step in the process, the team could have offered the superintendent or principal an assessment of each candidate's strengths and weaknesses before they extended a job offer.

Such an expanded selection process will certainly require more time than is devoted to hiring in the past. It will, however, reap several benefits. Teams will feel a greater sense of ownership in the success of their new colleague if members contribute to the selection process. The candidate will have a better sense of what it will be like to work with the team when he or she hears firsthand from its members about their collaborative process and their expectations for new members. The opportunity to observe a candidate teaching an essential skill provides greater insight into his or her instructional ability and whether or not it's a match with the PLC process.

The Need for Relevant Questions

Another problem with the interview process is that district and school administrators often use questions that are unlikely to elicit extended responses or differentiate among candidates. A question such as "Will you support our PLC process?" allows candidates to answer with a one-word response. Furthermore, that response is likely to be essentially the same—a variation on, "Absolutely!" Such a question that does not reveal the candidate's thinking and values or that does not distinguish between different candidates is essentially a waste of time. The best questions are presented as scenarios that call on candidates to explain how they would respond to given situations, the thinking that would guide their decisions, and how they have dealt with specific situations in the past. Questions could be organized to gain insight into the candidates' thinking about the three big ideas that drive the PLC process. See page 176, "Is This Candidate a Good Fit for Our PLC?" for sample questions.

Is This Candidate a Good Fit for Our PLC?

1. The purpose of our school is to ensure that all students learn, rather than to make sure they are taught.

   I'm going to present you with four statements. Please tell me which statement is closest to your personal philosophy and elaborate on your thinking.

   a. "I believe all students can learn based on their ability."

   b. "I believe all students can learn if they take advantage of the opportunities we give them to learn."

   c. "I believe all students can learn something, but it is more important that we create a warm and caring environment than fixating on academic achievement."

   d. "I believe all students can learn and we should be committed to doing whatever it takes to ensure all students learn at high levels."

2. If, at the end of the first semester, you discovered that 50 percent of your students were failing, would it trouble you? (*Then drop the percentage:* How about 25 percent? 15 percent? 10 percent?)

3. We have all encountered a student who simply does not want to work, but is not a behaviour problem and is not interfering with the learning of others. How have you responded to such a student?

4. One of your colleagues states that there is little a teacher can do to help a student who is just not interested in learning. Would you respond, and if so, how would you respond?

5. How would you respond to this assertion: "The major causes of learning do not fall within the teacher's sphere of influence. Student learning will be determined primarily by factors such as innate ability, parental support, the socioeconomic conditions in which the student lives, and the beliefs and behaviours of the student's peer group."

6. If we are to help all students learn, we must work collaboratively and collectively. How would you respond to the following statement:

   "A teacher is a professional who deserves wide-ranging autonomy regarding what to teach, how to teach, how to assess, and how to run his or her classroom. I would not presume to advise another teacher how to run his or her classroom, and I would not be receptive to a teacher offering unsolicited advice to me."

7. Think of a time when you were part of a group or team that led to better results for its members and a more satisfying professional experience. Think of another time when you were part of a group or team and it was a negative experience. What factors contributed to the difference?

8. Imagine you are on a team that is experiencing significant conflict. How would you respond?

9. If you were assigned to a teaching team and encouraged to collaborate, on what questions or issues do you believe the team should focus its efforts?

10. "Do you want to be the teacher with the highest student achievement in our school or a member of a team whose students all achieve at high levels?" (Smith, 2015, p. 6).

11. We say in our vision statement that we will work collaboratively and take collective responsibility for the success of our students. What does that phrase mean to you? Can you give me examples of how a staff might take collective responsibility for student success?

12. It is important to focus on results, rather than intentions. What is your understanding of the terms *formative assessment* and *summative assessment*? Can you cite examples of when and how you have used each of these assessments in your teaching experience? What do you feel is the primary purpose of assessing students?

13. What is your reaction to this statement: "Teachers of the same course or grade level should use common assessments so each member of the team can determine the achievement of his or her students compared to other students attempting to acquire the same knowledge and skills."

14. What is your reaction to the statement: "Teachers and students benefit when evidence of student learning is easily accessible and openly shared among members of the teaching team."

15. It has been said that in most schools the quality of a student's work is assessed primarily upon the idiosyncrasies of the teacher to whom that student is assigned. What is your reaction to that statement? Can you think of steps a school might take to provide more consistent feedback to students?

16. It's the end of your first year. I ask you to provide me with evidence you have been an effective teacher. What will you give me?

Other important questions to explore:

1. What is your understanding of the term *professional learning community*? How would you explain that term to someone completely unfamiliar with it? In what ways, if any, is the PLC process different from traditional schooling?

2. I'm a student in your class the first day. Help me understand your expectations regarding the classroom environment.

3. I'm one of your students. Help me understand the essential knowledge, skills, and dispositions I will acquire as a result of being in your classroom?

4. What does the research tell us about effective teaching strategies?

5. What should I have asked you that I didn't, a question you would want to ask a teaching candidate?

6. If you are offered this position, what could we do to make this a great school year for you?

7. What questions do you have for me?

The Need for a Common Vocabulary

The probability is that someone new to the organization will not understand the established common vocabulary. Terms such as *professional learning communities, collaborative teams, guaranteed and viable curriculum, common formative assessment,* and *transparent evidence of student learning* can certainly mean different things to different people. Candidates can't be held accountable for honouring a commitment if they are unclear as to what they are committing to.

To address this problem, the district administrator or principal should take the necessary time during the interview to explain key terms that capture the culture and processes of the school. An excellent way to accomplish this is to review the very foundation of the school—its written mission, vision, collective commitments, and goals. The district administrator or prinicpal could ask the candidate to read through the document and react to its contents or check for understanding of key terms by asking questions such as:

- "What is your understanding of the term *professional learning community?*"

- "How would you explain the PLC process to someone completely unfamiliar with it?"

- "In what ways, if any, is the PLC process different from traditional schooling?"

- "How would you distinguish between a group and a team?"

- "How familiar are you with the use of team-developed common formative assessments?"

- "What do you see as the advantages or disadvantages of teams using common formative assessments?"

Once the school year begins, engage the entire staff in reviewing the school's mission, vision, values, and goals.

Once the school year begins, engage the entire staff in reviewing the school's mission, vision, values, and goals. This helps the staff to refocus and recommit their collective efforts, while also allowing new staff members to be part of the process.

We have provided a Glossary of Key Terms and Concepts to assist you in building a shared understanding of a common vocabulary. You can access the glossary at **go.SolutionTree.com/ca/PLCbooks**. It is also available in the tools and resources section of the AllThingsPLC website (www.allthingsplc.info/tools-resources/search -result/view/id,70).

The Need for a More Thoughtful Orientation Program

In the traditional entry into the profession, teachers are pointed to their classrooms and wished good luck. Research has revealed the most common issues new teachers face: struggles with classroom management, a lack of instructional resources or guidance to assist in their planning, and unsupportive environments in which they are left to fend for themselves (Goodwin, 2012). Too often, new teachers are ill prepared to cope with these challenges along with instructional failures, student boredom, and the crushing sense of loneliness and isolation they are likely to encounter. As a result, for too many new teachers, their good intentions give way to a diminishing sense of self-efficacy and job satisfaction.

Doing a better job of clarifying expectations is an important step to address the problem of teacher turnover, but if new teachers are to meet those expectations, the school must provide a much more systematic and effective system of support—a system in which people throughout the school work together in an intentional, coordinated way to achieve the goal of greater teacher retention.

This coordinated induction system should include the following five characteristics.

1. **A mentor from the same field:** There is mixed evidence on the benefits of providing a new teacher with a mentor. An ongoing study of teacher retention finds that schools that assigned teachers an individual mentor did no better at improving the teacher's job satisfaction or retention rate (Johnson & Kardos, 2004). The National Commission on Teaching and America's Future (Carroll, 2007), the Alliance for Excellent Education (2014), and the National Center for Education Statistics (Raue & Gray, 2015) all conclude that having a mentor can improve teacher retention and providing a mentor from the same field should be part of a comprehensive induction program.

   It is evident that mentoring programs can differ greatly both in terms of the frequency of the interactions between the two teachers and the quality of their interactions. To increase the likelihood of a positive impact on retention, the elements of the mentoring process should be clearly defined and closely monitored, and mentors should embrace their responsibilities rather than view mentoring as an imposition.

2. **Common planning team with members of a grade-level or course-specific collaborative team:** The key factor in teacher retention is the school's culture. Schools that operate as true PLCs foster collaboration, collective responsibility, and commitment to supporting the ongoing learning of their members. These are the cultural characteristics that have proven most effective in cultivating teacher satisfaction and retention (Johnson & Kardos, 2004).

   Responsibility for a new teacher's success should not fall solely to a mentor; rather, every collaborative team member and the principal should share the responsibility. When new teachers are clear on the essential learning for each unit of instruction, when they know how students will be called on to demonstrate proficiency, when they are clear on the criteria students must meet to be deemed proficient, and when they know they have colleagues to turn to and talk to when they struggle, they are positioned to be successful. There is no better way to provide ongoing support for new teachers than to engage them in the work of a high-performing teacher team.

   To address the concern that new staff members often attend team meetings but fail to contribute, each team should review and revise its team commitments. Sample norms might include:

   ♦ We will share teamwork equally.

   ♦ Everyone must be a contributing team member.

   ♦ We will elicit all points of view before making decisions.

Responsibility for a new teacher's success should not fall solely to a mentor; rather, every collaborative team member and the principal should share the responsibility.

These norms create an expectation that every team member is expected to contribute. Even if a new teacher might not yet have the content expertise to take the lead on creating a team common assessment, for example, he or she can assist the process by offering to type up the final product. This division of labor will help new members feel like they are contributing, and veteran teachers will see the benefits of the new team member.

3. **Ongoing supportive communication from the principal:** In addition to district support, Superintendent Careen knows that at her schools her principals will need to schedule weekly individual meetings with new teachers during the first month of the year and monthly meetings during the remainder of the year. These meetings should focus on gaining insights into each teacher's perceptions, experiences, and concerns; celebrating progress; identifying problems; and offering support. Sample questions to ask might include:

   ♦ "Is teaching here different from what you expected it would be?"

   ♦ "What has gone well for you so far?"

   ♦ "What questions or concerns do you have?"

   ♦ "Tell me about the next unit you are going to teach. What student outcomes do you anticipate?"

   ♦ "What more can we do to help you have a great year?"

   This attention to new teachers' well-being should extend to such mundane issues as ensuring every new teacher has at least one person from his or her team with whom to eat lunch for the first few weeks of school. Each year, the number-one concern of new students at Rick's former high school, Adlai E. Stevenson, was the fear that they would enter the cafeteria and not have any friends to sit with at lunch. That concern is still present for adults, and a school with a supportive environment would eliminate the worry for teachers and students alike.

4. **A reduced course load or the support of a teacher aide:** In most schools, the responsibilities for first-year teachers are indistinguishable from those of a twenty-year veteran. Each will have the same preparation time, be assigned a similar number of students, and confront similar managerial responsibilities, such as communicating with parents, completing report cards, and responding to central office requests.

An environment that is supportive of new teachers recognizes that new teachers benefit from a lighter load in their first year of teaching.

An environment that is supportive of new teachers recognizes that new teachers benefit from a lighter load in their first year of teaching. At the secondary level, new teachers might be assigned a single preparation rather than multiple preparations. At the elementary level, new teachers could have the benefit of a teacher aide each day. At all levels, the school might consider a job-share arrangement in which two new teachers divide their teaching load and are assigned to assist with interventions when not teaching their classes. This arrangement not only reduces their classroom responsibilities but also gives them greater insight into the problems students are experiencing in mastering content.

Lightening a new teacher's responsibilities also includes not assigning new teachers an abnormally high number of students with potentially significant behaviour problems. Unfortunately, it is common for a new faculty member to inherit the most demanding classes, as most schools determine teacher assignments by seniority. The veteran teachers claim the classes with the most traditionally successful students, leaving the most challenging assignments to the new hires. This practice not only sets up new staff members to fail but also provides the students most at risk with teachers who are the least prepared to meet their needs and ensure their success.

5. **Ongoing professional development geared specifically toward new teachers' needs:** In addition to the other supports for new teachers, schools should provide their newest members with an ongoing professional development program focused on the issues and challenges they are likely to encounter. Superintendent Careen made great efforts as she continued to work with a PLC consultant who supported ongoing development of her teachers. This can also be done internally. We recommend a monthly program that teacher leaders and the principal jointly lead. Initial training follows a predetermined curriculum but also provides time for questions at each session. Topics for later sessions could be based on the results of surveys of the new teachers. Sample topics might include the following. Notice how April and May will be determined based on the new teachers' input.

Schools should provide their newest members with an ongoing professional development program focused on the issues and challenges they are likely to encounter.

- *September*—Keys to establishing effective classroom management

- *October*—Effective grading practices

- *November*—How to engage the unmotivated student

- *December*—Effective questioning in the classroom

- *January*—Evidence of student learning to inform instructional practice

- *February*—Strategies to promote higher-level thinking

- *March*—Effective cooperative learning structures for the classroom

- *April*—Topic to be determined based on new teacher input

- *May*—Topic to be determined based on new teacher input

- *June*—A great close to the school year

The Need to Address the Concerns of Experienced Staff Members

To improve retention, Superintendent Careen also needs to continue addressing any concerns and dissatisfaction among veteran staff members. Losing them before the PLC process is deeply embedded in the school's culture could represent a major setback. In many of our Canadian communities, geography can increase the feeling of isolation. Teachers who are not well supported are quick to leave their positions to join a district or school that is more centrally located. Retention in these schools is critically important. In many organizations, managers only become aware of the level of an employee's dissatisfaction during an exit interview when it is too late to solve the problem. We endorse the strategy of conducting *stay interviews* with staff to express appreciation, discover concerns, and jointly plan how to enrich their job and improve their satisfaction (Kaye & Jordan-Evans, 2014).

For example, Superintendent Careen could meet with key staff members individually and ask questions such as (Kaye & Jordan-Evans, 2014):

- "I want you to know how much I value your contribution to our district and your school. Is there anything you can think of that I could do that could enrich your work and improve your satisfaction?"

- "What is most satisfying aspect of your work? How can we build on that?"

- "Is there something you would like to do or learn to do that will energize your work?"

- "Can you identify specific problems that are getting in the way of your success and satisfaction?"

- "I know you and I are both concerned about the disruption new staff members create when they join a team. Do you have some ideas about how we might address this problem?"

- "What can I do differently to make your experience here better?"

One of the reasons a superintendent or principal may be reluctant to conduct stay interviews is the fear that teachers will ask for things that are impossible to provide. There are, however, ways to address this possibility that can make the teacher feel both heard and valued. Consider the following dialogue between Superintendent Careen and one of her key teachers during a stay interview.

> **Superintendent Careen:** *I want you to know how much I value your contributions to your students, your team, and your school and our district. I want you to spend your career here. Can you think of anything I might do to make your experience here more satisfying for you?*
>
> **Ms. Wantmore:** *Well, a $20,000 raise would certainly make me feel better.*
>
> **Superintendent Careen:** *In my mind, you are worth that and more. In fact, I wish all of our teachers could be better compensated for the important work they are doing. But as you know, the district salary schedule determines individual salaries, and we are both bound to honour it. There are, however, some ways that we might be able to increase your income. For example:*
>
> - *If there is a curriculum project you wanted to work on this summer, I could use your expertise and compensate you for it.*

- *If you have an interest in teaching summer school, I could give you that assignment.*

- *We all know you are an expert in integrating technology into the curriculum. I could recommend your approval to teach a course in that subject to interested teachers in the district's after-school professional development program.*

- *If you have an interest in starting a cocurricular club and generate student interest in that club, I could seek approval for you to receive a cocurricular stipend.*

- *We are planning to introduce a yearlong new teacher induction program next year, and I would love to have a veteran teacher like you play a role in creating and presenting that program. If the program and stipend are approved, would you be interested?*

These are some initial ideas we might explore. If you have other ideas, I would welcome hearing them, so give it some thought. In the meantime, what else can I do for you other than considering ideas for additional compensation?

The *What else?* question is an effort to help the teacher focus on things that are within the superintendent or principal's sphere of influence. It won't take long to establish that different teachers are interested in different things. For example, imagine different teachers asking the following questions.

- "I have been thinking about becoming a (counselor, dean, vice principal). Could you give me an opportunity to job shadow a person in that position for a semester?"

- "I would love to attend the national conference in my subject area. If I am approved to make a presentation there, will you help fund my participation?"

- "I am trying to finish my dissertation. Would you explore the possibility of me job sharing with a colleague next year?"

- "My commute is killing me. Would you support me transferring to another school in the district closer to my home?"

- "I feel we may be too focused on academic indicators to monitor student success and not focused enough on other important indicators we should be instilling in our students. I would like to lead a task force to explore what more we could be doing. Would you be willing to endorse such a task force and have me lead it?"

- "I feel I have a lot to offer new teachers. I would like to help with the new teacher induction program next year."

- "I would love to attend a workshop on how to make cooperative learning more effective."

- "I know some of the schools in our district have mathematics coaches to support classroom teachers. Would you consider me for that position in our school?"

Reasonable educators won't expect the superintendent or principal to provide all the answers, particularly if their requests lay outside of the administrator's sphere of influence. But a stay interview gives the administrator a chance to express admiration and appreciation, demonstrate an interest in the teacher as an individual, help the teacher identify and explore choices, and show a willingness to listen to the teacher's concerns and ideas. Most teachers will welcome this opportunity for dialogue.

Creating an effective recruitment and selection process to ensure candidates are a good fit both for the PLC process and their collaborative team should be a high priority on every superintendent and principal's agenda.

Creating an effective recruitment and selection process to ensure candidates are a good fit both for the PLC process and their collaborative team should be a high priority on every superintendent and principal's agenda. But "re-recruiting" key individuals is an equally important step in sustaining the PLC process over time.

Part Three

Here's Why

If a school can only be as good as the educators within it, it makes sense that schools would be intentional in recruiting, hiring, and retaining the very best people. In the forty-seventh annual *Phi Delta Kappan*/Gallup Poll (2015) on schooling, at least 94 percent of members identify the quality of teachers as "very important" for improving their schools. It was, by far, the most frequent factor cited as key to school improvement.

In some parts of Canada, skeptical administrators may object that teacher shortages prevent them from being selective when hiring new staff. There is some truth to that, but the greatest cause of the shortage has been the inability of schools to keep the people they hire rather than a general lack of interest in teaching. Almost 10 percent of new teachers quit before the end of their first year and approximately 16 percent of all teachers leave their posts every year (Riggs, 2013). As previously mentioned, Canada's geography, especially our northern communities, sometimes experience more difficulty when hiring and retaining quality educators. For this reason, it is even more crucial that effective practices such as professional learning communities are developed to prevent teacher isolation and strategic retention efforts are made to ensure our students have great teachers in front of them every day.

The problem is not an insufficient number of educators entering the education system, but the mass exodus of those within it. The group of teachers with the highest rate of turnover is beginners. Between 40 to 50 percent of those who enter teaching leave teaching within five years. Rates of leaving for first-year teachers rose from 9.8 to 13.1 percent from 1988 to 2008, a 34 percent increase. This increase in percentage, however, does not reveal the true extent of the problem. Since the teaching force has grown dramatically larger, and there are far more beginners than in the late 1980s, the actual numbers of teachers who quit the occupation after their first year on the job has also soared. After the 1987–1988 school year, about six thousand first-year teachers left teaching. Twenty years later, more than four times as many—about twenty-six thousand first-year teachers—left the occupation (Ingersoll & Merrill, 2012).

In 1988, the mode years of experience for the United States' teaching force was fifteen years in the profession. By 2008, the mode was one year. The economic turndown beginning in 2008 slowed the rate of new teachers entering the profession, so by 2012, the mode was five years, but with schools having difficulty filling vacancies, the mode is almost certain to drop again (Alliance for Excellent Education, 2014).

The financial costs associated with the recruiting, hiring, and training necessitated by teacher turnover are estimated at a staggering $7.3 billion per year (Carroll, 2007). The costs to replace a single teacher are estimated at $15,000 to $20,000 (Darling-Hammond, 2010). It is clear that every time a teacher leaves a school, it costs the district thousands of dollars to replace him or her.

Teacher turnover also carries significant *productivity costs*, which in education translates into lower student achievement. Several studies find that student achievement declines when a succession of new teachers teach students, yet students in high-poverty, high-minority schools are far more likely to be assigned to new teachers on a regular basis (Darling-Hammond, 2010; Hargreaves & Fullan, 2012; Mehta, 2014; Rice, 2010). As an analysis of those studies conclude, "Students in high-poverty or high-minority schools are in desperate need of expert, high-quality teachers if their achievement and attainment levels are to improve, yet they are almost twice as likely as other students to have novice teachers" (Watlington, Shockley, Guglielmino, & Felsher, 2010, p. 26). Another study finds that the educational achievement of students in at-risk schools is further jeopardized by chronic teacher turnover as teachers disproportionately leave schools with high-minority, low-performing student populations. Inexperienced new teachers who quickly turnover more frequently teach students in these schools, and thus, these at-risk schools spend a larger portion of their resources replacing teachers. In fact, in many of these schools, the teacher dropout rate is higher than the student dropout rate (Carroll, 2007).

Don't Forget the Experienced Teachers

Superintendent Careen is not solely focused on the needs of new teachers entering the district. It is imperative that she also address veteran staff members' needs and concerns. The relationship between an employee and his or her immediate supervisor is "the prime predictor of both daily productivity and the length of time people stay at their jobs" (Achor, 2010, p. 187). A study of twelve thousand white-collar workers finds that employees who felt that their supervisor cared about them and believed that their work served an important purpose were three times more likely to stay with their organizations (Schwartz & Porath, 2014). Another study of satisfaction levels of knowledge workers finds that the two most important things a leader can do to foster high morale are to create the conditions that allow people to succeed at what they are being asked to do and to recognize progress when it occurs (Amabile & Kramer, 2011).

Attention to re-recruiting experienced teachers as we have stressed in this chapter addresses the fundamental needs of feeling valued and appreciated.

Attention to re-recruiting experienced teachers as we have stressed in this chapter addresses the fundamental needs of feeling valued and appreciated. After three decades of studying keys to effective organization, Jim Kouzes and Barry Posner (2006) conclude, "There are few if any needs more basic than to be noticed, recognized, and appreciated for our efforts. . . . Extraordinary achievements never bloom in barren and unappreciative settings" (p. 44).

The stay-interview format also provides an opportunity to connect the daily work of educators to a larger purpose: making the world a better place by developing the full potential of every student. The one great advantage of a career in education is that it serves an unquestionably moral purpose. It is easy, however, for educators to lose sight of that fact when immersed in their day-to-day activities. The stay interview provides an opportunity for a superintendent or principal to reconnect the work of the district and school to its fundamental mission. As Daniel Pink (2011) notes, "Nothing bonds a team like a shared mission. The more that people share a common cause . . . the more your group will do deeply satisfying and outstanding work" (p. 174).

Finally, although a superintendent or principal is a critical figure in initiating a PLC process, that process will not be sustained unless shared leadership is fostered and there is a strong commitment to that process. Principals need the support of key teachers if the school is to develop a new culture. Therefore, the best systems are constantly developing widespread leadership to sustain improvement efforts (Mourshed et al., 2010). Superintendent Careen will want to ensure that her principals are cultivating that leadership among their experienced teachers. (See the reproducible, "Retaining Experienced Teachers.")

Good News: Consensus on the Solution

The single most significant factor in whether or not new teachers have a positive or negative experience is the culture of the school in which they work.

Given the costs and negative consequences of high teacher turnover and the need for widespread leadership to sustain an improvement process, educators can take heart in the fact that there is widespread consensus among researchers regarding how to address both issues. The single most significant factor in whether or not new teachers have a positive or negative experience is the culture of the school in which they work. When teachers have positive perceptions about their work environment, their principals, and the cohesion and support of their colleagues, they are more likely to remain in their schools because of their high levels of satisfaction with their work. These positive relationships have a more significant impact on teacher retention than student demographics or teacher salaries (Almy & Tooley, 2012). The researchers consistently describe the very conditions that characterize a PLC.

Retaining Experienced Teachers

Reflection: Consider what you are currently doing or not doing to intentionally retain your educators. Using the following sample list, create immediate next steps that you will take. Follow through on this action plan (be your own accountability partner!).

_____ Observe and build relationships with new teachers. Identify, address, and support the needs of new teachers entering the school or district. Make this an ongoing practice, not a one-off activity.

_____ Celebrate with staff often. Look for small wins, short-term SMART goals accomplished, and any other opportunity to share success together. Feeling valued and appreciated goes a long way in wanting to stay on the job.

_____ Create the conditions that allow people to succeed at what they are being asked to do and to recognize progress when it occurs.

_____ Ensure that all teachers are part of a collaborative team.

_____ Create many opportunities as a leader to connect, communicate, and build relationships with educators.

_____ As interesting as it is to conduct exit interviews, consider stay interviews allowing the educator to connect the daily work to a larger purpose. Talk with teachers about what they like and are challenged by in their work.

_____ Continue to build common understanding of the purpose and the _why_ of the work; help educators share a common cause.

_____ Provide well-planned, differentiated, and highly engaging professional development opportunities.

_____ Empower teachers to share in leadership.

Your immediate next steps:

Part Four

Assessing Your Place on the PLC Journey

It is important to help your staff build shared knowledge regarding your school's current status in addressing the critical step on the PLC journey of selecting, orienting, and retaining staff. We have created a tool to assist you in that effort. "The Professional Learning Communities at Work® Continuum: Selecting and Retaining New Instructional Staff Members" is available at **go.SolutionTree.com/ca/PLCbooks** as a free reproducible. Once your staff have established greater clarity regarding the current status of your collaborative teams, we urge you to turn your attention to the "Where Do We Go From Here?" worksheet that accompanies the continuum (also available for free to download at **go.SolutionTree.com/ca/PLCbooks**). It will prompt you to take the action necessary to close the knowing-doing gap.

Part Five

Tips for Moving Forward: Selecting and Retaining Staff

1 **Solicit input from experienced teachers:** Ask current teachers to reflect on their own orientation to the school and how the process can be improved, the skills and traits they feel are most important for new teachers to bring to the school and team, and the questions they feel will be most helpful in assessing a candidate's fit for the school.

2 **Determine what is essential to know about your school:** Clarify the most important aspects of the school culture that each candidate should be made aware of as a result of the interview process.

3 **Engage the prospective team in the selection:** Facilitate a process to help each team prepare to interview finalists and observe them in the classroom.

4 **Include staff members in orientation and ongoing professional development:** Solicit teacher leaders to help create the different elements of the curriculum for the monthly professional development program for new teachers.

5 **Conduct follow-up contact for new hires:** Require team leaders or mentors to contact new hires after the board of education has approved them and before the school year starts to welcome them to the team, answer any questions, and offer their assistance in helping the new teachers make the transition to the school.

6 **Respond to stay interview discussions:** Be certain to have a follow-up discussion after the stay interview with veteran staff. Let staff members know what actions you have taken as a result of the conversation.

Part Six

Questions to Guide the Work of Your Professional Learning Community

To promote the importance of selecting, orienting, and retaining staff for work in a PLC, ask:

1. If a candidate were to ask how is working in a PLC different from working in the traditional school setting, how would we respond?

2. What are the personal skills and traits that we hope our new colleagues will bring to our school?

3. How can we best determine who has those skills and traits?

4. How invested are we in the success of our new colleagues? How do we demonstrate our investment?

5. How would we like the orientation we provide our new colleagues to be similar to or different from our own orientation to the profession?

6. What steps can the administration take (that are within its sphere of influence) to help us succeed at what we are being asked to do?

7. How do we express appreciation and admiration to one another in our school? Can we do a better job in this area?

Part Seven

Dangerous Detours and Seductive Shortcuts

Selecting the right people for the PLC process is vitally important.

Stephen Covey (1989) points out that there is a difference between *urgent* and *important*. Urgent demands immediate attention and quick steps. Selecting the right people for the PLC process is vitally important. Every vacancy presents an opportunity to improve the school and improve a collaborative team. But if the vacancy remains unfilled the week before school opens, urgent will trump important. The priority becomes finding someone to assign to the classroom regardless of the fit. Avoid the temptation to procrastinate when it comes to hiring. Enter the market early and be thorough and thoughtful in the selection process. Attention in the front end of the hiring process can save hours of future grief if faced with the prospect of removing a bad hire. More importantly, students deserve the very best teacher a principal can find.

Particularly at the secondary level, principals are tempted to hire the candidate who helps plug the most holes. So the candidate with minimum certification in science and social studies who is willing to coach the hockey team or take on the school's musical production gets priority over a candidate with a stronger academic background who teachers feel is a better fit for their team and the school. Principals must remember that every hiring decision conveys their priorities and values to the staff. Administrative appeals for excellence will be muted if expediency is consistently the driving force in decisions.

Final Thoughts

Regardless of how carefully a school or district hires and supports new faculty, it is possible that a new hire might prove to be the wrong fit for the school or might not possess the innate qualities needed to be an exceptional teacher and teammate. When this is the case, it is critical that the principal has the courage to dismiss the teacher. Undoubtedly, taking this step can be uncomfortable and difficult. But if a school is committed to ensuring every student's success, then it must hire and retain exceptional educators. A weak link in the chain can break the progress of the entire team.

Once again, school leaders communicate most powerfully by what they say rather than what they do. In the next chapter, we consider two important forms of communicating what is important: (1) confrontation and (2) celebration.

CHAPTER 9

Addressing Conflict and Celebrating in a Professional Learning Community

Part One

The Case Study: Responding to Resistance

Maxine Hill had just completed her mandate as directrice of École élémentaire catholique Saint-Guillaume, proudly one of only seven Canadian schools, at the time, to be accepted as a model PLC school on the AllThingsPLC website. It was time to move on to a new challenge, and she was excited at the prospect of replicating this work at her new school, École élémentaire catholique La Vérendrye in Gloucester, Ontario. She was amazed at the culture and student success that she and her staff had accomplished at her previous school. Although she was the only person moving from the model school to the new school, she was confident that the PLC practices would soon be the work of her new staff.

At the beginning of the school year, Principal Hill set out her expectations, establishing what was tight around the three big ideas of PLCs; understanding that learning, collaboration, and results must drive the actions of all staff. With five years behind her as principal of a model PLC school, she understood what the end goal looked like and what the actions of the adults needed to be in order to get there. She established collaborative teams and helped teachers understand the four PLC critical questions and how they could impact their work.

It wasn't long, however, before she started to realize that some of her new staff members were resisting the journey. It wasn't that they were loudly or boldly opposing the work, but it felt like things were happening more out of compliance than understanding. Having left a school where collective capacity had been established, Principal Hill was disappointed that implementation was not happening as quickly as she thought that it should. It wasn't that she was afraid to have conversations with teachers if they were being ineffective; however, this wasn't her most pressing issue. The more she thought about it, the more she recognized that she was making a false assumption about common understanding. She started this new position assuming that her staff would share her values and beliefs about academic success for all students. She took for granted that others might have experience with the PLC journey and that implementation would be easier. Despite her understanding and experience with the work, she was working with a new staff that was not in the same place as she was with this collective wisdom.

As time passed, Principal Hill thought about several steps that she could take. She wondered if it would be best *to go backward to go forward* in order to build common messages and clarify the purpose of the work. Or, was it best to start by creating a trusting, safe environment for the adults to work in collaboratively? How important would it be to stop and celebrate successful steps in the implementation? Were these the right steps?

Reflection

Is Principal Hill considering the right actions to ensure that she is addressing resistance to deep implementation of the PLC process? How important is it for a leader to be aware of the adult culture of the building or district when asking others to join the PLC journey?

Part Two

Here's How

In chapter 2 (page 25), we offered suggestions for developing consensus: create a guiding coalition, build shared knowledge, and engage in dialogue with staff members in small groups to listen to and address concerns. Principal Hill understood the bigger picture but still needed to address the issues.

Recognize the Need to Confront

A staff that have built a solid foundation for a PLC by carefully crafting consensus regarding their purpose, the school they seek to create, their collective commitments, the specific goals they will use to monitor their progress, and the strategies for achieving those goals have not eliminated the possibility of conflict. The response to the disagreements that inevitably occur determine the real strength of a school committed to the PLC process. Every organization will experience conflict, particularly when the organization is engaged in significant change. Every collective endeavor will include instances when people fail to honour agreed-on priorities and collective commitments. The ultimate goal, of course, is to create a culture that is so strong and so open that members throughout the organization will use the violation as an opportunity to reinforce what is valued by bringing peer pressure to bear on the offender, saying, in effect, "That is not how we do it here." In the interim, however, it typically will be the responsibility of the leader (that is, principal or administrator) to communicate what is important and valued by demonstrating a willingness to confront when appropriate. Nothing will destroy the credibility of a leader faster than an unwillingness to address an obvious violation of what the organization contends is vital. A leader must not remain silent; he or she must be willing to act when people disregard the purpose and priorities of the organization.

Confrontation does not, however, involve screaming, demeaning, or vilifying. It is possible to be tough minded and adamant about protecting purpose and priorities while also being tender with people. Kerry Patterson and colleagues (2002) have been studying the challenge of conducting difficult conversations for over a decade. They contend that skillful communicators reject the false dichotomy of the "sucker's choice": I can either be honest and hurtful *or* be kind and withhold the truth. Instead, they search for the Genius of And—a way to be both honest *and* respectful and to say what needs to be said to the people who need to hear it without brutalizing them or causing undue offense (Patterson et al., 2002).

Ten strategies Patterson and colleagues (2002) offer for engaging in honest and respectful dialogue include the following.

1. Clarify what you want and what you do not want to result from the conversation—for yourself, for the other person, and for the relationship before initiating it.

2. Create a safe environment for honest dialogue.

3. Clarify if you will be addressing a specific incident of behaviour, a pattern of repeated behaviour, or the impact the behaviour is having on the individual's relationship with others.

4. Be concise when presenting the problem. Frame the conversation in terms of a gap between expectations and actions.

5. Attempt to find mutual purpose.

6. Use facts because "gathering facts is the homework required for holding an accountability discussion" (Patterson et al., 2013, p. 95).

7. Share your thought process that has led you to engage in the conversation.

8. Encourage recipients to share their facts and thought process.

9. Explain both the natural consequences and the potential for disciplinary action if the behaviour continues.

10. Clarify the specific behaviour that must be demonstrated and the process to be used both for monitoring and following up.

Let us think about the culture that Principal Hill wishes to create and apply these strategies to the situation.

Clarify Position

Prior to initiating the conversation with staff who might be resisting her vision for a collaborative school culture, Principal Hill should clarify her position in her own mind: "I want to reinforce the fact that, we as a staff, want to provide all students with the benefit of a teacher who is a member of a high-performing collaborative team. We

A leader must not remain silent; he or she must be willing to act when people disregard the purpose and priorities of the organization.

want a school that ensures students have access to a guaranteed curriculum and that monitors student learning through a process that includes team-developed common formative assessments and agreement about what represents proficient work. We want to create an environment in which educators are learning from each other. Therefore, I want my teachers to honour the commitments we make as a staff to the collaborative process by making a positive contribution to their teams. I do not want my teachers to think I am questioning their expertise or diminishing their contributions to the school. I will probably be working with most of these teachers for years to come, and I would like to establish a relationship based on clear expectations and mutual respect."

Create a Safe Environment

Principal Hill would then think of how she might achieve what she wants and avoid what she does not want through a meaningful, respectful dialogue with her teachers.

During the conversations with her teachers, the principal can attempt to find mutual purpose: "I believe we all want a school that is committed to helping all students achieve at high levels and to providing teachers with a satisfying and fulfilling professional experience." Principal Hill would want to ensure that the staff agreed with this with that assessment of their mutual purpose.

Principal Hill will want to create a safe environment for dialogue with her teachers by sharing facts, speaking tentatively, inviting her teachers to ask questions, reflect and to elaborate on their own thinking. She might say something like this: "I believe there is very compelling evidence that developing our capacity to work together collaboratively on significant issues centred in teaching and learning is vital to both raising student achievement and creating a rewarding workplace. I will continue to share that evidence with you. As you know, it is important for all of us to continue to live by our commitments to work together with our colleagues on their teams." If individual teachers continue to resist the implementation of the PLC process, Principal Hill will need to directly ask teachers if the commitments are problematic for them. She will want to explain events that cause her to raise this question. For example, "I understand you frequently do not attend the meetings of your collaborative team and that you have not made any contribution to creating common assessments. I received several complaints from students and parents that you had not taught the skills assessed on the last common test. I recognize the contribution you have made to this school over the years, and I don't want to diminish that contribution in any way. In fact, I think your teammates could benefit from your experience. So help me understand. Are my facts incorrect? Are there issues of which I am unaware? I'm very interested in hearing your perspective and your assessment of any factors that may be impacting your contribution to your collaborative team."

At this point, it is important for Principal Hill to listen carefully to any teacher she confronts, to make a good-faith effort to understand the teacher's perspective. In *Difficult Conversations*, another helpful study of how to address differences through dialogue, the authors advise, "Listening is not only the skill that lets you into the other person's world; it is the single most powerful move you can make to keep the conversation constructive" (Stone, Patton, & Heen, 2000, p. 202).

If teachers at Principal Hill's new school agree with the mutual purpose but cite conditions that are impeding their ability to contribute to the team, the principal and the teachers can brainstorm solutions and commit to carry out their agreed-on plan. If the teachers can express their reasons for resisting the actions needed, the principal may be able to modify the context of the plans in a way that resonates with the teachers. For example, we know of a teacher who asserted he would not work with his team because he was only two years from retirement and was already getting the best results in his department. The principal acknowledged those points and complimented the teacher on the craft knowledge he had developed over the years. The principal then pointed out that all that accumulated knowledge and wisdom would walk out the door with him on his retirement day unless he shared it with his colleagues. By shifting the focus from "participate to improve" to "participate to ensure your ongoing legacy," the principal convinced the teacher to commit to contribute to his team.

It is possible, however, that Principal Hill's teachers continue to reject the mutual agreed-on commitments and needed actions. They might say statements like, "My primary job is to give students the opportunity to demonstrate that they have learned what I taught, and I don't need to collaborate with peers to do my job. I see your insistence on collaboration as an attempt to deprive me of my autonomy. As a professional, I have a right to determine what I will teach, the instructional strategies I deem appropriate, and how I will assess my students. If others elect to collaborate, it is their choice, but I choose not to participate."

What options might Principal Hill resort to at this point? Howard Gardner (2004) offers the following seven strategies for changing someone's mind.

1. **Reasoning and rationale thinking:** "Doesn't it make sense that we can accomplish more by working together collaboratively rather than in isolation? If you and your colleagues are helping students acquire the same skills and knowledge, how logical is it that each of you would duplicate the work required to create lesson plans, search for supplementary materials, develop ways to integrate technology into the teaching and learning process, and construct authentic assessments? When people are engaged in the same work, isn't it more efficient for them to designate responsibilities to different members rather than replicate all that effort?"

2. **Research:** "The guiding coalition and I shared the research that supports this initiative with you and the entire faculty. We found it very compelling. Do you interpret the research another way? Do you have any contradictory research we could look at together that would support your position?"

3. **Resonance:** "I know you believe in equity and fairness. Wouldn't it be more equitable and fair if we could assure students they will have access to the same guaranteed curriculum, no matter who their teacher is, and that their work will be assessed according to the same criteria? Shouldn't we model the equity and fairness we say are important to us?"

4. **Representational redescription:** "I have presented you with the data regarding the large numbers of our students who are not being successful.

Now let me put those numbers into understandable terms; let me tell you some stories of the impact their failure to learn is having on their lives."

5. **Rewards and resources:** "I acknowledge this will be difficult. That is why I ask your help in identifying the resources you will need to be successful: time, training, materials, and support. Let's work together to identify the necessary resources, and I pledge I will do everything in my power to make them available."

6. **Real-world events:** "I understand you have misgivings and predict negative consequences if we implement this initiative. But let's visit some schools and districts that have done it successfully. You will hear teachers' enthusiasm as they explain how they and their students have benefited. Their observations will be based on experience rather than conjecture."

If teachers continue to refuse to participate in the process despite these efforts of persuasion, Principal Hill must resort to a seventh strategy.

7. **Requirement:** "I understand you remain unconvinced, but this is the direction in which we are going as a school, and this is what you must do to help us get us there. I hope you will have a good experience as you work through the process, and I hope you will come to have a more positive disposition toward it, but until then, you will do it because I am directing you to do it." Note that Howard Gardner did not include this seventh strategy in his work. He has acknowledged, however, that it might be required in some circumstances (H. Gardner, personal communication, August 14, 2013).

If it becomes necessary to resort to the strategy of *requirement*, Principal Hill should consider the following eight steps.

1. Continue to work with all teachers, including the resisters, in a respectful and professional manner. Losing her composure or arguing with a teacher serves no one's interest.

2. Acknowledge that there are fundamental differences in their perspectives; however, those differences do not exempt the teacher from participating in the collaborative process in a productive way. Principal Hill must send a clear message to her teachers that the need for change is immediate and imperative.

3. Clarify the specific behaviours she requires of her teachers. Admonitions such as "You need to do a better job with your team" or "You need to improve your attitude toward collaboration" do not provide teachers with clarity on what is tight or with the precise direction that is needed. A far more effective strategy might sound like this:

   "There are three things I need you to begin doing immediately. First, you must attend all of your team meetings. Second, you must honour each of the collective commitments your team has established regarding how members will fulfill their responsibilities and relate to one another. Third, you must provide me with specific evidence each week that you are teaching your students the team's essential learning outcomes and preparing your students to demonstrate their attainment of those outcomes on the team's common assessments. We can discuss different ways you might provide me with such evidence. To ensure that there are no misunderstandings, I will provide you with a written directive detailing these expectations."

4. Invite the teachers to offer any suggestions regarding support, training, or resources they might need to comply with the directive.

5. Clarify the specific consequences that will occur if the directive is ignored once it has been given.

   "I want to tell you that, if you disregard what I have directed you to do, I will have no choice but to consider your actions as insubordination. At that point, I will suspend you with pay and take the matter to the board of education."

6. Establish strategies to monitor a teacher's behaviour rather than his attitude. Attempts to talk a person into a new attitude are almost always unproductive when good-faith efforts to engage in meaningful dialogue reveal fundamental differences rather than common ground and when attempts to participate in crucial conversations lead to impasse rather than agreement.

7. Acknowledge and celebrate any efforts that the teacher makes to change his behaviour.

8. Apply the specified consequences if necessary.

In *Influencer: The Power to Change Anything*, Kerry Patterson and colleagues (2008) offer the following six recommendations in three areas—personal, social, and structural—taken from research in psychology, social psychology, and organizational theory to bring about a change in behaviour.

Influence Personal Motivation

Patterson and colleagues (2008) contend that "*the great persuader is personal experience . . . the mother of all cognitive map changes*" (p. 51, emphasis added) and that it is "the gold standard of change" (p. 57). They call for field trips to help people see the benefits of the behaviour in the real world. They also advise leaders to fight against all forms of moral disengagement such as justification ("We can't expect these students to learn given their socioeconomic status") or displaced responsibility ("I taught it; it is their job to learn it"). Leaders should focus on human rather than statistical consequences of failure to change (for example, stories of specific students rather than last year's test results). They should present the change as a personally defining moment within a larger moral issue.

Leaders should focus on human rather than statistical consequences of failure to change. . . . They should present the change as a personally defining moment within a larger moral issue.

Enhance the Personal Ability of Others

Because one of the pressing issues in the mind of someone being asked to change is often, "Can I do it?" effective leaders help build capacity by building confidence. They set aside time for deliberate practice, provide immediate feedback against a clear outcome, and break mastery into several specific ministeps.

Harness the Power of Peer Pressure

Effective leaders strive to create an environment where both formal and informal leaders constantly promote behaviour essential to the change and skillfully confront behaviours that are misaligned with the change.

Patterson and colleagues (2008) contend that "no resource is more powerful and accessible" than the power of peer influence and that the most effective leaders "embrace and enlist" that power rather than "denying it, lamenting it, or attacking it" (p. 138). Effective leaders strive to create an environment where both formal and informal leaders constantly promote behaviour essential to the change and skillfully confront behaviours that are misaligned with the change.

Find Strength in Numbers

Patterson and colleagues (2008) call for organizing people into interdependent teams in which the success or failure of the group depends on each member's contributions. When the organizational structure requires people to work together, share ideas and materials, support one another in difficult moments, and contribute to collective goals, those people are more likely to hold each other accountable. The result is "synergy through non-voluntary interaction" (Patterson et al., 2008, p. 183).

Design Rewards, and Demand Accountability

Effective leaders use rewards that are directly linked to vital behaviours and valued processes. They recognize and reward observable small improvement early in the change process because "even small rewards can be used to help people overcome some of the most profound and persistent problems" (Patterson et al., 2008, p. 198); however, "punishment sends a message, and so does its absence—so choose wisely" (p. 210). Failure to address those who refuse to engage in the vital behaviours sends a loud message to others that the behaviours aren't so vital after all. They recommend that punishment be preceded by a "shot across the bow"—a clear warning to an individual of what *will* happen if he or she continues with unacceptable behaviour.

Create Structures to Support the Change, and Provide Relevant Information

Changes in the structure and physical environment of an organization can make the right behaviour easier and the wrong behaviour more difficult. As Joseph Grenny, Kerry Patterson, David Maxfield, Ron McMillan, and Al Switzler (2013) write, "Often, all that is required to make good behaviour inevitable is to structure it into your daily routine" (p. 250). When the fundamental structure of the organization is the collaborative team, when time for collaboration is built in the weekly schedule, and when team members work in close proximity to one another, they are far more likely to collaborate and take collective responsibility for student learning. Finally, Patterson and colleagues (2008) advise leaders that they can change how people feel and act by creating systems to ensure relevant and timely information is easily accessible throughout the organization. The evidence of student learning—or lack thereof—from common formative assessments is a powerful tool for providing that information.

Finally, leaders are always in a better position to confront when they act as the promoters and protectors of the group's decisions, agreements, and commitments. Appeals to hierarchy—"Do it because I am the boss, and I said so"—may eventually become necessary on occasion, but in raising an issue initially, leaders are more effective utilizing the moral authority that comes with defending the articulated collective aspirations of the people within the organization.

Part Three

Here's Why

As we emphasized in chapter 2 (page 25), research consistently concludes that effective leaders build a shared vision and purpose that bind people together. But unless vision and purpose result in the desired action, nothing is accomplished. So what are leaders to do when some members of the organization are opposed to taking action that is critical to moving forward? Effective leaders do not wait for unanimity, but instead build shared knowledge until they have created a critical mass of those willing to act—and then they move the organization forward without expecting universal support. When they do move forward, they can expect conflict.

Managing Conflict

Transforming traditional schools and districts into PLCs "requires men and women to do things that they have never done before—not just to get better at what they have always done" (Schlechty, 2009, p. 4). Those leading the PLC process at any level must recognize that conflict is an inevitable by-product of this substantive change process (Evans, 1996; Lieberman, 1995; Louis, Kruse, & Marks, 1996). In fact, an absence of conflict suggests the changes are only superficial because "conflict and disagreements are not only inevitable but fundamental to successful change" (Fullan, 2007, p. 21).

The challenge, then, is not to eliminate or avoid conflict. The challenge is to learn how to manage conflict productively. Effective leaders will surface the conflict, draw out and acknowledge the varying perspectives, and search for a common ground that everyone can endorse (Goleman et al., 2004). When managed well, conflict can serve as an engine of creativity and energy (Saphier, 2005), clarify priorities (Bossidy & Charan, 2002), and develop stronger teams (Lencioni, 2005).

The challenge, then, is not to eliminate or avoid conflict. The challenge is to learn how to manage conflict productively.

Because conflict should not only be expected but desired in a PLC, it is critical to plan for this reality when creating a school mission and collective commitments. Members should agree that decisions in a learning-focused school must be based on what research and evidence have proven to best improve student learning. Subsequently, when disagreements arise regarding the specific actions the school or team should take, team members should not argue their individual opinions but should instead share research and evidence to advocate for their position.

When educational leaders at the district or school level avoid confrontation because they favour keeping the peace over productive conflict, they can do tremendous damage to any improvement process.

Repeated conflict over the same issues can certainly represent a drain on an organization's time and energy, and at some point, there is a need for closure. But when educational leaders at the district or school level avoid confrontation because they favour keeping the peace over productive conflict, they can do tremendous damage to any improvement process.

Responding to Resisters

So what is an effective way to respond when conflict turns into resistance—when efforts to build shared knowledge, answer questions, use effective strategies of persuasion, and develop consensus fail to bring about the desired changes in the behaviour of a few resistant staff? The most frequent question we hear as we work with educators is, "But how should we respond to the people in our organization who have bad attitudes?" Our advice is simple: don't focus on the attitude—focus on the *behaviour*. There is abundant evidence from the fields of psychology, organizational development, and education demonstrating that changes in attitudes follow rather than precede changes in behaviour (Champy, 1995; Elmore, 2003; Kotter, 1996; Kotter & Cohen, 2002; Pfeffer & Sutton, 2006; Reeves, 2006; Wheelis, 1973). Work that is designed to require people to *act* in new ways creates the possibility of new experiences. These new experiences, in turn, can lead to new attitudes over time.

We recognize that it is quite probable some people will *never* embrace the PLC process, regardless of what evidence of its benefits are presented and despite leaders' best efforts to bring them on board. Teachers who believe it is their job to teach and the students' job to learn, who are convinced that learning is a function of the student's aptitude rather than the teacher's expertise, who define professionalism as the autonomy to do as they please, or who take pleasure in wallowing in negativity will always find a way to dismiss the PLC process. Principals who define their job as maintaining order and keeping the adults happy are likely to resist a concept that requires them to lead.

Many educators conclude, perhaps rightly, that there is very little hope of changing these hard-core resisters, and so they begin to ignore the resisters' repeated disregard for implementing the improvement agenda and ongoing violations of their teams' collective commitments. Such salutary neglect is always a mistake. Leaders must persist and follow through on the specific consequences they have outlined to those who continue to fail to act in accordance with what has been established as tight. They must keep in mind that the goal in addressing these violations is not only to bring about change in the resister but also to communicate priorities throughout the organization. As Patterson and colleagues (2008) advise:

> The point isn't that people need to be threatened in order to perform. The point is that if you aren't willing to go to the mat when people violate a core value . . . that value loses its moral force in the organization. On the other hand, you do send a powerful message when you hold employees accountable. (p. 216)

Unwillingness to follow through sends mixed messages about what is important and valued. In fact, Patrick Lencioni (2003) contends that if leaders don't have the courage to insist that team members fulfill their responsibilities to teammates, they are better off avoiding the idea of collaborative teams altogether.

In his Pulitzer Prize–winning book on leadership, James MacGregor Burns (1979) offers advice to those faced with this dilemma: "No matter how strong the yearning for unanimity . . . [leaders] must settle for far less than universal affection. . . . They must accept conflict. They must be willing and able to be unloved" (p. 34). The recognition that they will not be universally loved despite their best efforts may trouble leaders initially; however, once they come to accept that truth, it can be quite liberating.

In every school that we have seen become a high-performing PLC, a defining moment has occurred when a leader chose to confront rather than avoid saboteurs. We are convinced their schools' improvement efforts could not have gone forward had they ignored violations of collective commitments.

Daniel Goleman is an ardent advocate of the importance of emotional intelligence, a concept anchored, in part, in having high levels of empathy and skillfully building relationships. Yet even Goleman (1998) advises:

> Persuasion, consensus building, and all the other arts of influence don't always do the job. Sometimes it simply comes down to using the power of one's position to get people to act. A common failing of leaders from supervisors to top executives is the failure to be *emphatically assertive* when necessary. (p. 190, emphasis added)

Leaders who face a scenario similar to the one described in this chapter should utilize every component of an effective change process and present the rationale for the proposed initiative using every available strategy. They must be willing to listen to concerns, seek common ground, and compromise on the details of implementation. Once they have reached a decision, however, they must be unequivocal in confronting resisters and demanding changes in behaviour. (See page 210, "Addressing Conflict as a Leader.")

Celebrating

The flip side of the confrontation coin as a means of communicating what is important is celebration (Amabile & Kramer, 2010; Kanold, 2011; Kouzes & Posner, 2006). When celebrations continually remind people of the purpose and priorities of their organizations, members are more likely to embrace the purpose and work toward agreed-on priorities. Regular public recognition of specific collaborative efforts, accomplished tasks, achieved goals, team learning, continuous improvement, and support for student learning remind staff of the collective commitment to create a PLC. The word *recognize* comes from the Latin "to know again." Recognition provides opportunities to say, "Let us all be reminded and let us all know again what is important, what we value, and what we are committed to do. Now let's all pay tribute to someone in the organization who is living that commitment."

Most schools and districts, however, will face a significant challenge as they attempt to integrate meaningful celebration into their cultures. The excessively egalitarian culture of schools makes it difficult to publicly recognize either individuals or teams. In most schools and districts, generic praise ("You are the best darn faculty in the province!") or private praise ("I want to send you a personal note of commendation") are acceptable—public recognition is not. Generic and private praise are ineffective in communicating priorities because neither conveys to the members at large what

When celebrations continually remind people of the purpose and priorities of their organizations, members are more likely to embrace the purpose and work toward agreed-on priorities.

specific actions and commitments are valued, and therefore neither is effective in shaping behaviour nor beliefs. As Peter Drucker (1992) advises, "Changing habits and behaviour requires changing recognition and rewards . . . [because] people in organizations tend to act in response to being recognized and rewarded" (p. 195). Tom Peters (1987) put it this way: "Well-constructed recognition settings provide the single most important opportunity to parade and reinforce the specific kinds of new behaviours one hopes others will emulate" (p. 307).

We offer the following four suggestions to those who face the challenge of incorporating celebration into the culture of their school or district.

1. **Explicitly state the purpose of celebration:** The rationale for public celebration should be carefully explained at the outset of every celebration. Staff members should be continually reminded that celebration represents—

   ◆ An important strategy for reinforcing the school or district's shared purpose, vision, collective commitments, and goals

   ◆ The most powerful tool for sustaining the improvement initiative

2. **Make celebration everyone's responsibility:** Recognizing extraordinary commitment should be the responsibility of everyone in the organization, and each individual should be called on to contribute to the effort. If the formal leader is the sole arbiter of who will be recognized, the rest of the staff can merely sit back and critique the choices. All staff members should have the opportunity to publicly report when they appreciate and admire the work of a colleague.

3. **Establish a clear link between the recognition and the behaviour or commitment you are attempting to encourage and reinforce:** Recognition must be specifically linked to the organization's purpose, vision, collective commitments, and goals if it is to play a role in shaping culture. As Rick and Bob write:

   > Recognition will have little impact if a staff believes the recognition is presented randomly, that each person deserves to be recognized regardless of his or her contribution to the improvement effort, or that rewards are given for factors unrelated to the goal of creating a learning community. (DuFour & Eaker, 1998, p. 145)

   It is imperative, therefore, to establish clear parameters for recognition and rewards. The answer to the question, "What behaviour or commitment are we attempting to encourage with this recognition?" should be readily apparent. Recognition should always be accompanied with a story relating the efforts of the team or individual back to the core foundation of the school or district. It should not only express appreciation and admiration but also provide others with an example they can emulate.

4. **Create opportunities to have many winners:** Celebration will not have a significant effect on the culture of a school if most people in the

organization feel they have no opportunity to be recognized. In fact, celebration can be disruptive and detrimental if there is a perception that recognition and reward are reserved for an exclusive few. Establishing artificial limits on appreciation—such as, "We honour no more than five individuals per meeting," or, "Only those with five or more years of experience are eligible"—lessens the impact celebration can have on a school or district. Developing a PLC requires creating systems specifically designed not only to provide celebrations but also to ensure that there are many winners.

Frequent public acknowledgements for a job well done and a wide distribution of small symbolic gestures of appreciation and admiration are far more powerful tools for communicating priorities than infrequent grand prizes that create a few winners and many losers. An effective celebration program will convince every staff member that he or she can be a winner and that his or her efforts can be noted and appreciated.

An effective celebration program will convince every staff member that he or she can be a winner and that his or her efforts can be noted and appreciated.

Four Keys for Incorporating Celebration Into the Culture of Your School or District

1. Explicitly state the purpose of celebration.

2. Make celebration everyone's responsibility.

3. Establish a clear link between the recognition and the behaviour or commitment you are attempting to encourage and reinforce.

4. Create opportunities for many winners.

Our U.S. example, Adlai E. Stevenson High School in Lincolnshire, Illinois, is often cited as a school that has used celebration to communicate purpose and priorities and to shape culture (Deal & Peterson, 1999; DuFour & Eaker, 1998; Kanold, 2006; Schmoker, 2006). Stevenson does not offer a Teacher of the Year program, but over several decades, it has distributed thousands of Super Pat awards (small tokens of appreciation that represent a pat on the back for a job well done) to hundreds of teachers. In fact, since 1995, Stevenson has *never* had a faculty meeting without celebrating the effort and commitment of individuals and teams. Stevenson also surveys its seniors each year to ask, "Which staff member has had the most profound impact on your life and why?" The students' heartfelt responses are then published in an internal Kudos Memorandum and distributed to the entire staff each quarter. Staff members have read thousands of testimonials citing specific examples of how they and their colleagues are making a difference in the lives of students. Stevenson employees receive ongoing reminders of the school's priorities and the commitments that are being honoured in order to achieve those priorities, and every staff member feels like he or she has the opportunity to be recognized and celebrated as a winner.

One of the most frequent concerns that educators raise when they are wary of making celebration a part of their school or district is that frequent celebration will lose its impact to motivate. Yet research has drawn the opposite conclusion; it reaffirms that frequent celebration communicates priorities, connects people to the organization and to each other, and sustains improvement initiatives (Amabile & Kramer, 2011; Kegan & Lahey, 2001; Kouzes & Posner, 2003; Peters, 1987).

A commendation should represent genuine and heartfelt appreciation and admiration. If that sincerity is lacking, celebration can be counterproductive.

Can celebration be overdone? Absolutely. The criterion for assessing the appropriateness of recognition for a team or individual should be the sincerity with which the recognition is given. A commendation should represent genuine and heartfelt appreciation and admiration. If that sincerity is lacking, celebration can be counterproductive.

Celebrations allow for expressions of both appreciation and admiration. Appreciation lets others know we have received something we value, something we are happy to have. Admiration conveys the message that we have been inspired or instructed by observing others' work and commitments. When admiration and appreciation are repeatedly expressed, organizations create a culture of ongoing regard that sustains effort because such language is "like pumping oxygen into the system" (Kegan & Lahey, 2001, p. 102).

Celebrations also provide an opportunity to use one of the oldest ways in the world to convey the values and ideals of a community: telling stories. As Kouzes and Posner (2003) write, "The intention of stories is not just to entertain. . . . They are also intended to teach. Good stories move us. They touch us, they teach us, and they cause us to remember" (p. 25). Good stories appeal to both the head and the heart and are more compelling and convincing than data alone. They bring data and evidence to life and persuade people to act in new ways (Pfeffer & Sutton, 2006). Good stories personify purpose and priorities. They put a human face on success by providing examples and role models that can clarify for others what is noted, appreciated, and valued. They represent one of the most powerful tools for shaping others' thinking and feelings (Grenny et al., 2013).

Finally, a multiyear study of what motivates knowledge workers concludes that the best motivator is celebration of progress (Amabile & Kramer, 2010). The study advises leaders to set clear overall goals, sustain the commitment to the pursuit of those goals, proactively create both the reality and the perception of progress, and celebrate even incremental progress (Amabile & Kramer, 2010).

An excellent predictor of future behaviour of any organization is to examine the people and events it elects to honour (Buckingham, 2005). This is true of schools in particular. In his study of school culture, sociologist Robert Evans (1996) concludes, "The single best low-cost, high-leverage way to improve performance, morale, and the climate for change is to dramatically increase the levels of meaningful recognition for—and among—educators" (p. 254).

Study after study of what workers want in their jobs offer the same conclusion: they want to feel appreciated (Kouzes & Posner, 2003). Yet Robert Kegan and Lisa Lahey (2001) conclude that "nearly every organization or work team we've spent time with astonishingly undercommunicates the genuinely positive, appreciative, and admiring experiences of its members" (p. 92).

One challenge every organization will face in implementing a comprehensive improvement effort is sustaining the momentum of that effort over time. Experts on the process of organizational change offer very consistent advice regarding that question (see the reproducible, "Why Should Celebration Be a Part of Our Culture?").

Why Should Celebration Be a Part of Our Culture?

"In successful change efforts, empowered people create short-term wins—victories that nourish faith in the change effort, emotionally reward the hard workers, keep the critics at bay, and build momentum. Without sufficient wins that are visible, timely, unambiguous, and meaningful to others, change efforts inevitably run into serious problems" (Kotter & Cohen, 2002, p. 125).

"Milestones that are identified, achieved, and celebrated represent an essential condition for building a learning organization" (Thompson, 1995, p. 96).

"Remembering to recognize, reward, and celebrate accomplishments is a critical leadership skill. And it is probably the most underutilized motivational tool in organizations" (Kanter, 1999, p. 20).

"Win small. Win early. Win often" (Hamel, 2002, p. 202).

"The most effective change processes are incremental—they break down big problems into small, doable steps and get a person to say 'yes' numerous times, not just once. They plan for small wins that form the basis for a consistent pattern of winning that appeals to people's desire to belong to a successful venture. A series of small wins provides a foundation of stable building blocks for change" (Kouzes & Posner, 1987, p. 210).

"Specific goals should be designed to allow teams to achieve small wins as they pursue their common purpose. Small wins are invaluable to building members' commitment and overcoming the obstacles that get in the way of achieving a meaningful, long-term purpose" (Katzenbach & Smith, 1993, p. 54).

"When people see tangible results, however incremental at first, and see how the results flow from the overall concept, they will line up with enthusiasm. People want to be a part of a winning team. They want to contribute to producing visible, tangible results. . . . When they feel the magic of momentum, when they can begin to see tangible results—that's when they get on board" (Collins, 2001, p. 178).

"Reward small improvements in behavior along the way. Don't wait until people achieve phenomenal results" (Patterson et al., 2008, p. 205).

"Small successes stimulate individuals to make further commitments to change. Staffs need tangible results in order to continue the development of their commitment to the change program and small steps engender understanding as well" (Eastwood & Louis, 1992, p. 219).

"Visible measures of progress are critical for motivating and encouraging educators to persist in the challenging work of improvement. Even the most dedicated and optimistic among us will stop if there's no sign that what we're doing is making a difference, or might make a difference eventually" (Elmore & City, 2007).

"When you set small, visible goals, and people achieve them, they start to get it into their heads that they can succeed. They break the habit of losing and begin to get into the habit of winning" (Heath & Heath, 2010, p. 144).

One of the most important things leaders can do is to create the conditions that allow people to experience progress in their work and then recognize and celebrate their accomplishments, even small accomplishments (Amabile & Kramer, 2011).

Part Four

Assessing Your Place on the PLC Journey

It is important to help your staff build shared knowledge regarding your school's current status in addressing the critical step on the PLC journey of responding to conflict and celebration. We have created a tool to assist you in that effort. "The Professional Learning Communities at Work® Continuum: Responding to Conflict" is available at **go.SolutionTree.com/ca/PLCbooks** as a free reproducible. Once your staff have established greater clarity regarding the current status of your collaborative teams, we urge you to turn your attention to the "Where Do We Go From Here?" worksheet that accompanies the continuum (also available for free to download at **go.SolutionTree.com/ca/PLCbooks**). It will prompt you to take the action necessary to close the knowing-doing gap.

Part Five

Tips for Moving Forward: Addressing Conflict and Celebrating

1   **Practice the skill of difficult conversations:** Teach and practice skills for dealing with conflict.

2   **Create cues you can use to refocus when participants seem to be resorting to fight or flight:** Signal time-out or simply ask, "Are we moving away from dialogue?"

3   **Remember that gathering facts is the prerequisite homework for any crucial conversation:** What are the facts you can bring to the dialogue?

4   **Build shared knowledge when faced with contrasting positions:** Seek agreement on what research or evidence could help lead to a more informed conclusion.

5   **Use action research to explore differences:** Create strategies that allow participants to put their theories to the test.

6   **Refer to your shared foundation:** Recognize that resolving conflict is more productive when members find common ground on major issues and approach one another with an assumption of good intentions.

Be patient: Remember that you are attempting to develop new skills that will require practice. Therefore, "Don't expect perfection; aim for progress" (Patterson et al., 2002, p. 228). Be tender with one another.

Use what you know about celebration: Apply each of the suggestions presented earlier in the chapter when attempting to introduce celebration as part of your school culture: explicitly state the purpose of celebration, make celebration everyone's responsibility, establish a clear link between the recognition and the behaviour or commitment you are attempting to encourage and reinforce, and create opportunities to have many winners.

Part Six

Questions to Guide the Work of Your Professional Learning Community

To assess how your school addresses conflict, ask . . .

1. Has a conflict emerged in our school in the past? How was that conflict addressed?

2. Are we building shared knowledge and conducting action research in an effort to address conflict productively? Can we cite an example in which we resolved a difference of opinion through examining the research or conducting our own action research?

3. What is the process we currently use to resolve conflict? What skills could we identify and practice to become more effective in this important area?

4. Do we view conflict as something to be avoided?

5. Do we expect administrators to resolve conflict or do we work together to address it in ways that improve our effectiveness?

6. Are we developing our skills to hold crucial conversations?

To assess the presence of celebration in your school, ask . . .

7. What gets publicly celebrated in our school?

8. Do our public celebrations reinforce our purpose and priorities?

9. Have we created opportunities for lots of people in our organization to be recognized and celebrated?

page 2 of 2

Addressing Conflict as a Leader

Using the suggestions in this chapter and considering your current reality, identify an area of concern in your school or district where conflict is causing dysfunction. Reflect on your actions to date. Review the content of chapter 9 (page 191) to make an immediate plan of action.

Conflict: Area of concern (who, what, and why)	What I have tried to do to resolve the conflict	What I need to do next to resolve the conflict	Follow-up and notes

Part Seven

Dangerous Detours and Seductive Shortcuts

Don't assign responsibility for confrontation to others. In *Crucial Conversations*, Patterson and his colleagues (2002) conclude it was not the absence of conflict that made teams effective but rather how the team dealt with the conflict. Bad teams ignored it, letting it fester until the situation deteriorated into fight or flight— unproductive bickering or people not attending meetings. Good teams went to the boss and asked him or her to resolve the problem. Great teams dealt with the issue themselves, recommitting to norms or establishing new norms to address the issue.

Principals cannot expect every team to start off as a great team. Principals will inevitably be called on to intervene when teams experience problems, and they should not shirk that responsibility. As teams become more mature and sophisticated in the process, they should assume greater responsibility for addressing their own problems.

Another example of deflecting responsibility to others is a leader who addresses an issue with a staff member but explains that he or she is doing someone else's bidding. For example, the principal who advises a teacher of the need for change because "the central office wants you to do this" is abdicating responsibility and undermining a systematic effort.

Don't use blanket announcements to deal with individual problems. Ineffective leaders will sometimes seek to avoid personal confrontation by sending out general admonitions regarding inappropriate behaviour. Not only does this typically fail to impact the inappropriate behaviour, but it also is offensive to those who are not acting in that way.

Principals cannot expect every team to start off as a great team. . . . As teams become more mature and sophisticated in the process, they should assume greater responsibility for addressing their own problems.

Final Thoughts

As we have stressed throughout this book, how people behave is a much more powerful way to communicate their priorities than what they say or write in documents that are too often filed away and forgotten. One of the ways leaders best convey their priorities is by what they pay attention to. Confronting behaviour that violates the purpose and priorities of the school or district and publicly celebrating behaviour that reflects purpose and priorities are very effective ways to communicate what is important. The use of skillful confrontation and celebration has not traditionally been a part of the culture of most schools; however, effective leaders of PLCs will develop and model these skills if they hope to sustain the PLC process.

Although we have referenced district leadership at various points throughout the book, most of the case studies have focused on the school site. Districts can, however, play a very important role in implementing the PLC process in all of their schools. We turn our attention to a district's attempt to do so in the next chapter.

CHAPTER 10
Implementing the PLC Process Districtwide

Part One

The Case Study: The High Cost of Failing to Speak With One Voice

Located in a remote northern indigenous region of the Northwest Territories, the Tłı̨chǫ Community Services Agency serves a student population with high socioeconomic and health needs. The agency also experienced high teacher turnover. Director of Education Shannon Aikman knew she needed a regional approach to address historically low academic student performance and a siloed approach to teaching. After attending a PLC at Work Institute with a lead principal and two regional staff members, she believed she had found the vehicle for necessary change in the region. Energized and inspired, she brought the regional leadership team consisting of principals, regional coordinators, program support teachers, and community board members to a workshop to establish the regional team culture. She anticipated that this start-up along with other training would create a team dedicated to using PLC processes to drive student achievement, so she developed a strategic plan that outlined a three-year process to entrench PLCs as a way of improving student achievement.

Over the next year, the leadership team focused on the first PLC question, "What is it we want our students to know and be able to do?" Director Aikman led her team to establish essential learning outcomes, provided professional development on PLCs to all staff, and led the leadership team through data-driven decision making. Each time it worked together, the leadership team was focused and intentional in its thinking. Members left their time together feeling confident that they were working on the right work. At the end of the year, Director Aikman and her team were disappointed. There was very little change to the main objective of improving student reading scores. Why weren't they seeing the improvements that they all seemed to be wanting and working toward?

The leadership team reassembled and reviewed student achievement data. Some members offered that there were students with very low attendance bringing down the data, others suggested that the district should look at trauma-informed practices and focus more on social supports, and still others thought that PLC might not be the right approach after all since they had been "doing PLC" all year without results. These were not the conversations that Director Aikman envisioned having after a year of hard work; however, she arrived at the conclusion that the process had been driven by a small committed leadership team (a guiding coalition) but that it really had not built the capacity of the entire adult community.

Reinvigorated, the leadership team cycled back to its purpose: *high student achievement for every student*. Director Aikman and her team recognized that they would need to start where the adults were on their learning journey. Director Aikman worried that some of her teachers held beliefs that were contrary to working as a team: moving from "my students" to "our students," using evidence to drive decisions, sharing their assessment results, and collaborating on assessments. She wondered if this would all prove to be too challenging for this region. And, finally, would this bring about the changes that she wanted to see in student achievement?

Reflection

Are Director Aikman and her leadership team on the right track, revisiting purpose and taking steps to build collective understanding of the purpose of the work? Is it possible to successfully implement a substantive improvement initiative in schools through a region or district, or is school improvement something that can only occur one building at a time?

Part Two

Here's How

Director Aikman did a lot of things right in this scenario. She made an effort to build shared knowledge about PLCs within her region and with her administrators through articles, books, visitations, professional development, and dialogue. She worked to foster a district culture that was simultaneously loose and tight by publicly articulating what was to be tight—all schools were to function as PLCs. She provided training to assist her leaders from each school in implementing the process. She directed resources to support the initiative. What went wrong? What more could she have done? Is she on the right track now?

Talking is not doing. Planning is not doing. Goal setting is not doing. Training is not doing.

Despite her well-intentioned efforts, Director Aikman had forgotten the central message of this book. Talking is not doing. Planning is not doing. Goal setting is not doing. Training is not doing. Even directing resources to support a plan is not doing. It is not until people are doing differently that any organization can expect different results, and she was correct to revisit what it would take to ensure that the talking, planning, and training actually resulted in action.

Thus, those who hope to lead implementation of the PLC process on a districtwide basis must be prepared to address the following questions.

- What are our priorities?

- What are the specific conditions we expect to see in every school?

- What must we do to build the capacity of people throughout the organization to create these conditions?

- What indicators of progress will we monitor?

- What attitudes and behaviours will we publically recognize and celebrate?

- What current district practices and leadership behaviours are not aligned with the purpose and priorities we have articulated?

- What could we stop doing to provide more time for implementation of the PLC process in all of our schools?

The challenge for Director Aikman, and for any leader who hopes to improve student achievement, is to engage all members of the organization in processes to:

- Clarify priorities

- Clarify the specific conditions that must be created in each school to achieve the priorities

- Build the capacity of people throughout the organization to succeed in what they are being called on to do

- Establish indicators of progress to be monitored carefully

- Align leadership behaviours with the articulated purpose and priorities

- Publically recognize and celebrate incremental success

- Identify high-time, low-impact practices that should be discontinued

Establishing Clear Purpose and Priorities

It is commonplace for districts and regions to adopt a mission statement articulating a commitment to helping all students learn. It is not unusual for the district or region to announce that it intends to help all students learn by transforming their schools into PLCs. What is very rare, however, is for district leaders to articulate exactly what they expect to see in schools that are functioning as PLCs.

In *Raising the Bar and Closing the Gap* (DuFour et al., 2010), we examine three very diverse districts that raised student achievement in every one of their schools. In every instance, the superintendent not only emphasized that the district was committed to helping all students learn by transforming schools into PLCs but also was very specific about the conditions leaders expected to see in each school. They established specific parameters and priorities for what was to occur in each school, and then provided the staff at individual schools with a degree of autonomy regarding how the school would address the priorities within the parameters. These leaders were masterful at what we have called simultaneous loose-tight leadership or the "defined autonomy" characteristic of effective district leaders (Marzano & Waters, 2009).

After taking time to build shared knowledge about the PLC process throughout their districts, all three of the superintendents stipulated that they expected every school to:

- Organize staff into collaborative teams

- Ensure each team—

  - Created a guaranteed and viable curriculum, unit by unit, that provided all students with access to essential knowledge, skills, and dispositions regardless of the teacher to whom they were assigned

  - Used an assessment process that included frequent team-developed common formative assessments to monitor the learning of each student on a timely basis and to inform and improve professional practice.

  - Applied a data-analysis protocol to use transparent evidence of student learning to inform and improve the individual and collective practice of its members

- Create a schoolwide plan for intervention and extension that guaranteed students who experienced difficulty would receive additional time and support for learning in a timely, directive, and systematic way and that those who were proficient would be given the opportunity to extend their learning

The superintendents presented a detailed rationale for their directives, and provided the resources and training necessary for administrators, faculty, and staff. Ultimately, however, they were tight on what they expected to see in each school at the same time that they were loose in terms of implementation. Each school had a significant degree of autonomy regarding how it would create the conditions, but no school could ignore the stipulation that it would address this district priority.

In a study comparing districts that had implemented the PLC process, we examined the differences between high-leverage districts that experienced significant gains in student achievement and low-leverage districts that saw little or no gains. The one thing that was common to both sets of districts was that teachers were provided with time to collaborate, reinforcing the point that how educators use collaborative time will determine the impact of collaboration. There were marked differences in how the two types of districts elected to use that time.

High-leverage districts:

- Were four times more likely to devote ongoing time to building shared knowledge with staff regarding key terms and concepts within the PLC process

- Were more than five times more likely to have teams establish a guaranteed and viable curriculum, unit by unit

- Were four times more likely to have teams develop and administer common formative assessments

- Were more than five times more likely to share evidence of student learning among teammates from common formative assessments

- Monitored student learning more frequently and intervened more promptly and systematically

Once again, school and district leaders must do more than urge teachers to go collaborate. They must provide the priorities and parameters that help teachers focus their collective effort on the right work.

Build Principal Capacity to Lead the PLC Process

Like Director Aikman, each of the superintendents in our highly successful districts recognized that the principal plays the pivotal role in implementing the PLC process in the school setting. They also recognized that if they were to hold principals accountable for developing their staffs into high-performing PLCs, reciprocal accountability demanded that central office leaders provide principals with the knowledge, skills, resources, and training to be successful in what they were being called on to do.

The superintendents of these effective districts began by helping principals develop a deeper understanding of the PLC process by providing them with training, sending them to visit schools that were functioning as high-performing PLCs, and leading them in reading books and articles on the process. Even more importantly, they turned the district principals' meetings into a collaborative and collective effort to identify and resolve any implementation challenges.

The focus of principal meetings shifted from "nuts and bolts" details of administration to gaining shared knowledge and understanding of the PLC process. As Eaker and Keating (2012) observe:

> One of the most important cultural shifts a district can make is to refocus the district's own work on learning—to parallel and model what the district expects from teachers in the classroom. For example, most district leaders want their teachers to move from focusing on low-level memorization of facts to promoting higher levels of thinking, such as analyzing, synthesizing, and evaluating. Yet often in meetings, what do administrators do? Focus on low-level communication. Meetings are constantly in danger of degenerating into traditional, low-level information exchanges. Not only is this an inefficient use of time, it's a misuse of limited resources. (p. 62)

The effective districts used meetings to rehearse and role-play what principals would be called on to do back in their buildings. For example, prior to asking teams to establish norms, a principals' meeting would be devoted to helping principals articulate a rationale for team norms and gathering the tools, templates, and resources they could use to help their teams complete this task.

Most importantly, each principal was called on to present a progress report to the central office cabinet and to their fellow principals on how implementation was proceeding in his or her school. The presentation began with an explanation as to how

School and district leaders must do more than urge teachers to go collaborate. They must provide the priorities and parameters that help teachers focus their collective effort on the right work.

the particular school had addressed the specific conditions expected of all schools. Principals were to explain how teachers had been organized into teams, how they were given time to collaborate, how the principal was monitoring the work of the teams to ensure they were creating a guaranteed curriculum and common formative assessments, how the results of the assessments were being used by teams, and how the school was providing for systematic interventions and enrichment. Principals also presented artifacts and evidence of the work of teams, a comprehensive analysis of student achievement data, and the specific strategies the school had identified to build on strengths and resolve concerns related to student achievement. The central office staff and other principals then provided suggestions to help the principal succeed. In short, these superintendents were asking principals to model what they were asking of teachers by working collaboratively with colleagues rather than independently, making student achievement data easily accessible and openly shared among team members, seeking best practices, helping each other build on strengths and address weaknesses, and taking an interest in and contributing to one another's success. Thus, administrative meetings blended both pressure to hold principals accountable and support to help them meet the challenge of leading a PLC.

Monitor Progress

Merely announcing new priorities, strategies, or goals does nothing to improve a school or district.

Each of the superintendents recognized that merely announcing new priorities, strategies, or goals does nothing to improve a school or district. District leaders should follow the example of effective classroom teachers and constantly monitor not only student achievement—are the students learning and how do we know?—but also the implementation of those things about which the district is tight (Eaker & Keating, 2012).

The new format for principals' meetings was one very effective way to monitor implementation, as principals had to demonstrate to the central office cabinet and their peers exactly what they had done to lead the PLC process in their schools. But since the very purpose of helping schools function as PLCs was to improve results, the central office leaders also monitored progress by establishing a few results-oriented improvement goals for the district and calling on schools and teams to establish goals that aligned with the district goals.

Aligning Leadership Behaviour With the District's Purpose and Priorities

As Director Aikman recognized, it was necessary to build collective capacity throughout the region and she had to make sure that she and her leaders were "doing" not just "saying." Theologian Albert Schweitzer insisted, "Example isn't the main thing in influencing others, it's the only thing." In every instance of effective systemwide implementation of the PLC process we have witnessed, central office leaders visibly modeled the commitment to learning for all students, collaboration, collective inquiry, and results orientation they expected to see in other educators throughout the district. They created structures and processes to help principals and teachers function as collaborative teams. They celebrated progress and confronted individuals whose actions did not reflect the district's priorities. They recognized the need to "impose on themselves congruence between deeds and words, between behaviour and professed beliefs and values" (Drucker, 1992, p. 117). In this chapter's scenario, it was very important for Director Aikman and her leadership team to speak with one voice and take the time to build and model common purpose for the region. Once specific priorities were established in the high-performing districts, the superintendents pledged to protect schools from competing initiatives so educators throughout the district could focus on creating these conditions for an extended period of time. In *Cultures Built to Last: Systemic PLCs at Work,* Rick DuFour and Michael Fullan (2013) identify "pursuing too many initiatives rather than sustaining a focus on continuous improvement" as one of the common "mistakes leaders make that inhibit the evolution of shared coherence" in schools and school districts (p. 23).

Experienced educators have become inured to the sheer volume of frequent, fragmented, and uncoordinated new projects, programs, and reforms that wash upon them in waves. They suffer from what Doug Reeves (2004) has called the "irrefutable law of initiative fatigue" (p. 59) as each new improvement scheme they are called on to adopt saps energy, resources, and attention from those that preceded it. These highly effective superintendents avoided initiative fatigue by stipulating that building the capacity of staff to function as PLCs was not one of many strategies for improving student achievement but instead represented *the* district strategy for accomplishing that goal. Furthermore, they announced that they would sustain their commitment to and focus on that strategy for years to come.

A corollary to the idea of limiting initiatives is to sustain the district's focus on the implementation of PLCs for an extended period of time. Effective central office leaders will recognize that the implementation of PLCs is not a program to complete but a process to perfect. Director Aikman and her team are on the right track by going back and building common purpose and collective understanding. This will ensure that it is about process not a "program." Doug Reeves (2015) conducted an analysis of the impact of PLC implementation in districts that experienced dramatic gains versus those that did not. He found that the PLC process could lead to much higher levels of student achievement, *but only if the process was implemented deeply and sustained for an extended period of time.* The longer the district maintained its focus on becoming better at the PLC process, the greater the gains in student learning.

In November 2016, delegates from thirty-two school-leader associations from across the globe participated in the third annual International Symposium on the Role of Professional Associations for School Leaders held in Toronto, Ontario. The symposium explored research on work intensification, generational theory and its influence on principal work and aspirations, and work-life balance and well-being. Work-life balance and well-being of school leaders is becoming an even larger concern beyond individuals and schools; in many jurisdictions, it is an emerging issue for recruitment and retention. "Ontario Principals' Council International Symposium White Paper: Principal Work-Life Balance and Well-Being Matters" summarizes the findings of the symposium and underscores the problem that "the principalship has become undesirable" (Ontario Principals' Council, 2017).

The need for sustained focus is undermined by the fact that the average tenure of principals in the United States is between three and four years. One quarter of U.S. principals leave their schools each year. More than half of newly hired principals stay for three years or less, and fewer than 30 percent stay beyond five years (School Leaders Network, 2014). Although we don't have national statistics for Canada, we know that most districts and regions in Canada are concerned about principal retention. When asked what they needed to sustain themselves in the position, principals overwhelmingly reported the practices being used by the high-performing districts—ongoing support with peers, collaborative settings, focus on questions of leadership practice, and reflective activities (School Leaders Network, 2014).

In many districts, however, not only does the central office fail to provide support for principals but also routinely rotates principals from school to school every few years. There is no research to support this practice. In fact, the constant shuffling of leaders has a significantly negative impact on student achievement, interferes with the attempt to create a sense of shared purpose, generates cynicism among staff, and makes it impossible to maintain a school improvement focus long enough to actually accomplish meaningful change (Hargreaves & Fullan, 2012; Leithwood et al., 2009). The most effective districts are more likely to heed the advice of researchers who recommend that principals who are making progress in implementing the PLC process should remain in their positions at least five to seven years because it takes that long to have a sustainable impact on a school (Wallace Foundation, 2012).

Part Three

Here's Why

The first two decades of research on how to improve student learning focused, for the most part, on the individual teacher and individual school rather than the district. In the late 1970s, researchers pursued the question, "Do specific teacher instructional behaviours affect student learning?" The answer was a resounding "Absolutely!" This led to the logical research question of the 1980s and 1990s: "If student achievement is affected by the teacher to which a student is assigned, does it matter which school a student attends?" Again, the answer proved to be, "Yes!" In the 2000s, these two bodies of research have led researchers to the question, "Does school district leadership matter." Again, the answer is, "Yes, it does!"

A meta-analysis of research studies to determine the influence of school district leadership on student achievement confirms that effective leadership at the central office level has a statistically significant impact on student achievement (Marzano & Waters, 2009). A later study concludes, "School districts shape the conditions in which schools operate and as such can support or undermine school success and thus student success. All of which is to say—to steal a phrase—school districts matter" (Chenoweth, 2015, p. 14).

The Need for Central Office Leadership

In *Cultures Built to Last*, DuFour and Fullan (2013) assert that the fundamental challenge of district leadership is the too-loose, too-tight dilemma we referenced earlier. Tight, top-down leadership that dictates and micromanages every detail of the process is ineffective because it fails to generate the necessary commitment, ownership, and clarity vital to sustainable improvement. Loose, bottom-up leadership that leaves every aspect of school improvement to the discretion of each school site has proven to be even less effective (Elmore, 2003; Kruse, Louis, & Bryk, 1994). In fact, in some studies, site-based management has been found to have a negative correlation with improved student achievement (Marzano & Waters, 2009).

The solution to the too-tight, too-loose leadership dilemma does come from the top. Districts that create a simultaneously loose and tight culture "do not require less leadership at the top, but rather more—more of a different kind" (Fullan, 2007, p. 41). Effective district leadership fosters continuous improvement and purposeful peer interaction in the pursuit of clear priorities within specific parameters. These districts then hold school leadership teams responsible for addressing the priorities; however, they also provide school leadership teams with a great deal of freedom for operating within the parameters at the school site and with ongoing support to foster their success (DuFour & Fullan, 2013; Elmore, 2003; Marzano & Waters, 2009).

A synthesis of research studies on improved school districts reinforces both the importance of strong district leadership and the need for loose-tight leadership. It concludes that effective district leaders establish a "clear understanding of the district and school roles" characterized by a "*balance between district control and school autonomy*" (Shannon & Bylsma, 2004, p. 45, emphasis added).

Effective district leadership fosters continuous improvement and purposeful peer interaction in the pursuit of clear priorities within specific parameters.

In his three decades of work examining school improvement, Larry Lezotte arrived at a similar conclusion regarding the significance of central office leadership in school improvement. The initial focus on the Effective Schools movement was the individual school site. Over time, however, Lezotte (2002) and his colleagues recognized that school improvement resulting in increased student achievement could only be sustained with strong district direction and support. Lezotte (2011) summarizes the critical nature of district leadership and support, noting:

> If creating and maintaining schools as effective isn't a district-wide priority, the school will likely not be able to maintain its effectiveness status. Without broader based organizational support, school effectiveness tends to depend too heavily on the heroic commitment of the school leader or only a few staff. We have [seen] numerous cases where the principal of any effective school moved on for one reason or another and was replaced by someone who did not share the passion, vision or values. When this happened the school usually, and quickly I might add, returned to its earlier state. (p. 14)

Not surprisingly, the themes that run through the literature on district effectiveness are similar to those found in the research on effective schools. These include findings that clear academic essential outcomes, high expectations for student achievement, aligned curricula, coherent organizational structures, strong instructional leadership, frequent monitoring, and focused professional learning lead to higher student achievement (Trujillo, 2013).

In reviewing the ways in which many districts improved student achievement across the entire system, DuFour and Fullan (2013) observe:

> In each case, district leaders maintained a commitment to and focus on building the individual and collective capacity of educators

throughout the district. In each case, the district provided educators with the ongoing clarity and support to help them succeed at what they were being asked to do. In short, they worked to ensure that every school was functioning as a PLC. (p. 6)

Shannon Dulaney, Pamela Hallam, and Gary Wall (2013) echo DuFour and Fullan (2013), writing:

Our findings suggest that to realize sustainable improvement districts must (1) develop a common language and framework for implementation, (2) work collaboratively within the PLC structure to meet the needs of all students, and (3) purposefully build capacity within the district organization. (pp. 42–43)

John Hattie (2015b) contends that the best system leaders create a culture of "collaborative expertise" within and between schools. In such a culture, there is clarity regarding the priorities and purpose of the district, an intense focus on student learning, ready access to evidence of student learning that allows educators to intervene for students who are struggling, professional dialogue regarding the effectiveness of different instructional strategies based on evidence of student learning, and a recognition of the power of collective wisdom to help teachers have a positive impact on student learning.

Fullan and Quinn (2016) echo similar thoughts when summarizing what they consistently found in high-performing districts, writing:

First, all of these examples had a clear and focused sense of direction. They articulated a small number of goals directly linked to improved student learning and then persisted in working toward them. . . . Second, they built a collaborative culture by focusing on capacity building. . . . Third, they have a deep commitment to the learning and teaching nexus. They are not looking for a quick fix but rather to create collaborative communities of inquiry that deeply examine instructional practices and student results. . . . In these places of deep learning for the adults as well as the students, there is a professionalism that permeates relationships and decisions. (p. 107)

DuFour and Marzano (2011) summarize the importance of districtwide leadership by noting:

Leadership from the central office matters—both in terms of raising student achievement and in terms of creating the conditions for adult learning that lead to higher levels of student achievement. Without effective leadership from the central office, the PLC process will not become deeply embedded in schools throughout a district. (p. 45)

A region or district's simultaneous loose and tight culture will impact student and adult learning in a positive way only if the system is tight on the right things.

The Need for Specificity

Of course, a region or district's simultaneous loose and tight culture will impact student and adult learning in a positive way only if the system is tight on the right things.

We listed those right things in the previous section. A study of districts that were able to double student achievement should sound familiar. Researchers found that those districts clarified what students were to learn, used formative assessments to monitor their learning, intervened for struggling students with extended learning time, used evidence of student learning to inform and improve their professional practice, and established collaborative relationships with widely dispersed leadership. As the authors conclude:

> It should be no surprise that one result of the multiplicity of activities was a collaborative, professional school culture—what some refer to as a "professional learning community." . . . Leaders understood that the way to attain their ambitious goals was to develop what is commonly called a "professional learning community" today. (Odden & Archibald, 2009, p. 78)

However, many district-level leaders that call for the schools to function as PLCs "lack a clear understanding of how they could engage in the work or provide the system-level supports necessary to sustain learning communities" (Annenberg Institute for School Reform, 2005, p. 6). Director Aikman needs to continue to develop the specific expectations of the practices and processes she expects in each school. It is not imperative that district leaders use the term *professional learning community* in clarifying how schools are to operate. It is imperative, however, that when stipulating the specific conditions they expect to see in each school, those conditions reflect the practices of PLCs.

In their study of high-performing districts, Allan Odden and Sarah Archibald (2009) found central office leaders helped create the culture of PLCs in schools throughout the district by insisting educators do what PLCs do. These leaders didn't change existing assumptions, beliefs, and expectations in order to get people to act in new ways: they got people to act in new ways in order to change assumptions, beliefs, and expectations. As organizational theorists John Kotter and Dan Cohen (2002) conclude:

> It is essential to understand a fundamental and widely misunderstood aspect of organizational change. In a change effort, culture comes last, not first. . . . A culture truly changes only when a new way of operating has been shown to succeed over some minimum period of time. . . . You can create new behaviours that reflect the desired culture. But those new behaviours will not become norms, will not take hold, until the very end of the process. (pp. 175–176)

The Need for a Common Language (Once Again)

But even if district or regional leaders themselves are aware of what must be tight, they face the challenge of communicating so effectively that people all throughout the organization are clear on priorities and parameters. This will not happen unless leaders help to establish a common language with widely shared meanings of key

It is not imperative that district leaders use the term professional learning community in clarifying how schools are to operate. It is imperative, however, that when stipulating the specific conditions they expect to see in each school, those conditions reflect the practices of PLCs.

terminology. If key terms are only vaguely understood or represent different things to people throughout the district, it will be impossible to implement the PLC process across a district. The best indicator of a districtwide common language and clear understanding of the specific implications for action regarding key terms is when people *throughout* the system can "talk the walk." They can explain what they are doing and why (Fullan, 2014). This is Director Aikman's goal, and she is committed to making it happen.

The Need to Monitor

What gets monitored gets done.

What gets monitored gets done. Tłı̨chǫ Community Services Agency, under Director Aikman's leadership, was decisive about establishing the PLC process in schools throughout the region, but she soon recognized that a decision, by itself, changes nothing unless there are mechanisms in place to monitor implementation (Pfeffer & Sutton, 2000). She needed her principals and leadership team to deeply implement and monitor what everyone was doing to support the initiative. She put no process in place to assess progress that schools were making. By slowing down and revisiting the common understanding of vision, mission, and common language, the region is now moving in the right direction. Once again, one of the most powerful ways leaders communicate priorities is by clarifying the indicators of progress they will track, and the specific actions members can take immediately to begin making that progress (Buckingham, 2005). A key characteristic of learning-centred leadership is establishing processes for monitoring priorities (Goldring, Porter, Murphy, Elliott, & Cravens, 2007), and effective districts continually monitor progress toward clearly defined goals (Marzano & Waters, 2009).

The Need to Develop the Capacity of Principals to Lead the PLC Process

One of the most consistent findings of the research on PLCs is the vital role the principal plays in implementing the PLC process at the school site (see the reproducible, "Why Is Principal Leadership So Important?").

Given the vital importance of the principalship, it only makes sense that district and regional leaders establish the clear expectation that leading the PLC process is a key requirement of and priority for every principal. Central office leaders would also, however, (1) devote time and resources to developing the capacity of principals to lead the process through initial training and ongoing support and (2) work to remove high-time, low-impact strategies that make demands on principals' time but have little impact on student learning.

District leadership that has a positive impact on student achievement will be intentional in providing the ongoing training, support, and monitoring to ensure that every principal is developing the knowledge, skills, and dispositions vital to leading the PLC process in their schools.

Why Is Principal Leadership So Important?

"Principals are widely seen as indispensable to innovation. No reform effort, however worthy, survives a principal's indifference or opposition. When they are asked to lead projects they don't fully grasp or endorse, they are likely to be ambivalent. Central office must remember the importance of allowing time for principals to thrash out their questions as they relate to changes" (Evans, 1996, p. 202).

"If you take the principal and other key building leaders out of the picture as a committed and skillful force for these qualities, then no successful PLC will form. The possibilities of all other forces combined (state education law and policy, standardized testing and accountability, central office staff development, parent and community pressure) to raise student achievement are fatally weakened" (Saphier, 2005, p. 38).

"Principals arguably are the most important players affecting the character and consequence of teachers' school-site professional communities. Principals are culture-makers, intentionally or not" (McLaughlin & Talbert, 2006, p. 80).

"I know of no improving school that doesn't have a principal who is good at leading improvement" (Fullan, 2007, p. 160).

"[Positive] outcomes are unlikely in the absence of building leadership that supports and holds teacher teams accountable for sustaining the inquiry process until they see tangible results" (Gallimore et al., 2009, p. 544).

"In developing a starting point for this six-year study, we claimed, based on a preliminary review of research, that leadership is second only to classroom instruction as an influence on student learning. After six additional years of research, we are even more confident about this claim. To date we have not found a single case of a school improving its student achievement record in the absence of talented leadership" (Leithwood et al., 2009, p. 9).

"Our empirical results also attest strongly to the centrality of school leadership as a catalyst for change. . . . A major practical "take-away": the centrality of principal leadership in initiating and sustaining the organizational changes necessary to improve student learning. Quite simply, school improvement is highly unlikely to occur in its absence" (Bryk, Sebring, Allensworth, Luppescu, & Easton, 2010, pp. 199, 204).

"A particularly noteworthy finding . . . is the empirical link between school leadership and improved student achievement" (Wallace Foundation, 2012, p. 3).

"Everyone shares a common aspiration for all students to attend high-quality schools. Yet, as the research definitively illustrates, that goal will remain out of reach without a similar commitment to high-quality principal leadership" (National Association of Secondary School Principals & National Association of Elementary School Principals, 2013, p. 11).

"Principals who are strong, effective, responsive leaders help to inspire and enhance the abilities of their teachers and other school staff to do excellent work. . . . In short, principals, through their actions, can be powerful multipliers of effective teaching and leadership practices in schools. And those practices can contribute much to the success of the nation's students" (Manna, 2015, p. 7).

The Need for the Principal as a Leader of Learning

While research confirming that principals can play an important role in improving student achievement has been abundant, the nature of the role remains somewhat vague and seems to constantly expand. One study identified twenty-one different responsibilities principals must fulfill (Marzano et al., 2005). New, additional responsibilities continue to be layered on top of old ones making the job nearly impossible to do well (Manna, 2015). Three-quarters of principals agree that their job has become too complex, a view shared by principals regardless of demographic characteristics such as school level, location, or proportion of low-income or minority students (Markow & Pieters, 2010). It is a job that requires miracles that "a few can pull it off, but mere mortals have little chance" (Fullan, 2014, p. 7).

The challenges of the principalship have expanded exponentially with the current emphasis on the principal as instructional leader who will somehow do everything he or she has always done and yet find the time to spend hours in classrooms supervising and evaluating individual teachers into better performance. Even if, somehow, principals find the time to observe teachers much more frequently, it is not the best use of their time. DuFour and Mattos (2013) merely stated the obvious when they wrote:

> An algebra teacher has a better chance of becoming more effective when he or she works with other algebra teachers weekly to improve student learning than when he or she is observed by a former social studies teacher four times a year. (p. 40)

In an *Educational Leadership* article published in 2002, Rick called on principals to shift their focus from watching teaching to using the PLC process to monitor learning, to abandon the idea of instructional leadership, and to embrace the idea of principal as lead learner. Principals facilitate the learning of educators throughout the building not by serving as the lead evaluator of teaching but by fully supporting the ongoing learning of the PLC process (DuFour & Mattos, 2013). As Sharon Kramer (2015) points out:

> The fact is that leadership is always a collective endeavor. No one person has all the expertise, skill, and energy to improve a school or meet the needs of every student in his or her classroom. In a professional learning community, instead of being the instructional leader in charge of all things important, the principal becomes the lead learner of the school. In this role, the goal is to build the capacity of the people within the school to ensure high levels of learning for all students. (p. 44)

One of the strongest proponents of the role of principal as a leader of learners is Canadian Michael Fullan. In *The Principal: Three Keys to Maximizing Impact*, Fullan (2014) argues that the old paradigm of the "principal as instructional leader" is a recipe for failure since it simply requires too much of and is far too complex for any one person. Instead, he proposes that a principal be a "*learning leader—one who models learning, but also shapes the conditions for all to learn on a continuous basis*" (Fullan, 2014, p. 9). The very term *professional learning community* implies a "community of learners." And, in such a community, the principal is the leader of learning, the one who leads the school community in learning about and implementing best practices and ensuring a culture of continuous learning and improvement.

This is precisely what effective superintendents do in developing the leadership capacity of principals. They work with principals to identify the specific skills and vital behaviours that are essential to leading the PLC process in schools. They then call on principals to demonstrate those skills and behaviours in the context of their ongoing work in schools. They align the processes and structures of the organization to support the new skills and behaviours, engage in collective study to address challenges, construct situations that allow for deliberate practice, and provide ongoing coaching and support. They establish specific goals and expectations that stretch individuals, they use the power of positive peer pressure to challenge each individual, and they also are attentive to providing the assistance to help their people succeed. They demonstrate reciprocal accountability at its best.

> *Effective superintendents . . . work with principals to identify the specific skills and vital behaviours that are essential to leading the PLC process in schools.*

Part Four

Assessing Your Place on the PLC Journey

It is important to help your staff build shared knowledge regarding your school's current status in addressing the critical step on the PLC journey of implementing the PLC process districtwide. We have created a tool to assist you in that effort. "The Professional Learning Communities at Work® Continuum: Implementing the PLC Process Districtwide" is available at **go.SolutionTree.com/ca/PLCbooks** as a free reproducible. Once your staff have established greater clarity regarding the current status of your collaborative teams, we urge you to turn your attention to the "Where Do We Go From Here?" worksheet that accompanies the continuum (also available for free to download at **go.SolutionTree.com/ca/PLCbooks**). It will prompt you to take the action necessary to close the knowing-doing gap.

Part Five

Tips for Moving Forward: Implementing a Districtwide PLC Process

 Train principals: Principals should be trained together in how to lead the PLC process. In large districts, training may take place in cohorts. As the former assistant superintendent in one model of a districtwide PLC writes:

To create collaborative districts, district leaders must provide principals with training opportunities that allow them to collaborate, learn together, and find best practices. In this way, principals have the opportunity to discuss and find meaning in the new PLC concepts presented to them. As practitioners, principals need time to collaborate to clearly see how implementation might look in their schools. They need to bounce ideas off one another and hear what others are planning. (Smith, 2015, pp. 31–32)

2 **Don't assume a common verbiage means common understanding:** The fact that people use the same terms does not mean that they have a shared understanding of a term's meaning or implications. Remember the advice of Jeffrey Pfeffer and Robert Sutton (2000), based on their research on high-performing organizations:

The use of complex language hampers implementation . . . when leaders or managers don't really understand the meaning of the language they are using and its implications for action. It is hard enough to explain what a complex idea means for action when you understand it and others don't. It is impossible when you use terms that sound impressive but you don't really understand what they mean. (p. 52)

Develop formal and informal processes to determine people's interpretation of the key terms in the PLC lexicon. "Help me understand what you mean by that term" should be a phrase you use routinely in conversations with others. A portion of district-led principals' meetings should ask members to clarify terms that are essential to the PLC process. Principals, in turn, should use the same strategies in their buildings until there is a truly common language. Remember that in high-performing PLCs, people not only "walk the talk" by acting in accordance to the process, they can "talk the walk" by explaining what they are doing and why (Fullan, 2014).

3 **Don't assume that others share or understand your interpretation of what is tight:** Develop formal and informal processes to provide you with feedback on what people throughout the organization believe are the priorities. For example, at a principals' meeting, the superintendent could ask principals to write down the two or three things they believe are tight in the district. The responses should be gathered, read aloud, and discussed. How consistent are the responses? Principals should repeat this process in their schools.

Link what is tight to board policy: Work with the school board to codify expectations of priorities through adoption of board policy. As seen in the First Nations Schools Association of British Columbia (n.d.) example cited in the preface of this book, it is helpful when boards establish policy and expectations of effective school improvement strategies, such as addressing the four critical questions of a PLC—

a. What do students need to know and be able to do?

b. How will we know when they have learned it?

c. What will we do when they haven't learned it?

d. What will we do when they already know it?

A great American example is Schaumberg District 54 in suburban Chicago, which has adopted a board policy that states:

> An exemplary district is a professional learning community that includes all employees working together on a variety of collaborative teams for the benefit of students . . . As a professional learning community, all employees will—
>
> ♦ Plan/support instruction, analyze data, and establish intervention and enrichment opportunities in a collaborative manner
>
> ♦ Commit to continuous improvement with knowledge, purpose, and efficiency
>
> ♦ Seek appropriate resources and support
>
> ♦ Be dedicated to continuous learning and student achievement
>
> ♦ Treat everyone with courtesy, dignity, and respect, while maintaining all necessary confidences

Of course, merely adopting policy does not ensure change in professional practice. It can, however, demonstrate a public commitment to certain expectations, and it allows leaders to serve as promoters and protectors of district policy.

Recognize the need for specificity regarding what people throughout the organization must do: Telling educators to operate their schools as PLCs will almost certainly have no impact unless there is a clear understanding of the specific actions people take in a PLC. The goal is not to have educators in a district refer to their school as a PLC; the goal is to have them do what members of a PLC do. In many instances, we have seen the adoption of language substitute for meaningful action. It is far more effective to stipulate exactly what must be done and then provide some latitude regarding how it is done.

Create systems to monitor conditions that are vital to the success of a PLC: One of the most important and frequent questions effective district leaders of the PLC process ask is, "How do we know?" They identify elements they believe must be in place for the process to be effective, and then they develop specific strategies to gather ongoing evidence of the presence of those elements.

 Demonstrate reciprocal accountability: Work with leaders throughout the organization to identify the specific support and resources staff will need in order to accomplish what they are being called to do, and then provide the necessary support and resources. Remember that part of the responsibility of leadership is helping others develop the capacity to succeed at what they are asked to accomplish.

Part Six

Questions to Guide the Work of Your Professional Learning Community

To assess the commitment to districtwide PLC implementation, ask:

1. How do we know if we have a common language that is widely understood throughout the district?

2. How do we know if educators throughout the district understand what must be tight in our organization and in each school?

3. How do we know if educators are organized into collaborative teams (not merely groups) whose members are working interdependently on the right work?

4. How do we know if each student's learning is being monitored on a frequent and timely basis and that the quality of his or her work is being assessed according to the same criteria?

5. How do we know if we're using assessment results to inform and improve professional practice?

6. How do we know if every student who experiences difficulty in acquiring essential knowledge and skills will receive additional time and support for learning in a timely, directive, and systematic way?

7. How do we know what resources and support people need throughout the organization to help them succeed at what they are being called on to do?

8. How do we know if we are providing the necessary resources and support?

9. How do we know our ongoing efforts to train and support principals in the PLC process are impacting school practices?

10. Have we limited initiatives and sustained a collective focus in building our collective capacity to function as a PLC?

Part Seven

Dangerous Detours and Seductive Shortcuts

No one person can lead the PLC process at either the building or district level; effective leaders must delegate responsibility and authority to others. There are some things, however, that they cannot delegate. As Director Aikman and her team determined, clarifying purpose and priorities, establishing systems to monitor specific indicators of progress, ensuring steps are taken to build capacity of people to be successful, and aligning their own behaviour with the priorities are among those nontransferable responsibilities.

Conversely, some well-intentioned districts have attempted to implement the PLC process in a way that removes educators at the building level from doing the work. Central office leaders think:

- We won't ask teachers to identify essential outcomes. We will do it for them.

- We won't ask teachers to create assessments. We will do it for them.

- We won't ask teachers to analyze evidence of student learning. We will do it for them.

- We won't ask principals to create systems of intervention. We will buy a computer program that will provide interventions for them.

Remember this fundamental truth about implementing the PLC process: *When you remove educators from doing the work, you remove them from the learning.* It is the process of *engaging* in this collective learning that begins to transform traditional schools into PLCs.

Some leaders have interpreted the adage "What gets monitored gets done" to mean, "The more things we monitor, the more we get done." This is absolutely wrong. Clarify a few key priorities, and focus your sustained efforts on them. Limit initiatives. Engage in what Peter Drucker (1992) has called "organizational abandonment" by periodically looking at every process, procedure, and activity and asking, "If we stopped doing this, would our organization suffer or benefit?" For example, successful Canadian districts use surveys and ask questions such as, "What tasks that are required by the district or regional office would you recommend be simplified or eliminated to give you more time to focus on student achievement? As a district, are we effectively monitoring the right and important things? Does the central office provide a sense of coherence, speak with one voice, and help you in clarifying the important issues or send mixed messages? Please provide specific examples."

No one person can lead the PLC process at either the building or district level; effective leaders must delegate responsibility and authority to others.

Final Thoughts

Coordination, collaboration, and interdependence between the district office and schools are essential to districtwide implementation of the PLC process. Unproductive conflict and ongoing resistance interfere with that coordination, collaboration, and interdependence.

CONCLUSION

The Fierce Urgency of Now

As we have stressed throughout this book, transforming a traditional school into a true professional learning community is not a program to implement; rather, it is an ongoing, never-ending process specifically designed to change the very culture and structure of the school. We summarize some of these shifts in the free reproducible on pages 236–238.

When We Know Better We Have an Obligation to Do Better

We acknowledge that this transformation is not easy. It requires a sustained, focused, and collective effort over an extended period of time. Yet despite the difficulty of the challenge, we are at a point in time when educators must embrace that challenge because it is so clearly the right thing to do.

In Canada, Prince Edward Island introduced the first provincewide common schooling system in 1852. By 1873, all provinces but three funded their schools through taxation. Alberta and Saskatchewan adopted a free-school act in the early half of the 20th century. Newfoundland began legislation in 1942 (Oreopoulos, 2005).

For most of Canada's history, providing the opportunity for all children to learn was sufficient because those who were unsuccessful in school had access to the middle class through good-paying jobs in factories, farms, and mines that did not require a high school education. In the 21st century, that access no longer exists. As we established in chapter 1 (page 9), those unable to succeed in the K–12 system have limited employment opportunities, suffer economically, have shortened life expectancies, and are a drain on society. The consequences for those individuals have never been more dire. If we are to fulfill the moral imperative of our profession, we can no longer settle for simply giving students the chance to learn; we must ensure high levels of learning for each student in our collective care.

There has never been greater consensus on the most promising strategy to improve our schools. Researchers from around the world have cited the collaborative culture, collective responsibility, transparency of practice, and unrelenting focus on each student's learning that are central to the PLC process as vital to transforming our schools. As discussed in the preface of this book and through the case studies, there are schools and districts that are models of the PLC process spread throughout Canada just as there are in the United States and increasingly the world. Given the ongoing impact of failure in the K–12 system for our students, there is simply no justification for inaction.

If we are to fulfill the moral imperative of our profession, we can no longer settle for simply giving students the chance to learn; we must ensure high levels of learning for each student in our collective care.

Cultural Shifts in a Professional Learning Community

A Shift in Fundamental Purpose	
From a focus on teaching . . .	to a focus on learning
From emphasis on what was taught . . .	to a fixation on what students learned
From coverage of content . . .	to demonstration of proficiency
From providing individual teachers with curriculum documents such as province or territory learning outcomes and curriculum guides . . .	to engaging collaborative teams in building shared knowledge regarding essential curriculum

A Shift in Use of Assessments	
From infrequent summative assessments . . .	to frequent common formative assessments
From assessments to determine which students failed to learn by the deadline . . .	to assessments to identify students who need additional time and support
From assessments used to reward and punish students . . .	to assessments used to inform and motivate students
From assessing many things infrequently . . .	to assessing a few things frequently
From individual teacher assessments . . .	to collaborative team-developed assessments
From each teacher determining the criteria to use in assessing student work . . .	to collaborative teams clarifying the criteria and ensuring consistency among team members when assessing student work
From an over-reliance on one kind of assessment . . .	to balanced assessments
From focusing on average scores . . .	to monitoring each student's proficiency in every essential skill

A Shift in the Response When Students Don't Learn	
From individual teachers determining the appropriate response . . .	to a systematic response that ensures support for every student
From fixed time and support for learning . . .	to time and support for learning as variables
From remediation . . .	to intervention
From invitational support outside of the school day . . .	to directed (that is, required) support occurring during the school day
From one opportunity to demonstrate learning . . .	to multiple opportunities to demonstrate learning

page 1 of 3

A Shift in the Work of Teachers

From isolation . . .	to collaboration
From each teacher clarifying what students must learn . . .	to collaborative teams building shared knowledge and understanding about essential learning
From each teacher assigning priority to different learning outcomes . . .	to collaborative teams establishing the priority of respective learning outcomes
From each teacher determining the pacing of the curriculum . . .	to collaborative teams of teachers agreeing on common pacing
From individual teachers attempting to discover ways to improve results . . .	to collaborative teams of teachers helping each other improve
From privatization of practice . . .	to open sharing of practice
From decisions made on the basis of individual preferences . . .	to decisions made collectively by building shared knowledge of best practice
From "collaboration lite" on matters unrelated to student achievement . . .	to collaboration explicitly focused on issues and questions that most impact student achievement
From an assumption that these are "my students, those are your students" . . .	to an assumption that these are "our students"

A Shift in Focus

From an external focus on issues outside of the school . . .	to an internal focus on steps the staff can take to improve the school
From a focus on inputs . . .	to a focus on results
From goals related to completion of projects and activities . . .	to SMART goals demanding evidence of student learning
From teachers gathering data from their individually constructed tests in order to assign grades . . .	to collaborative teams acquiring information from common assessments in order to inform their individual and collective practice and respond to students who need additional time and support

A Shift in School Culture

From independence . . .	to interdependence
From a language of complaint . . .	to a language of commitment
From long-term strategic planning . . .	to planning for short-term wins
From infrequent generic recognition . . .	to frequent specific recognition and a culture of celebration that creates many winners

page 2 of 3

Learning by Doing © 2020 Solution Tree Press • SolutionTree.com
Visit **go.SolutionTree.com/ca/PLCbooks** to download this free reproducible.

A Shift in Professional Development

From external training (workshops and courses) . . .	to job-embedded learning
From the expectation that learning occurs infrequently (on the few days devoted to professional development) . . .	to an expectation that learning is ongoing and occurs as part of routine work practice
From presentations to entire faculties . . .	to team-based action research
From learning by listening . . .	to learning by doing
From learning individually through courses and workshops . . .	to learning collectively by working together
From assessing impact on the basis of teacher satisfaction ("Did you like it?") . . .	to assessing impact on the basis of evidence of improved student learning
From short-term exposure to multiple concepts and practices . . .	to sustained commitment to limited focused initiatives

Mike Schmoker (2004a) writes that we will know when our profession has committed to substantive instructional improvement when the absence of a strong PLC in a school is an embarrassment. Sadly, effective PLCs are not yet the norm in Canadian schools, nor will they be unless members of our profession acknowledge and act on three facts.

1. We have, within our sphere of influence, everything we need to create conditions that lead to higher levels of learning for both students and adults through the PLC process.

2. No one has forbidden us to create those conditions.

3. We must accept some responsibility for the fact that these conditions are not yet the norm in our schools.

There is no simple answer to improving all schools in Canada. Public discourse continues to focus on external factors such as class size, decreasing or increasing funding, teacher cuts or shortages, language rights, the needs of our indigenous people, and new policies and initiatives as provincial and territorial governments come and go. This is our current reality. This dialogue calls on *others* to improve our schools, not us, the educators. And while these factors are important and necessary conversations, their impact on student achievement is far less than the six conditions that we have listed as tight in a PLC.

1. Educators work collaboratively rather than in isolation, take collective responsibility for student learning, and clarify the commitments they make to each other about how they will work together.

2. The fundamental structure of the school becomes the collaborative team, in which members work interdependently to achieve common goals for which all members are mutually accountable.

3. The team establishes a guaranteed curriculum, unit by unit, so all students have access to the same knowledge and skills regardless of the teacher to whom they are assigned.

4. The team develops common formative assessments to frequently gather evidence of student learning.

5. The school has created systems of intervention and extensions to ensure students who struggle receive additional time and support for learning in a way that is timely, directive, diagnostic, and systematic and students who demonstrate proficiency can extend their learning.

6. The team uses evidence of student learning to inform and improve the individual and collective practice of its members.

Even when educators endorse the PLC process, too often they look for others to lead it. A superintendent or director will lament the lack of provincial or territorial support for PLCs when, in the same province or territory, another district or region has been highly successful in implementing the process throughout its schools. A

Sadly, effective PLCs are not yet the norm in Canadian schools

principal cites the lack of district support for the PLC process, overlooking the fact that most districts that have embraced the process only did so after one of its schools provided such compelling evidence of its benefits that the district leadership had to take notice. Teachers cite a lack of leadership from the principal, ignoring the fact that they have the opportunity to lead their principals. Teachers can clarify what they are willing to do to bring the process to life in their school and instruct the principal about the things he or she must be tight about. They can adopt the PLC process in their grade level or department to demonstrate its impact. This tendency to look for others to solve our problems ignores the fact that we have the power to bring about the necessary changes in our school.

It is time that we act with a sense of urgency, as if the very lives of our students depend on us, because, more so than any other time in our history, they do depend on us.

The 13th century Persian poet Rumi writes, "Yesterday I was clever, so I wanted to change the world. Today I am wise, so I am changing myself." It is time for our profession to become wise. It is time to stop waiting for others. It is time for every Canadian educator to take *personal* responsibility for helping bring the PLC process to life in his or her school or district. And it is time that we act with a sense of urgency, as if the very lives of our students depend on us, because, more so than any other time in our history, they do depend on us.

Final Thoughts

This book has attempted to address some of the challenges that prevent schools and districts from making progress as PLCs. We have attempted to draw on research from organizational development, education, leadership, psychology, and sociology to suggest alternative strategies for dealing with those challenges. We have attempted to give you the preliminary awareness, knowledge, and tools to help you begin the PLC journey—but you will only develop your skill and capacity to build a PLC by engaging in the work. You must learn by doing.

Thus, we have not presented you with a how-to book. The history, cultures, and contexts of each school and district are unique and must be considered in the improvement process. Furthermore, challenges to education will arise in the coming years that we could not possibly anticipate when we wrote this book. We remain convinced, however, that when educators learn to clarify their priorities, to assess the current reality of their situation, to work together, and to build continuous improvement into the very fabric of their collective work, they create conditions for the ongoing learning and self-efficacy essential to solving whatever problems they confront. We hope every school or district that begins the PLC journey will come to believe deeply in and, more importantly, act on the advice attributed to Ralph Waldo Emerson: "What lies behind us and what lies ahead of us are tiny matters compared to what lies within us."

References and Resources

Achor, S. (2010). *The happiness advantage: The seven principles of positive psychology that fuel success and performance at work.* New York: Crown Business.

Ainsworth, L. (2014). *Common formative assessments 2.0: How teacher teams intentionally align standards, instruction, and assessment* (2nd ed.). Thousand Oaks, CA: Corwin Press.

Ainsworth, L. (2015a, February 24). *Priority standards: The power of focus.* Accessed at http://blogs.edweek.org/edweek/finding_common_ground/2015/02/priority_standards_the_power_of_focus.html?qs=larry+ainsworth on November 14, 2015.

Ainsworth, L. (2015b, March 25). *Unwrapping the standards: A simple way to deconstruct lesson outcomes.* Accessed at http://blogs.edweek.org/edweek/finding_common_ground/2015/03/unwrapping_the_standards_a_simple_way_to_deconstruct_learning_outcomes.html?qs=larry+ainsworth on November 14, 2015.

Ainsworth, L., & Viegut, D. (2006). *Common formative assessments: How to connect standards-based instruction and assessment.* Thousand Oaks, CA: Corwin Press.

Alberta Education. (n.d.). *Alberta Education leadership quality standard.* Accessed at https://education.alberta.ca/media/3739621/standardsdoc-lqs-_fa-web-2018-01-17.pdf on November 4, 2019.

Alliance for Excellent Education. (2014, July). *On the path to equity: Improving the effectiveness of beginning teachers.* Washington, DC: Author. Accessed at http://all4ed.org/wp-content/uploads/2014/07/PathToEquity.pdf on September 9, 2015.

AllThingsPLC. (n.d.a). *Pollard Meadows.* Accessed at www.allthingsplc.info/evidence/details/id,1101 October 1, 2019.

AllThingsPLC. (n.d.b). *See the evidence.* Accessed at www.allthingsplc.info/evidence/?level=&enrollment=&lunch_percent=&english_percent=&special_percent=&country=CA&state= on October 5, 2019.

AllThingsPLC. (n.d.c). *South Kamploos Secondary.* Accessed at www.allthingsplc.info/evidence/details/id,1027l on October 1, 2019.

Almy, S., & Tooley, M. (2012, June). *Building and sustaining talent: Creating conditions in high-poverty schools that support effective teaching and learning.* Washington, DC: Education Trust.

Amabile, T., & Kramer, S. (2010). What really motivates workers: Understanding the power of progress. *Harvard Business Review, 88*(1), 44–45.

Amabile, T., & Kramer, S. (2011). *The progress principle: Using small wins to ignite joy, engagement, and creativity at work.* Boston: Harvard Business Review Press.

American Society for Quality. (n.d.). *Vision, mission, values statements.* Accessed at http://asq.org/service/body-of-knowledge/tools-vision-mission-values on September 24, 2015.

Annenberg Institute for School Reform. (2005). *Professional learning communities: Professional development strategies that improve instruction.* Accessed at www.annenberginstitute.org/pdf/ProfLearning.pdf on January 18, 2010.

Anrig, G. (2013). *Beyond the education wars: Evidence that collaboration builds effective schools.* New York: Century Foundation Press.

Autry, J. A. (2001). *The servant leader: How to build a creative team, develop great morale and improve bottom-line performance.* New York: Three Rivers Press.

Axelrod, R. H. (2002). *Terms of engagement: Changing the way we change organizations.* San Francisco: Berrett-Koehler.

Bailey, K., & Jakicic, C. (2012). *Common formative assessment: A toolkit for Professional Learning Communities at Work.* Bloomington, IN: Solution Tree Press.

Barber, M., & Mourshed, M. (2007, September). *How the world's best-performing school systems come out on top.* New York: McKinsey. Accessed at www.mckinsey.com/App_Media/Reports?SSO/Worlds_School_Systems_Final.pdf on January 1, 2010.

Barber, M., & Mourshed, M. (2009, July). *Shaping the future: How good education systems can become great in the decade ahead* (Report on the International Education Roundtable). New York: McKinsey & Company. Accessed at www.mckinsey.com/locations/southeastasia/knowledge/Education_Roundtable.pdf on January 1, 2010.

Battelle for Kids. (2015). *Five strategies for creating a high-growth school.* Accessed at www.battelleforkids.org/docs/default-source/publications/soar_five_strategies_for_creating_a_high-growth_school.pdf?sfvrsn=2 on September 10, 2015.

Bennis, W., & Biederman, P. W. (1997). *Organizing genius: The secrets of creative collaboration.* New York: Basic Books.

Berry, L. L., & Seltman, K. D. (2008). *Management lessons from Mayo Clinic: Inside one of the world's most admired service organizations.* New York: McGraw-Hill.

Black, P., Harrison, C., Lee, C., Marshall, B., & Wiliam, D. (2004). Working inside the black box: Assessment for learning in the classroom. *Phi Delta Kappan, 86*(1), 9–21.

Black, P., & Wiliam, D. (1998). The formative purpose: Assessment must first promote learning. In M. Wilson (Ed.), *Towards coherence between classroom assessment and accountability* (103rd Yearbook of the National Society for the Study of Education, pp. 20–50). Chicago: National Society for the Study of Education.

Black, P., & Wiliam, D. (2009). Developing the theory of formative assessment. *Educational Assessment, Evaluation and Accountability, 21*(1), 5–31.

Blanchard, K. (2007). *Leading at a higher level: Blanchard on leadership and creating high performing organizations.* Upper Saddle River, NJ: Prentice Hall.

Block, P. (2003). *The answer to how is yes: Acting on what matters.* San Francisco: Berrett-Koehler.

Blythe, T., Allen, D., & Powell, B. S. (1999). *Looking together at student work: A companion guide to assessing student learning.* New York: Teachers College Press.

Bossidy, L., & Charan, R. (2002). *Execution: The discipline of getting things done.* New York: Crown Business.

Boston Consulting Group. (2014, December). *Teachers know best: Teachers' view on professional development.* Seattle, WA: Bill and Melinda Gates Foundation. Accessed at http://collegeready.gatesfoundation.org/sites/default/files/Gates -PDMarketResearch-Dec5.pdf on February 20, 2015.

Breslow, J. M. (2012, September 21). *By the numbers: Dropping out of high school.* Accessed at www.pbs.org/wgbh/pages/frontline/education/dropout-nation/by -the-numbers-dropping-out-of-high-school on September 21, 2012.

Bryant, A. (2014, January 4). Management be nimble. *New York Times.* Accessed at www.nytimes.com/2014/01/05/business/management-be-nimble.html?_r=0 on September 10, 2015.

Bryk, A. S., Sebring, P. B., Allensworth, E., Luppescu, S., & Easton, J. Q. (2010). *Organizing schools for improvement: Lessons from Chicago.* Chicago: University of Chicago Press.

Buckingham, M. (2005). *The one thing you need to know . . . about great managing, great leading, and sustained individual success.* New York: Free Press.

Buffum, A., & Mattos, M. (Eds.). (2015). *It's about time: Planning interventions and extensions in elementary school.* Bloomington, IN: Solution Tree Press.

Buffum, A., Mattos, M., & Malone, J. (2018). *Taking action: A handbook for RTI at Work.* Bloomington, IN: Solution Tree Press.

Buffum, A., Mattos, M., & Weber, C. (2009). *Pyramid response to intervention: RTI, professional learning communities, and how to respond when kids don't learn.* Bloomington, IN: Solution Tree Press.

Buffum, A., Mattos, M., & Weber, C. (2012). *Simplifying response to intervention: Four essential guiding principles.* Bloomington, IN: Solution Tree Press.

Buffum, A., Mattos, M., Weber, C., & Hierck, T. (2015). *Uniting academic and behavior interventions: Solving the skill or will dilemma.* Bloomington, IN: Solution Tree Press.

Burns, J. M. (1979). *Leadership.* New York: Harper & Row.

Canadian Assessment for Learning Network. (2019). *Moving assessment forward in strong and wise ways.* Accessed at https://cafln.ca/2019-conference-and-symposium on October 1, 2019.

Canadian Education Association. (2012). *Public survey results.* Accessed at www.edcan.ca/wp-content/uploads/cea-2012-public-survey-results.pdf on November 4, 2019.

Canadians for 21st Century Learning and Intervention. (2015, May). *Shifting minds 3.0: Redefining the learning landscape in Canada.* Accessed at www.c21canada.org /wp-content/uploads/2015/05/C21-ShiftingMinds-3.pdf on October 1, 2019.

Canadian Teachers' Federation. (2004). *Education accountability with a human face.* Accessed at www.ctf-fce.ca/Research-Library/EducationalAccountability _HumanFace_Eng.pdf on October 1, 2019.

Carroll, T. (2007). *Policy brief: The high cost of teacher turnover.* Washington, DC: National Commission on Teaching and America's Future. Accessed at http:// nctaf.org/wp-content/uploads/2012/01/NCTAF-Cost-of-Teacher-Turnover -2007-policy-brief.pdf on December 21, 2015.

Carroll, T. (2009). The next generation of learning teams. *Phi Delta Kappan, 91*(2), 8–13.

Champy, J. (1995). *Reengineering management: The mandate for new leadership.* New York: HarperBusiness.

Chenoweth, K. (2009). It can be done, it's being done, and here's how. *Phi Delta Kappan, 91*(1), 38–43.

Chenoweth, K. (2015). Teachers matter. Yes. Schools matter. Yes. Districts matter— really? *Phi Delta Kappan, 97*(2), 14–20.

Childress, S. M., Doyle, D. P., & Thomas, D. A. (2009). *Leading for equity: The pursuit of excellence in Montgomery County Public Schools.* Cambridge, MA: Harvard Education Press.

Christman, J. B., Neild, R. C., Bulkley, K., Blanc, S., Liu, R., Mitchell, C., et al. (2009, June). *Making the most of interim assessment data: Lessons from Philadelphia.* Philadelphia: Research for Action. Accessed at https://files.eric.ed.gov/fulltext/ED 505863.pdf on December 10, 2019.

Collins, J. (1996). Aligning action and values. *Leader to Leader, 1,* 19–24.

Collins, J. (1999). Aligning actions and values. In F. Hesselbein & P. M. Cohen (Eds.), *Leader to leader: Enduring insights on leadership from the Drucker Foundation's award-winning journal* (pp. 237–266). San Francisco: Jossey-Bass.

Collins, J. (2001). *Good to great: Why some companies make the leap . . . and others don't.* New York: HarperBusiness.

Collins, J. (2009). *How the mighty fall: And why some companies never give in.* New York: HarperBusiness.

Collins, J., & Porras, J. I. (1994). *Built to last: Successful habits of visionary companies.* New York: HarperBusiness.

Conference Board of Canada. (2019). High-school completion. *How Canada Performs.* Accessed at https://www.conferenceboard.ca/hcp/Details/education /high-school-graduation-rate.aspx?AspxAutoDetectCookieSupport=1 on December 17, 2019.

Consortium on Productivity in the Schools. (1995). *Using what we have to get the schools we need.* New York: Teachers College Press.

Conzemius, A., & O'Neill, J. (2014). Handbook for *SMART* school teams: *Revitalizing best practices for collaboration.* Bloomington, IN: Solution Tree Press.

Cotton, K. (2000). *The schooling practices that matter most.* Portland, OR: Northwest Regional Educational Laboratory.

Coughlin, S. (2017, August 2). How Canada became an education superpower. *BBC News.* Accessed at www.bbc.com/news/business-40708421 on October 1, 2019.

Council of Canadians With Disabilities. (2013). *Human rights.* Accessed at www.ccdonline.ca/en/humanrights on October 1, 2019.

Council of Ministers of Education, Canada. (n.d.). *Celebrating 50 years of pan-Canadian leadership in education.* Accessed at www.cmec.ca/299/Education_in_Canada__An_Overview.html on September 13, 2019.

Covey, S. R. (1989). *The seven habits of highly effective people: Powerful lessons in personal change.* New York: Fireside.

Covey, S. R. (2006). *The speed of trust: The one thing that changes everything.* New York: Free Press.

Cree School Board. (2018). *Mission, vision and values.* Accessed at www.cscree.qc.ca/en/our-organization/mission-vision-and-values on October 5, 2019.

Darling-Hammond, L. (1996). What matters most: A competent teacher for every child. *Phi Delta Kappan, 78*(3), 193–200.

Darling-Hammond, L. (2010). *The flat world and education: How America's commitment to equity will determine our future.* New York: Teachers College Press.

D'Auria, J. (2015). Learn to avoid or overcome leadership obstacles. *Phi Delta Kappan, 96*(5), 52–54.

David, J. (2008, October). What research says about pacing guides. *Educational Leadership, 66*(2), 87–88.

Deal, T. E., & Peterson, K. D. (1999). *Shaping school culture: The heart of leadership.* San Francisco: Jossey-Bass.

Dolan, W. P. (1994). *Restructuring our schools: A primer on systemic change.* Kansas City, MO: Systems and Organization.

Dolejs, C. (2006). *Report on key practices and policies of consistently higher performing high schools.* Washington, DC: National High School Center. Accessed at www.betterhighschools.org/docs/ReportOfKeyPracticesandPolicies_10–31–06.pdf on January 10, 2010.

Drucker, P. F. (1992). *Managing for the future: The 1990s and beyond.* New York: Truman Talley Books.

Druskat, V. U., & Wolff, S. B. (2001). Group emotional intelligence and its influence on group effectiveness. In C. Cherniss & D. Goleman (Eds.), *The emotionally intelligent workplace: How to select for, measure, and improve emotional intelligence in individuals, groups, and organizations* (pp. 132–158). San Francisco: Jossey-Bass.

Duffett, A., Farkas, S., Rotherham, A. J., & Silva, E. (2008, May). *Waiting to be won over: Teachers speak on the profession, unions, and reform.* Washington, DC: Education Sector.

DuFour, R. (2002). The learning-centered principal. *Educational Leadership, 59*(8), 12–15.

DuFour, R. (2003). *Through new eyes: Examining the culture of your school* [Video]. Bloomington, IN: Solution Tree Press.

DuFour, R. (2015). *In praise of American educators: And how they can become even better.* Bloomington, IN: Solution Tree Press.

DuFour, R., & DuFour, R. (2012). *The school leader's guide to Professional Learning Communities at Work.* Bloomington, IN: Solution Tree Press.

DuFour, R., DuFour, R., Eaker, R., & Karhanek, G. (2010). *Raising the bar and closing the gap: Whatever it takes.* Bloomington, IN: Solution Tree Press.

DuFour, R., & Eaker, R. (1998). *Professional Learning Communities at Work: Best practices for enhancing student achievement.* Bloomington, IN: Solution Tree Press.

DuFour, R., & Fullan, M. (2013). *Cultures built to last: Systemic PLCs at Work.* Bloomington, IN: Solution Tree Press.

DuFour, R., & Marzano, R. J. (2011). *Leaders of learning: How district, school, and classroom leaders improve student achievement.* Bloomington, IN: Solution Tree Press.

DuFour, R., & Mattos, M. (2013). How do principals really improve schools? *Educational Leadership, 70*(7), 34–40.

Dulaney, S. K., Hallam, P. R., & Wall, G. (2013). Superintendent perceptions of multi-tiered systems of support (MTSS): Obstacles and opportunities for school system reform. *AASA Journal of Scholarship and Practice, 10*(2), 30–45.

Dweck, C. S. (2006). *Mindset: The new psychology of success.* New York: Ballantine Books.

Dweck, C. S. (2007). The perils and promises of praise. *Educational Leadership, 65*(2), 34–39.

Eaker, R., & Keating, J. (2012). *Every school, every team, every classroom: District leadership for growing Professional Learning Communities at Work.* Bloomington, IN: Solution Tree Press.

Eaker, R., & Sales, D. (2016). *A new way: Introducing higher education to Professional Learning Communities at Work.* Bloomington, IN: Solution Tree Press.

Eastwood, K. W., & Louis, K. S. (1992). Restructuring that lasts: Managing the performance dip. *Journal of School Leadership, 2*(2), 212–224.

Edmondson, A. C. (2013, December 17). The three pillars of a teaming culture. *Harvard Business Review.* Accessed at https://hbr.org/2013/12/the-three-pillars -of-a-teaming-culture on November 11, 2015.

Elmore, R. F. (2000). *Building a new structure for school leadership.* Washington, DC: Albert Shanker Institute. Accessed at http://citeseerx.ist.psu.edu/viewdoc /download?doi=10.1.1.103.7688&rep=rep1&type=pdf on January 20, 2010.

Elmore, R. F. (2003). *Knowing the right thing to do: School improvement and performance-based accountability.* Washington, DC: National Governors Association Center for Best Practices.

Elmore, R. F. (2010). "I used to think . . . and now I think . . ." *Harvard Education Letter, 26*(1), 7–8.

Elmore, R. F., & City, E. (2007). The road to school improvement. *Harvard Education Newsletter, 23*(3). Accessed at www.hepg.org/hel/article/229#home on January 15, 2010.

Erkens, C., Schimmer, T., & Vagle, N. D. (2019). *Growing tomorrow's citizens in today's classrooms: Assessing seven critical competencies.* Bloomington, IN: Solution Tree Press.

Erkens, C., & Twadell, E. (2012). *Leading by design: An action framework for PLC at Work leaders.* Bloomington, IN: Solution Tree Press.

Evans, R. (1996). *The human side of school change: Reform, resistance, and the real-life problems of innovation.* San Francisco: Jossey-Bass.

Farbman, D. A., Goldberg, D. J., & Miller, T. D. (2014, January). *Redesigning and expanding school time to support Common Core implementation.* Washington, DC: Center for American Progress. Accessed at https://cdn.americanprogress.org /wp-content/uploads/2014/01/CommonCore-reprint.pdf on October 20, 2015.

Ferlazzo, L. (2014, November 29). *Response: Formative assessments are powerful* [Blog post]. Accessed at http://blogs.edweek.org/teachers/classroom_qa_with_larry _ferlazzo/2014/11/response_formative_assessments_ are_powerful.html on April 11, 2015.

First Nations Schools Association of British Columbia. (n.d.). *About First Nations School Professional Learning Communities.* Accessed at www.fnsa.ca/programs/plc on October 5, 2019.

Fullan, M. (2001). *Leading in a culture of change.* San Francisco: Jossey-Bass.

Fullan, M. (2005). *Leadership and sustainability: System thinkers in action.* Thousand Oaks, CA: Corwin Press.

Fullan, M. (2007). *The new meaning of educational change* (4th ed.). New York: Teachers College Press.

Fullan, M. (2008). *The six secrets of change: What the best leaders do to help their organizations survive and thrive.* San Francisco: Jossey-Bass.

Fullan, M. (2010). *Motion leadership: The skinny on becoming change savvy.* Thousand Oaks, CA: Corwin Press.

Fullan, M. (2011). *The moral imperative realized.* Thousand Oaks, CA: Corwin Press.

Fullan, M. (2014). *The principal: Three keys to maximizing impact.* San Francisco: Jossey-Bass.

Fullan, M., & Quinn, J. (2016). *Coherence: The* right *drivers in action for schools, districts, and systems.* Thousand Oaks, CA: Corwin Press.

Fulton, K., & Britton, T. (2011, June). *STEM teachers in professional learning communities: From good teachers to great teaching.* Washington, DC: National Commission on Teaching and America's Future.

Fulton, K., Yoon, I., & Lee, C. (2005, August). *Induction into learning communities.* Washington, DC: National Commission on Teaching and America's Future. Accessed at www.nctaf.org/documents/NCTAF_Induction_Paper_2005.pdf on January 10, 2010.

Gabriel, J. G., & Farmer, P. C. (2009). *How to help your school thrive without breaking the bank.* Alexandria, VA: Association for Supervision and Curriculum Development.

Gallimore, R., Ermeling, B. A., Saunders, W. M., & Goldenberg, C. (2009). Moving the learning of teaching closer to practice: Teacher education implications of school-based inquiry teams. *Elementary School Journal, 109*(5), 537–553.

Gardner, H. (2004). *Changing minds: The art and science of changing our own and other people's minds.* Boston: Harvard Business School Press.

Garmston, R. J. (2007). Results-oriented agendas transform meetings into valuable collaborative events. *Journal of Staff Development, 28*(2), 55–56.

Georgiades, W., Fuentes, E., & Snyder, K. (1983). *A meta-analysis of productive school cultures.* Houston, TX: University of Texas.

Goldberg, M., & Cross, C. T. (2005). *Time out.* Edutopia. Accessed at http://email.e-mailnetworks.com/ct/ct.php?t=1018842&c=561784071&m=m&type=3 on August 18, 2005.

Goldring, E., Porter, A. C., Murphy, J., Elliott, S. N., & Cravens, X. (2007, March). *Assessing learning-centered leadership: Connections to research, professional standards, and current practices.* New York: Wallace Foundation. Accessed at https://wallacefoundation.org/knowledge-center/Documents/Assessing-Learning-Centered-Leadership.pdf on December 10, 2019.

Goldsmith, M. (1996). Ask, learn, follow up, and grow. In F. Hesselbein, M. Goldsmith, & R. Beckhard (Eds.), *The leader of the future: New visions, strategies, and practices for the next era* (pp. 227–237). San Francisco: Jossey-Bass.

Goleman, D. (1998). *Working with emotional intelligence.* New York: Bantam Books.

Goleman, D., Boyatzis, R., & McKee, A. (2004). *Primal leadership: Learning to lead with emotional intelligence.* Boston: Harvard Business Review Press.

Good, T. L., & Brophy, J. E. (2002). *Looking in classrooms* (9th ed.). Boston: Allyn & Bacon.

Goodwin, B. (2012). Research says / New teachers face three common challenges. *Educational Leadership, 69*(8), 84–85.

Government of New Brunswick. (2013) *Department of Education and Early Childhood Development: Policy 322—Inclusive education.* Accessed at www2.gnb.ca/content/dam/gnb/Departments/ed/pdf/K12/policies-politiques/e/322A.pdf on October 1, 2019.

Grenny, J., Patterson, K., Maxfield, D., McMillan, R., & Switzler, A. (2013). *Influencer: The new science of leading change* (2nd ed.). New York: McGraw-Hill.

Grissom, J. A., Loeb, S., & Master, B. (2013). Effective instructional time use for school leaders: Longitudinal evidence from observations of principals. *Educational Researcher, 42*(8). Accessed at https://cepa.stanford.edu/sites/default/files/grissom%20loeb%20%26%20master%20instructional%20time%20use_0.pdf on December 21, 2015.

Guskey, T. R. (2014). Planning professional learning. *Educational Leadership, 71*(8). Accessed at www.ascd.org/publications/educational-leadership/may14/vol71/num08/Planning-Professional-Learning.aspx on December 21, 2015.

Halvorson, G. C. (2014). Getting to "us." *Harvard Business Review, 92*(9), 38.

Hamel, G. (2002). *Leading the revolution: How to thrive in turbulent times by making innovation a way of life.* Boston: Harvard Business School Press.

Hargreaves, A., & Fullan, M. (2012). *Professional capital: Transforming teaching in every school.* New York: Teachers College Press.

Hattie, J. (2009). *Visible learning: A synthesis of over 800 meta-analyses relating to achievement.* New York: Routledge.

Hattie, J. (2012). *Visible learning for teachers: Maximizing impact on learning.* New York: Routledge.

Hattie, J. (2015a, October 28). *The effective use of testing: What the research says.* Accessed at www.edweek.org/ew/articles/2015/10/28/we-arent-using -assessments-correctly.html on November 17, 2015.

Hattie, J. (2015b, June). *What works best in education: The politics of collaborative expertise.* London: Pearson. Accessed at www.pearson.com/content/dam /corporate/global/pearson-dot-com/files/hattie/150526_ExpertiseWEB_V1.pdf on September 30, 2015.

Heath, C., & Heath, D. (2010). *Switch: How to change things when change is hard.* New York: Broadway Books.

Herman, J., & Linn, R. (2013). *On the road to assessing deeper learning: The status of Smarter Balanced and PARCC assessment consortia* (CREST Report 823). Los Angeles: University of California's National Center for Research on Evaluation, Standards, and Student Testing.

Hirsch, E. D., Jr. (1996). *The schools we need and why we don't have them.* New York: Doubleday.

Inclusive Education Canada. (2017). *What is inclusive education?* Accessed at https://inclusiveeducation.ca/about/what-is-ie on November 4, 2019.

Individuals with Disabilities Education Act (IDEIA) 20 U.S.C. §§ 1400 *et. seq.* (2004).

Ingersoll, R. M., & Merrill, L. (2012, November). *Seven trends: The transformation of the teaching force.* Philadelphia: Consortium for Policy Research in Education. Accessed at https://researchgate.net/publication/304049650_Seven_Trends_The _Transformation_of_the_Teaching_Force on December 10, 2019.

Institute for Education Leadership. (2013, September). *The Ontario leadership framework: A school and system leader's guide to putting Ontario's leadership framework into action.* Accessed at www.education-leadership-ontario.ca /application/files/8814/9452/4183/Ontario_Leadership_Framework_OLF.pdf on November 4, 2019.

Jacobs, H. H. (2001). New trends in curriculum: An interview with Heidi Hayes Jacobs. *Independent School, 61*(1), 18–22.

Johnson, S. M., & Kardos, S. M. (2004). Professional culture and the promise of colleagues. In S. M. Johnson (Ed.), *Finders and keepers: Helping new teachers survive and thrive in our schools* (pp. 139–166). San Francisco: Jossey-Bass.

Kanold, T. D. (2006). The continuous improvement wheel of a professional learning community. *Journal of Staff Development, 27*(2), 16–21.

Kanold, T. D. (2011). *The five disciplines of PLC leaders.* Bloomington, IN: Solution Tree Press.

Kanter, R. M. (1999). The enduring skills of change leaders. *Leader to Leader, 13,* 15–22.

Kanter, R. M. (2004). *Confidence: How winning streaks and losing streaks begin and end.* New York: Crown Business.

Kanter, R. M. (2005). How leaders gain (and lose) confidence. *Leader to Leader, 35,* 21–27.

Katzenbach, J. R., & Smith, D. K. (1993). *The wisdom of teams: Creating the high-performance organization.* Boston: Harvard Business School Press.

Kaye, B., & Jordan-Evans, S. (2014). *Love 'em or lose 'em: Getting good people to stay* (5th ed.). San Francisco: Berrett-Koehler.

Kegan, R., & Lahey, L. L. (2001). *How the way we talk can change the way we work: Seven languages for transformation.* San Francisco: Jossey-Bass.

Kotter International. (2015). *Eight steps to accelerate change in 2015.* Accessed at www.kotterinternational.com/ebook/Kotter-8-steps-ebook.pdf on January 26, 2016.

Kotter, J. P. (1996). *Leading change.* Boston: Harvard Business School Press.

Kotter, J. P. (2012). *Leading change.* Boston: Harvard Business Review.

Kotter, J. P., & Cohen, D. S. (2002). *The heart of change: Real-life stories of how people change their organizations.* Boston: Harvard Business School Press.

Kouzes, J. M., & Posner, B. Z. (1987). *The leadership challenge: How to get extraordinary things done in organizations.* San Francisco: Jossey-Bass.

Kouzes, J. M., & Posner, B. Z. (2003). *Encouraging the heart: A leader's guide to rewarding and recognizing others.* San Francisco: Jossey-Bass.

Kouzes, J. M., & Posner, B. Z. (2006). *A leader's legacy.* San Francisco: Jossey-Bass.

Kramer, S. V. (2015). *How to leverage PLCs for school improvement.* Bloomington, IN: Solution Tree Press.

Kruse, S., Louis, K. S., & Bryk, A. (1994). *Building professional community in schools.* Madison, WI: Center on Organization and Restructuring of Schools.

Larner, M. (2007). *Tools for leaders: Indispensable graphic organizers, protocols, and planning guidelines for working and learning together.* New York: Scholastic.

Learning Disabilities Association of Canada. (2017). *Prevalence of learning disablilities.* Accessed at https://ldac-acte.ca/prevalence-of-learning-disabilities on November 4, 2019.

Leithwood, K., Louis, K. S., Anderson, S., & Wahlstrom, K. (2004). *How leadership influences student learning.* New York: Wallace Foundation.

Leithwood, K., Louis, K. S., Wahlstrom, K., Anderson, S., Mascall, B., Michlin, M., et al. (2009). *Learning from district efforts to improve student achievement.* New York: Wallace Foundation.

Lencioni, P. (2003). The trouble with teamwork. *Leader to Leader, 29*, 35–40.

Lencioni, P. (2005). *Overcoming the five dysfunctions of a team: A field guide for leaders, managers, and facilitators.* San Francisco: Jossey-Bass.

Lencioni, P. (2012). *The advantage: Why organizational health trumps everything else in business.* San Francisco: Jossey-Bass.

Lezotte, L. W. (1991). *Correlates of effective schools: The first and second generation.* Okemos, MI: Effective Schools Products. Accessed at www.effectiveschools.com/Correlates.pdf on January 6, 2006.

Lezotte, L. W. (2002). *Revolutionary and evolutionary: The effective schools movement.* Accessed at www.effectiveschools.com/images/stories/RevEv.pdf on January 10, 2010.

Lezotte, L. W. (2005). More effective schools: Professional learning communities in action. In R. DuFour, R. Eaker, & R. DuFour (Eds.), *On common ground: The power of professional learning communities* (pp. 177–191). Bloomington, IN: Solution Tree Press.

Lezotte, L. W. (2011). Effective schools: Past, present, and future. *Journal of Effective Schools, 10*(1), 3–21.

Lieberman, A. (1995). Restructuring schools: The dynamics of changing practice, structure, and culture. In A. Lieberman (Ed.), *The work of restructuring schools: Building from the ground up* (pp. 1–17). New York: Teachers College Press.

Little, J. W. (2006, December). *Professional community and professional development in the learning-centered school.* Washington, DC: National Education Association. Accessed at www.nea.org/assets/docs/mf_pdreport.pdf on January 18, 2010.

Looney, J. (2005). *Formative assessment: Improving learning in secondary classrooms.* Paris: Organisation for Economic Co-operation and Development.

Louis, K. S., Kruse, S. D., & Marks, H. M. (1996). Schoolwide professional community. In F. M. Newmann & Associates (Eds.), *Authentic achievement: Restructuring schools for intellectual quality* (pp. 179–204). San Francisco: Jossey-Bass.

Louis, K. S., Leithwood, K., Wahlstrom, K. L., & Anderson, S. E. (2010, July). *Investigating the links to improved student learning: Final report of research findings.* New York: Wallace Foundation.

Lucie and André Chagnon Foundation. (n.d.). *Project CAR (collaborer, apprendre, réussir).* Accessed at https://fondationchagnon.org/initiatives-soutenues/reseaux /projet-car on November 8, 2019.

Manna, P. (2015). *Developing excellent school principals to advance teaching and learning: Considerations for state policy.* New York: Wallace Foundation. Accessed at www.wallacefoundation.org/knowledge-center/school-leadership/state-policy /Documents/Developing-Excellent-School-Principals.pdf on October 10, 2015.

Many, T. W., & Sparks-Many, S. K. (2015). *Leverage: Using PLCs to promote lasting improvement in schools.* Thousand Oaks, CA: Corwin Press.

Marchildon, J. (2017). *How Canada has quietly risen to the top of international rankings for education.* Accessed at https://globalcitizen.org/en/content/canada-international -education/ on October 5, 2019.

Markow, D., Macia, L., & Lee, H. (2013, February). *The Metlife survey of the American teacher: Challenges for school leadership.* New York: MetLife. Accessed at www.metlife.com/assets/cao/foundation/MetLife-Teacher-Survey-2012.pdf on December 8, 2015.

Markow, D., & Pieters, A. (2010, April). *The Metlife survey of the American teacher: Collaborating for student success.* New York: MetLife. Accessed at http://files.eric .ed.gov/fulltext/ED509650.pdf on December 15, 2015.

Marshall, K. (2015). How principals can reshape the teaching bell curve. *Journal of Staff Development, 36*(4), 34–37.

Martin, M., Mullis, I., Foy, P., & Stanco, G. (2012). TIMSS international results in science. Amsterdam: International Association for the Evaluation or Educational Achievement. Accessed at http://timssandpirls.bc.edu/timss2011/downloads/T11 _IR_Science_FullBook.pdf on January 27, 2016.

Marzano, R. J. (2003). *What works in schools: Translating research into action.* Alexandria, VA: Association for Supervision and Curriculum Development.

Marzano, R. J. (2006). *Classroom assessment and grading that work.* Alexandria, VA: Association for Supervision and Curriculum Development.

Marzano, R. J. (2009). Setting the record straight on "high-yield" strategies. *Phi Delta Kappan, 91*(1), 30–37.

Marzano, R. J. (2010). When students track their progress. *Health and Learning, 67*(4), 86–87.

Marzano, R. J., Warrick, P. B., & Simms, J. A. (2014). *A handbook for high reliability schools: The next step in school reform.* Bloomington, IN: Marzano Resources.

Marzano, R. J., & Waters, T. (2009). *District leadership that works: Striking the right balance.* Bloomington, IN: Solution Tree Press.

Marzano, R. J., Waters, T., & McNulty, B. A. (2005). *School leadership that works: From research to results.* Alexandria, VA: Association for Supervision and Curriculum Development.

Mattos, M., & Buffum, A. (Eds.). (2015). *It's about time: Planning interventions and extensions in secondary school.* Bloomington, IN: Solution Tree Press.

Mattos, M., DuFour, R., DuFour, R., Eaker, R., & Many, T. W. (2016). *Concise answers to frequently asked questions about Professional Learning Communities at Work.* Bloomington, IN: Solution Tree Press.

McDonald, J. P., Mohr, N., Dichter, A., & McDonald, E. C. (2007). *The power of protocols: An educator's guide to better practice* (2nd ed.). New York: Teachers College Press.

McLaughlin, M. W., & Talbert, J. E. (2006). *Building school-based teacher learning communities: Professional strategies to improve student achievement.* New York: Teachers College Press.

McLuhan, M. (1994). *Understanding media: The extensions of man.* Cambridge, MA: MIT Press.

Mehta, J. (2014, July 16). *Five inconvenient truths for reformers* [Blog post]. Accessed at http://blogs.edweek.org/edweek/learning_deeply/2014/07/five_inconvenient _truths_for_reformers.html on December 20, 2014.

Mintzberg, H. (1994). *The rise and fall of strategic planning.* New York: Free Press.

Mourshed, M., Chijioke, C., & Barber, M. (2010, November). *How the world's most improved school systems keep getting better.* New York: McKinsey & Company. Accessed at www.mckinsey.com/~/media/mckinsey/dotcom/client_service/social %20sector/pdfs/how-the-worlds-most-improved-school-systems-keep-getting -better_download-version_final.ashx on December 17, 2015.

Muhammad, A., & Hollie, S. (2012). *The will to lead, the skill to teach: Transforming schools at every level.* Bloomington, IN: Solution Tree Press.

Mullis, I., Martin, M., Foy, P., & Arora, A. (2012). TIMSS 2011 results in mathematics. Amsterdam: International Association for the Evaluation of Educational Achievement. Accessed at http://timssandpirls.bc.edu/timss2011/downloads/T11_IR_Mathematics_FullBook.pdf on January 26, 2016.

Nanus, B. (1992). *Visionary leadership*. San Francisco: Jossey-Bass.

National Association of Secondary School Principals & National Association of Elementary School Principals. (2013). *Leadership matters: What the research says about the importance of principal leadership*. Alexandria, VA: National Association of Elementary School Principals.

National Center for Educational Achievement. (2009, January). *Core practices in math and science: An investigation of consistently higher performing school systems in five states*. www.act.org/content/dam/act/unsecured/documents/NCEA-core_practices _in_math_and_science-01-01-09.pdf on December 3, 2019.

National Center on Response to Intervention. (2008, May 12). *What is response to intervention?* [Webinar]. Accessed at www.rti4success.org/index. php?option=com_content&task=blogcategory&id=22&Itemid=79 on January 18, 2010.

National Commission on Teaching and America's Future. (2003, January). *No dream denied: A pledge to America's children*. Washington, DC: Author.

National Governors Association Center for Best Practices & Council of Chief State School Officers. (2008). *Benchmarking for success: Ensuring U.S. students receive a world-class education*. Washington, DC: Author. Accessed at www.achieve.org /files/BenchmarkingforSuccess.pdf on December 17, 2015.

National Governors Association Center for Best Practices & Council of Chief State School Officers. (2010a). *Common Core State Standards for English language arts and literacy in history/social studies, science, and technical subjects*. Washington, DC: Authors. Accessed at www.corestandards.org/assets/CCSSI_ELA%20 Standards.pdf on March 10, 2015.

National Governors Association Center for Best Practices & Council of Chief State School Officers. (2010b). *Common Core State Standards for mathematics*. Washington, DC: Authors. Accessed at www.corestandards.org/assets/CCSSI _Math%20Standards.pdf on December 10, 2019.

National Policy Board for Educational Administration. (2015). *Policy standards for educational leaders*. Reston, VA. Accessed at www.ccsso.org/Documents/2015 /ProfessionalStandardsforEducationalLeaders2015forNPBEAFINAL.pdf on January 24, 2016.

National Turning Points Center. (2001). *Turning points: Guide to collaborative culture and shared leadership*. Boston: Author.

New Teacher Project. (2015). *The mirage: Confronting the hard truth about our quest for teacher development*. Accessed at http://tntp.org/assets/documents /TNTP-Mirage_2015.pdf on January 26, 2016.

Newmann, F. M., & Wehlage, G. G. (1995). *Successful school restructuring: A report to the public and educators*. Madison, WI: Center on Organization and Restructuring of Schools.

Newmann, F. M., & Wehlage, G. G. (1996). Conclusion: Restructuring for authentic student achievement. In F. M. Newmann & Associates (Eds.), *Authentic achievement: Restructuring schools for intellectual quality* (pp. 286–301). San Francisco: Jossey-Bass.

Odden, A. R., & Archibald, S. J. (2009). *Doubling student performance . . . and finding the resources to do it.* Thousand Oaks, CA: Corwin Press.

O'Hora, D., & Maglieri, K. A. (2006). Goal statements and goal-directed behavior: A relational frame account of goal setting in organizations. *Journal of Organizational Behavior Management, 26*(1), 131–170.

Ontario Principals' Council. (2017). *Ontario Principals' Council International Symposium white paper: Principal work-life balance and well-being matters.* Accessed at https://www.edu.uwo.ca/faculty-profiles/docs/other/pollock /PrincipalWellBeing-17-FINAL-with-Acknowledgement-1.pdf on December 3, 2019.

Oreopoulos, P. (2005). *Canadian compulsory school laws and their impact on educational attainment and future earnings.* Accessed at https://www150.statcan .gc.ca/n1/en/catalogue/11F0019M2005251 on December 3, 2019.

Organisation for Economic Co-operation and Development. (2009, December). *21st century skills and competencies for new millennium learners in OECD countries* (Working Paper No. 41). Paris: Author. Accessed at www.oecd.org /officialdocuments/publicdisplaydocumentpdf/?cote=EDU/WKP(2009)20 &doclanguage=en on February 14, 2015.

Organisation for Economic Co-operation and Development. (2012). *Equity and quality in education: Supporting disadvantaged students and schools.* Accessed at www.oecd.org/education/school/50293148.pdf on November 4, 2019.

Organisation for Economic Co-operation and Development. (2014). *Education at a glance: Country note—United States.* Paris: Author. Accessed at www.oecd.org /edu/United%20States-EAG2014-Country-Note.pdf on December 13, 2015.

Organisation for Economic Co-operation and Development. (2018). *PISA 2015: Results in focus.* Accessed at www.oecd.org/pisa/pisa-2015-results-in-focus.pdf on October 5, 2019.

Patterson, K., Grenny, J., Maxfield, D., McMillan, R., & Switzler, A. (2008). *Influencer: The power to change anything.* New York: McGraw-Hill.

Patterson, K., Grenny, J., Maxfield, D., McMillan, R., & Switzler, A. (2013). *Crucial accountability: Tools for resolving violated expectations, broken commitments, and bad behavior* (2nd ed.). New York: McGraw-Hill.

Patterson, K., Grenny, J., McMillan, R., & Switzler, A. (2002). *Crucial conversations: Tools for talking when stakes are high.* New York: McGraw-Hill.

Pellegrino, J. W., & Hilton, M. L. (Eds.). (2012). *Education for life and work: Developing transferable knowledge and skills in the 21st century.* Washington, DC: National Academies Press.

Perkins, D. (2003). *King Arthur's round table: How collaborative conversations create smart organizations.* New York: Wiley.

Peters, T. (1987). *Thriving on chaos: A handbook for a management revolution.* New York: Knopf.

Peters, T., & Austin, N. (1985). *A passion for excellence: The leadership difference.* New York: Random House.

Pfeffer, J., & Sutton, R. I. (2000). *The knowing-doing gap: How smart companies turn knowledge into action.* Boston: Harvard Business School Press.

Pfeffer, J., & Sutton, R. I. (2006). *Hard facts, dangerous half-truths and total nonsense: Profiting from evidence-based management.* Boston: Harvard Business School Press.

Phi Delta Kappan/Gallup Poll. (2014). *Archive of responses regarding quality of education.* Accessed at www.pdkmembers.org/members_online/publications /GallupPoll/k_q_quality_1.htm#519 on January 25, 2016.

Phi Delta Kappan/Gallup Poll. (2015). Testing doesn't measure up for Americans: The 47th annual PDK/Gallup poll of the public's attitudes toward the public schools. *Phi Delta Kappan, 97*(1), k1–k32.

Pinchot, G., & Pinchot, E. (1993). *The end of bureaucracy and the rise of the intelligent organization.* San Francisco: Berrett-Koehler.

Pink, D. H. (2011). *Drive: The surprising truth about what motivates us.* New York: Riverhead Books.

Popham, W. J. (2008). *Transformative assessment.* Alexandria, VA: Association for Supervision and Curriculum Development.

Popham, W. J. (2009). Curriculum mistakes to avoid. *American School Board Journal, 196*(11), 36–38.

Popham, W. J. (2013). Formative assessment's "advocatable moment." *Education Week, 32*(15), 29.

President's Commission on Excellence in Special Education. (2002, July). *A new era: Revitalizing special education for children and their families.* Washington, DC: U.S. Department of Education Office of Special Education and Rehabilitative Services. Accessed at http://ectacenter.org/~pdfs/calls/2010/earlypartc/revitalizing _special_education.pdf on December 17, 2015.

Purkey, S. C., & Smith, M. S. (1983). Effective schools: A review. *Elementary School Journal, 83*(4), 427–452.

Quate, S. (n.d.). *Conductive conversations leading to results using protocols and structures in professional learning communities.* Denver, CO: University of Colorado Denver School of Education.

Ragland, M. A., Clubine, B., Constable, D., & Smith, P. A. (2002, April). *Expecting success: A study of five high performing, high poverty schools.* Washington, DC: Council of Chief State School Officers.

Rand Corporation (n.d.). *Teachers matter: Understanding teachers' impact on student achievement.* Accessed at www.rand.org/pubs/corporate_pubs/CP693z1-2012 -09.html on January 26, 2016.

Raue, K., & Gray, L. (2015, September). *Career paths of beginning public school teachers: Results from the first through fifth waves on the 2007–08 beginning teacher longitudinal study* (NCES 2015-196). Washington, DC: National Center for Education Statistics. Accessed at http://nces.ed.gov/pubs2015/2015196.pdf on October 10, 2015.

Reeves, D. B. (2002). *The leader's guide to standards: A blueprint for educational equity and excellence*. San Francisco: Jossey-Bass.

Reeves, D. B. (2004). *Accountability for learning: How teachers and school leaders can take charge*. Alexandria, VA: Association for Supervision and Curriculum Development.

Reeves, D. B. (2005). Putting it all together: Standards, assessment, and accountability in successful professional learning communities. In R. DuFour, R. Eaker, & R. DuFour (Eds.), *On common ground: The power of professional learning communities* (pp. 45–63). Bloomington, IN: Solution Tree Press.

Reeves, D. B. (2006). *The learning leader: How to focus school improvement for better results*. Alexandria, VA: Association for Supervision and Curriculum Development.

Reeves, D. B. (2009). *Leading change in your school: How to conquer myths, build commitment, and get results*. Alexandria, VA: Association for Supervision and Curriculum Development.

Reeves, D. B. (2015). *Inspiring creativity and innovation in K–12*. Bloomington, IN: Solution Tree Press.

Rice, J. K. (2010, August). *The impact of teacher experience: Examining the evidence and policy implications* (Brief No. 11). Washington, DC: National Center for Analysis of Longitudinal Data in Education Research. Accessed at www.urban.org/uploadedpdf/1001455-impact-teacher-experience.pdf on March 21, 2015.

Riggs, L. (2013, October 18). Why do teachers quit? And why do they stay? *Atlantic*. Accessed at https://theatlantic.com/education/archive/2013/10/why-do-teachers-quit/280699 on December 10, 2019.

Robinson, M. A. (2010, November). *School perspectives on collaborative inquiry: Lessons learned from New York City, 2009–2010*. Philadelphia: Consortium for Policy Research in Education.

Saphier, J. (2005). *John Adams' promise: How to have good schools for all our children, not just for some*. Acton, MA: Research for Better Teaching.

Saphier, J., King, M., & D'Auria, J. (2006). 3 strands form strong school leadership. *Journal of Staff Development, 27*(2), 51–57.

Sarason, S. B. (1996). *Revisiting "the culture of the school and the problem of change."* New York: Teachers College Press.

Schaffer, R. H., & Thomson, H. A. (1992). Successful change programs begin with results. *Harvard Business Review, 70*(1), 80–89.

Schein, E. H. (1996). Leadership and organizational culture. In F. Hesselbein, M. Goldsmith, & R. Beckhard (Eds.), *The leader of the future: New visions, strategies, and practices for the next era* (pp. 59–69). San Francisco: Jossey-Bass.

Schlechty, P. C. (2009). *Leading for learning: How to transform schools into learning organizations*. San Francisco: Jossey-Bass.

Schmoker, M. (2004a). Learning communities at the crossroads: A response to Joyce and Cook. *Phi Delta Kappan, 86*(1), 84–89.

Schmoker, M. (2004b). Start here for improving teaching. *School Administrator, 61*(10), 48.

Schmoker, M. (2006). *Results now: How we can achieve unprecedented improvements in teaching and learning*. Alexandria, VA: Association for Supervision and Curriculum Development.

School Leaders Network. (2014). *CHURN: The high cost of principal turnover*. Accessed at https://connectleadsucceed.org/sites/default/files/principal_turnover _cost.pdf on November 20, 2015.

Schwartz, T., & Porath, C. (2014, May 30). Why you hate work. *New York Times*. Accessed at www.nytimes.com/2014/06/01/opinion/sunday/why-you-hate-work .html on December 15, 2015.

Senge, P., Ross, R., Smith, B., Roberts, C., & Kleiner, A. (1994). *The fifth discipline fieldbook: Strategies and tools for building a learning organization*. New York: Doubleday.

Shannon, G. S., & Bylsma, P. (2004, October). *Characteristics of improved school districts: Themes from research*. Olympia, WA: Office of Superintendent of Public Instruction.

Smith, W. R. (2015). *How to launch PLCs in your district*. Bloomington, IN: Solution Tree Press.

Southern Regional Education Board. (2000). *Things that matter most in improving student learning*. Atlanta, GA: Author.

Sparks, D. (2007). *Leading for results: Transforming teaching, learning, and relationships in schools* (2nd ed.). Thousand Oaks, CA: Corwin Press.

Spiller, J., & Power, K. (2019). *Leading with intention: Eight areas for reflection and planning in your PLC at Work*. Bloomington, IN: Solution Tree Press.

Statistics Canada. (2013). *The educational attainment of Aboriginal peoples in Canada*. Accessed at www12.statcan.gc.ca/nhs-enm/2011/as-sa/99-012-x/99-012-x201 1003_3-eng.pdf on November 4, 2019.

Statistics Canada. (2016). *Data products, 2016 census*. Accessed at www12.statcan .gc.ca/census-recensement/2016/dp-pd/index-eng.cfm on October 5, 2019.

Statistics Canada. (2017). *Education indicators in Canada: An international perspective 2017*. Accessed at www150.statcan.gc.ca/n1/pub/81-604-x/81-604-x2017001 -eng.htm on November 4, 2019.

Statistics Canada. (2019). *Education indicators in Canada: Report of the Pan-Canadian Education Indicators Program*. Accessed at www150.statcan.gc.ca/n1 /en/catalogue/81-582-X on November 4, 2019.

Stevenson, H. W., & Stigler, J. W. (1992). *The learning gap: Why our schools are failing and what we can learn from Japanese and Chinese education*. New York: Touchstone.

Stiggins, R. (1999). Assessment, student confidence, and school success. *Phi Delta Kappan, 81*(3), 191–198.

Stiggins, R. (2004). New assessment beliefs for a new school mission. *Phi Delta Kappan, 86*(1), 22–27.

Stiggins, R. (2005). Assessment FOR learning: Building a culture of confident learners. In R. DuFour, R. Eaker, & R. DuFour (Eds.), *On common ground: The power of professional learning communities* (pp. 65–83). Bloomington, IN: Solution Tree Press.

Stiggins, R., & DuFour, R. (2009). Maximizing the power of formative assessments. *Phi Delta Kappan, 90*(9), 640–644.

Stigler, J. W., & Hiebert, J. (2009). Closing the teaching gap. *Phi Delta Kappan, 91*(3), 32–37.

Stone, D., Patton, B., & Heen, S. (2000). *Difficult conversations: How to discuss what matters most.* New York: Penguin.

Tavernise, S. (2012, February 9). Education gap grows between rich and poor, studies say. *New York Times.* Accessed at https://www.nytimes.com/2012/02/10/education/education-gap-grows-between-rich-and-poor-studies-show.html?mtrref=www.google.com&gwh=5FFDD5CA9A83776F77B4959CC642E8DE&gwt=pay&assetType=REGIWALL on December 3, 2019.

Thompson, J. W. (1995). The renaissance of learning in business. In S. Chawla & J. Renesch (Eds.), *Learning organizations: Developing cultures for tomorrow's workplace* (pp. 85–100). New York: Productivity Press.

Tichy, N. M. (1997). *The leadership engine: How winning companies build leaders at every level.* New York: HarperBusiness.

Tomlinson, C. A., & McTighe, J. (2006). *Integrating differentiated instruction and understanding by design.* Alexandria, VA: Association for Supervision and Curriculum Development.

Trujillo, T. (2013). The reincarnation of the effective schools research: Rethinking the literature on district effectiveness. *Journal of Educational Administration, 51*(4), 426–452.

Tucker, M. S. (2014). *Fixing our national accountability system.* Washington, DC: National Center for Education and the Economy. Accessed at www.ncee.org/wp-content/uploads/2014/08/FixingOurNationalAccountabilitySystemWebV4.pdf on December 17, 2015.

UNICEF. (2019). *Every child learns: UNICEF education strategy 2019–2030.* New York: Author. Accessed at https://www.unicef.org/media/59856/file/UNICEF-education-strategy-2019-2030.pdf on December 17, 2019.

United Nation's Children's Fund. (2019, April). *A world ready to learn: Prioritizing quality early childhood education.* New York: Author. Accessed at https://unicef.org/media/57926/file/A-world-ready-to-learn-advocacy-brief-2019.pdf on December 3, 2019.

Vagle, N. D. (2015). *Design in five: Essential phases to create engaging assessment practice.* Bloomington, IN: Solution Tree Press.

Vander Ark, T., & Schneider, C. (2012). *Deeper learning: For every student every day.* Menlo Park, CA: Hewlett Foundation. Accessed at http://cdno.gettingsmart.com/wp-content/uploads/2013/12/DLForEveryStudent_FINAL.pdf on December 21, 2015.

Wagner, T. (2007, August 14). Five "habits of mind" that count. *Education Week.* Accessed at www.edweek.org/ew/articles/2007/08/15/45wagner.h26.html on November 11, 2015.

Wallace Foundation. (2012, January). *The school principal as leader: Guiding schools to better teaching and learning.* New York: Author. Accessed at www.wallacefoundation.org/knowledge-center/school-leadership/effective-principal-leadership/Documents/The-School-Principal-as-Leader-Guiding-Schools-to-Better-Teaching-and-Learning.pdf on January 7, 2012.

Watlington, E., Shockley, R., Guglielmino, P., & Felsher, R. (2010). The high cost of leaving: An analysis of the cost of teacher turnover. *Journal of Education Finance, 36*(1), 22–37.

Wei, R. C., Darling-Hammond, L., Andree, A., Richardson, N., & Orphanos, S. (2009, February). *Professional learning in the learning profession: A status report on teacher development in the U.S. and abroad.* Dallas, TX: National Staff Development Council.

Weisberg, D., Sexton, S., Mulhern, J., & Keeling, D. (2009, June). *The widget effect: Our national failure to acknowledge and act on differences in teacher effectiveness.* New York: New Teacher Project: Accessed at http://widgeteffect.org/downloads /thewidgeteffect_execsummary.pdf on January 10, 2010.

WestEd. (2000). *Teachers who learn, kids who achieve: A look at schools with model professional development.* San Francisco: Author.

Wheatley, M. (1999). Goodbye, command and control. In F. Hesselbein & P. M. Cohen (Eds.), *Leader to leader: Enduring insights on leadership from the Drucker Foundation's award-winning journal* (pp. 151–162). San Francisco: Jossey-Bass.

Wheelis, A. (1973). *How people change.* New York: Harper & Row.

White, K. (2017a). *Softening the edges: Assessment practices that honor K–12 teachers and learners.* Bloomington, IN: Solution Tree Press.

White, K. (2017b, February 16). *The unbreakable bond: Assessment and instruction* [Blog post]. Accessed at https://allthingsassessment.info/2017/02/16/the -unbreakable-bond-assessment-and-instruction on October 1, 2019.

Wiggins, G. (2012, January 4). *On pacing guides.* Accessed at https://grantwiggins .wordpress.com/2012/01/04/on-pacing-guides on January 24, 2016.

Wiliam, D. (2007). Content then process: Teacher learning communities in the service of formative assessment. In D. Reeves (Ed.), *Ahead of the curve: The power of assessment to transform teaching and learning* (pp. 183–204). Bloomington, IN: Solution Tree Press.

Wiliam, D. (2011). *Embedded formative assessment.* Bloomington, IN: Solution Tree Press.

Wiliam, D., & Thompson, M. (2007). Integrating assessment with instruction: What will it take to make it work? In C. A. Dwyer (Ed.), *The future of assessment: Shaping teaching and learning* (pp. 53–82). Mahwah, NJ: Erlbaum.

Williams, K. C., & Hierck, T. (2015). *Starting a movement: Building culture from the inside out in professional learning communities.* Bloomington, IN: Solution Tree Press.

Williams, T., Perry, M., Studier, C., Brazil, N., Kirst, M., Haertel, E., et al. (2005). *Similar students, different results: Why do some schools do better?* Mountain View, CA: EdSource.

World Population Review. (2019). *Canada population 2019.* Accessed at http://worldpopulationreview.com/countries/canada-population on November 4, 2019.

Index

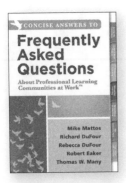

Concise Answers to Frequently Asked Questions About Professional Learning Communities at Work®
Mike Mattos, Richard DuFour, Rebecca DuFour, Robert Eaker, and Thomas W. Many

Get all of your PLC questions answered. Designed as a companion resource to *Learning by Doing: A Handbook for Professional Learning Communities at Work®* (3rd ed.), this powerful, quick-reference guidebook is a must-have for teacher teams working to build and sustain a PLC.

BKF705

Leading with Intention
Jeanne Spiller and Karen Power

Designed as a guide and reflective tool, *Leading With Intention* will help focus your invaluable everyday work as a school leader. Discover actionable steps for creating a highly effective school community in which staff collaborate, make evidence-based decisions, and believe students are the top priority.

BKF829

Amplify Your Impact
Thomas W. Many, Michael J. Maffoni, Susan K. Sparks, and Tesha Ferriby Thomas

Now is the time to improve collaboration in your PLC. Using the latest research on coaching and collaboration, the authors share concrete action steps your school can take to adopt proven collaborative coaching methods, fortify teacher teams, and ultimately improve student learning in classrooms.

BKF794

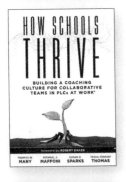

How Schools Thrive
Thomas W. Many, Michael J. Maffoni, Susan K. Sparks, and Tesha Ferriby Thomas

A companion to *Amplify Your Impact*, this resource drills deeper into the more complex aspects of PLC at Work®. Coaches and leaders will acquire new insights and strategies for improving their team's professional practice around the essential elements of the PLC process.

BKF855

Enriching the Learning
Michael Roberts

Rely on *Enriching the Learning* to help your school community address question four of the PLC at Work® process. The book's wide range of strategies, templates, and tools is designed to fully prepare collaborative teams to plan and execute engaging extensions for students who have already demonstrated proficiency.

BKF889

Solution Tree | Press *a division of* Solution Tree

Visit SolutionTree.com or call 800.733.6786 to order.

"Tremendous, tremendous, tremendous!

The speaker made me do some very deep internal reflection about the **PLC process** and the personal responsibility I have in making the school improvement process work **for ALL kids."**

—Marc Rodriguez, teacher effectiveness coach, Denver Public Schools, Colorado

PD Services ·

Our experts draw from decades of research and their own experiences to bring you practical strategies for building and sustaining a high-performing PLC. You can choose from a range of customizable services, from a one-day overview to a multiyear process.

Book your PLC PD today!
888.763.9045

Solution Tree